| Oxford Shakespeare Topics

Shakespeare and Biography

OXFORD SHAKESPEARE TOPICS

Published and Forthcoming Titles Include:

Lawrence Danson, *Shakespeare's Dramatic Genres*
Paul Edmondson and Stanley Wells, *Shakespeare's Sonnets*
Gabriel Egan, *Shakespeare and Marx*
Andrew Gurr and Mariko Ichikawa, *Staging in Shakespeare's Theatres*
Douglas Lanier, *Shakespeare and Modern Popular Culture*
Jill L. Levenson, *Shakespeare and Modern Drama*
Ania Loomba, *Shakespeare, Race, and Colonialism*
Raphael Lyne, *Shakespeare's Late Work*
Russ McDonald, *Shakespeare and the Arts of Language*
Steven Marx, *Shakespeare and the Bible*
Robert S. Miola, *Shakespeare's Reading*
Phyllis Rackin, *Shakespeare and Women*
Catherine Richardson, *Shakespeare and Material Culture*
Bruce R. Smith, *Shakespeare and Masculinity*
Zdeněk Stříbrný, *Shakespeare and Eastern Europe*
Michael Taylor, *Shakespeare Criticism in the Twentieth Century*
Stanley Wells, ed., *Shakespeare in the Theatre: An Anthology of Criticism*
Martin Wiggins, *Shakespeare and the Drama of His Time*

Oxford Shakespeare Topics

Shakespeare and Biography

DAVID BEVINGTON

OXFORD
UNIVERSITY PRESS

Great Clarendon Street, Oxford OX2 6DP

Oxford University Press is a department of the University of Oxford.
It furthers the University's objective of excellence in research, scholarship,
and education by publishing worldwide in

Oxford New York

Auckland Cape Town Dar es Salaam Hong Kong Karachi
Kuala Lumpur Madrid Melbourne Mexico City Nairobi
New Delhi Shanghai Taipei Toronto

With offices in

Argentina Austria Brazil Chile Czech Republic France Greece
Guatemala Hungary Italy Japan Poland Portugal Singapore
South Korea Switzerland Thailand Turkey Ukraine Vietnam

Oxford is a registered trade mark of Oxford University Press
in the UK and in certain other countries

Published in the United States
by Oxford University Press Inc., New York

British Library Cataloguing in Publication Data
Data available

Library of Congress Cataloging in Publication Data
Library of Congress Control Number: 2009941585

Typeset by SPI Publisher Services, Pondicherry, India
Printed in Great Britain by
Clays Ltd, St Ives plc

ISBN 978-0-19-958648-6 (hbk.)
ISBN 978-0-19-958647-9 (pbk.)

1 3 5 7 9 10 8 6 4 2

For Stanley Wells and Peter Holland

Of Shakespeare biographies we have many, both in recent years and over the centuries. The present book is not another contribution to that list. It is instead a study of the art of Shakespeare biography: its fascinations, its changing preoccupations, and above all the challenges that biographers face in writing about a hugely gifted author who chose not to talk about himself. I have learned a great deal about Shakespeare and biography from working on this topic. If I can convey some of my excitement about the importance of the idea, I will have had my wish.

I am grateful to Stanley Wells and Peter Holland for inviting me to join their distinguished Oxford University Press series, Oxford Shakespeare Topics, of which they are the General Editors. They have been enormously helpful to me in conceptualizing the topic. They have read drafts and have rescued me from many a potential error. They have encouraged lucidity of style, aiming at a readership of students at all levels of expertise and of lay persons interested in Shakespeare. My greatest pleasure has been to aim at writing the kind of book they envisaged, and for this special reason I am honoured to dedicate the book to them.

I wish to thank my colleagues, Richard Strier, Michael Murrin, and Joshua Scodel, together with the members of the Renaissance Workshop at the University of Chicago, for their careful reading of parts of this study, especially the chapter on religion.

My wife Peggy has listened thoughtfully to me as I have read the chapters of this book to her, often on long summer drives to see our family and our farm in Ohio, where, in the quiet of the countryside, I have done most of the writing. Her observations and corrections, along with her encouragement and support, have been more helpful than I can easily say.

Contents

The Biographical Problem

'If his biography is to be found', writes Barbara Everett about William Shakespeare in a *Times Literary Supplement* commentary, 17 August 2006, 'it has to be here, in the plays and poems, *but never literally and never provably*'. Ralph Waldo Emerson holds a similar view: 'Shakespeare is the only biographer of Shakespeare, and even he can tell nothing, except to the Shakespeare in us' ('Shakespeare, or, The Poet', quoted in part in Jonathan Bate, *Soul of the Age*, pp. ix and xix). Germaine Greer is openly sceptical of the very enterprise: 'All biographies of Shakespeare are houses built of straw', she declares, 'but there is good straw and rotten straw, and some houses are better built than others' (*Shakespeare's Wife*, 9). Yet, as Katherine Duncan-Jones insists, the widely held view that 'virtually nothing is known about Shakespeare's life' is a serious overstatement: 'We do possess a remarkably substantial body of documents relating to Shakespeare's life' (*Ungentle Shakespeare*, p. ix).

We do in fact know more about Shakespeare than about any of his contemporaries in the early modern theatre, since researchers have been indefatigable in tracking down as much information as possible about England's most famous writer. To cite one instance, an attractive portrait of a man from about 1610 has recently come to light, having been for nearly 300 years in the possession of an aristocratic Anglo-Irish family named Cobbes with historic family links to Shakespeare's only patron, the third Earl of Southampton. The portrait shows a bearded man in a high lace collar. The pose, the intelligent facial expression, the eyes all suggest to Stanley Wells and some other scholars that this portrait may have been the original of the Folger Library's painting of Shakespeare and of the engraving by Martin Droeshout in the Shakespearean First Folio of 1623. (The posthumous portrait bust in Holy Trinity Church, Stratford-upon-Avon, also shows a resemblance, in Wells's view, but seems to have been produced from other sources of information.) To be sure, Katherine Duncan-Jones has forcefully argued, in the *Times Literary Supplement*, that the painting is more probably a portrait of Sir Thomas Overbury. We may not have a new Shakespeare portrait after all. The incident points, more than anything else, to our eagerness to know what Shakespeare was like.

Despite all this eagerness to learn more, the information we have is disappointingly thin regarding him as a person. What was he like? What were his beliefs, his ideals, his hopes, his fears? Was he happily married? What did he do during the so-called 'dark years' after the births of his twins in 1585 until the time his name shows up in London records in 1592? Is it true that he left his family in Stratford-upon-Avon for the whole of his career in London as a dramatist and actor, from the early 1590s until 1611 or so? Did he retire to Stratford then, or may he have done so earlier? What did he look like? We would love to know more about how Shakespeare got into acting, what company or companies he acted and wrote plays for, how he got the money in 1594 to become a sharer in the newly formed Lord Chamberlain's Men, and what his relationship to the Earl of Southampton was like. Did he aspire to be a poet like Edmund Spenser, depending on patronage? Might he have preferred that to the theatre? When his only son Hamnet died in 1596, where was he, and how did he take this terrible news? Was his instituting proceedings for a coat of arms for his father John in that same year related to his son's death? Why is there so little dramatization of the death of a son in the plays immediately following 1596?

Over the centuries, biographers of Shakespeare have asked whether one can responsibly discuss the plays and poems as a means of determining what Shakespeare may have been like as a person. They have wondered about his reticence in talking about himself, and whether or not the great tragedies of the early and mid-1600s were prompted by adverse personal experience, or whether the late romances relate to his retirement to a life with Anne Hathaway in Stratford.

A central problem is that Shakespeare wrote essentially nothing about himself. Unlike Ben Jonson, his younger contemporary, who loudly proclaimed in prologues, manifestos, essays, and private conversations his views on the arts and writers from antiquity down to the Renaissance, and who has left us vivid testimonials of his feelings about the death of a son, about his wife ('a shrew, but honest'), about his conversion to Catholicism, and much more, Shakespeare has left us his plays and poems. Even here, he seems not to have been involved in the publication of his Sonnets in 1609, and was content to see publication of only about half his plays during his lifetime. We do have the dedications to his two non-dramatic poems, addressed to the Earl of Southampton, published in Shakespeare's name when the poems appeared in print: *Venus and Adonis* in 1593 and *The Rape of Lucrece* in 1594. That is the sum total of writings to which he affixed his name, other than a few legal documents that have no relation to his artistic career, and his last will and testament drawn up for him in 1616 as he neared death. He may have composed his fine poem the 'Phoenix and Turtle' as a compliment to Sir John and Lady Salusbury in 1601, but even if so he did not accompany it with a dedicatory letter. His name appears on a number of title pages of plays in quarto and in the 1623 First Folio, but again without any statement by him as author. No manuscripts in his handwriting have survived, other than, purportedly, a scene that he added to the play of *Sir Thomas More* in a revision needed to placate the censor.

The problem for the biographer centres implicitly on Shakespeare's view of himself as an artist. He presents himself first and foremost as a dramatist, whose job is to entertain and edify audiences. He characteristically effaces himself as a storyteller and dramatist. He writes not about himself but through his characters. He draws his plot materials from literary sources: from a long narrative poem for *Romeo and Juliet*, from Italian short stories (*Othello, The Merchant of Venice, Much Ado About Nothing, Twelfth Night, All's Well That Ends Well*), from pastoral romance (*As You Like It, The Two Gentlemen of Verona*), from the Latin drama of Plautus and from neoclassical comedy (*The Comedy of Errors, The Taming of the Shrew*), from Raphael Holinshed's *Chronicles of England, Scotland, and Ireland* and other historical accounts for his English history plays and also *Macbeth*, from Plutarch's *Lives of the Noble Grecians and Romans* for his Roman and Greek plays (*Julius Caesar, Antony and Cleopatra, Timon of Athens, Coriolanus*), from an ancient Scandinavian saga for *Hamlet*, from legendary British history (*Cymbeline, King Lear*), from earlier plays that had been acted in London (*King John, Measure for Measure, Hamlet* again, and *King Lear*), from a fictional prose chapbook for *Titus Andronicus*, from post-Homeric legends of the Trojan War as well as from Homer's *Iliad* (*Troilus and Cressida*), from prose romances (*The Winter's Tale, Pericles*), and from Chaucer (*The Two Noble Kinsmen, Troilus and Cressida* again). Only in a very few plays, notably *Love's Labour's Lost, A Midsummer Night's Dream, The Merry Wives of Windsor,* and *The Tempest,* does Shakespeare invent his own plot, and even here the materials are often an amalgam of the kinds of plot devices he uses elsewhere.

Drama as a genre can of course be polemical in expressing its author's point of view, but it also affords a very different model of authorial near-anonymity that Shakespeare evidently found congenial to his purposes. Drama of this sort can provide a forum in which many opposing points of view are expressed through characters who disagree with one another about matters of vital public or private interest. Is Prince Hal, in the *Henry IV* plays, to be admired or deplored for his companionship with Falstaff? King Henry IV and Falstaff, among others, hold radically opposite points of view on this important question. Can Shakespeare be said to be in favour of public order and self-disciplined devotion to duty, or does he plead the case for personal expression and restive dislike of restraint? The question is essentially impossible to answer with any assurance, since Shakespeare's job as dramatist is to present opposing sides with rare insight. Is Antony's infatuation with Cleopatra to be regretted as the undoing of a great warrior, as he is presented in Plutarch's *Life of Antony,* or are we to resonate to Cleopatra's description of him, after he has died, as a demigod whose 'legs bestrid the ocean' and whose 'reared arm / Crested the world' (*Antony and Cleopatra,* V. ii. 81)? Can both be true in the suspended animation of this great play?

Is Hamlet mad, or only pretending to be mad? Is Jaques right to defend literary satire as a powerful artistic vehicle for attacking human folly, or is Duke Senior, his interlocutor in a debate on the subject, right to suspect that many satirists are really only getting back at people they dislike (*As You Like It,* II. vii. 47–87)? Are Iago in

Othello and Edmund in *King Lear* out-and-out villains, or are we invited to perceive something disturbingly persuasive in their impatience with the follies of parents and other figures of authority? Is Julius Caesar, in the play named for him, a would-be dictator deservedly overthrown in the name of republican self-rule, or is he a clear-sighted strongman who knows what is best for Rome? Conversely, is Brutus a champion of resistance to tyranny, or is he a well-meaning but myopic statesman who does not fathom his own personal ambitions and does not foresee that the assassination plot he joins will end up by destroying the very liberties that he so cherishes? Is Coriolanus something of a fascist in his sneering contempt for the common people, or is he a thoughtful conservative whose mistrust of populism is confirmed by the course of events in that play?

John Keats famously ascribed to Shakespeare (in a letter to Keats's brother Thomas, 17 December 1817) a 'negative capability', by which Keats meant a creative state of mind 'when a man is capable of being in uncertainties, mysteries, doubts, without any irritable reaching after fact or reason'. Keats, as a romantic poet, was greatly attracted to what he admiringly understood to be the way in which imaginative uncertainties can liberate the poet's creative powers. The phrase has come to signify Shakespeare's (or, potentially, any other writer's) skill in setting aside his own point of view in order to focus on what his characters may be thinking at any given moment. Thus 'negative capability' has come to be a way of describing Shakespeare's uncanny ability for showing, through dramatic dialogue and action, what his characters are thinking, not what the dramatist wishes to prove. The characterization is apt, and it helps explain a part of Shakespeare's remarkable appeal as a dramatist, since this quality of 'negative capability' affords him such an extraordinary range of opportunities to see into varied aspects of the human condition. At the same time, for our present purposes it erects a barrier between the work of art and the artist who created it, since it affords little opportunity or desire for the artist to speak in his own behalf. How can a biographer proceed to tell the story of a dramatist who refuses to be overtly biographical?

Should we even care about the artist's personal life and preferences? The so-called New Critical movement, originating in the 1930s and afterwards in the work of G. Wilson Knight, L. C. Knights, Derek Traversi, Cleanth Brooks, and others, mounted a frontal assault on historical criticism by insisting that critics pay close attention to poetry and language without the distractions of historical background, including biographical information about the author. The critic should focus instead on tone, image patterns, and persona. 'A poem should not mean, but be', intoned Archibald MacLeish, in a dictum meant to apply to drama and fiction as well as to lyric poetry. This corrective to the austerely factual approaches of much traditional historicism made an important point, of course, and is one that is not forgotten today, but criticism has also broadened its sympathies in such a way as to make room for both biography and close textual analysis. Cannot biographical information provide us with significant insights as to how a work of art came into being, how the artist appears to have shaped personal experience into a work of enduring beauty? One can hardly imagine understanding *Ulysses* without knowing a lot about Dublin and James Joyce's combative relation to that city's culture. W. B. Yeats wrote many of his best poems in response to the exigencies of civil strife in Ireland and his own place in that conflict. Eugene O'Neill's finest play, *A Long Day's Journey into Night*, is so agonizingly autobiographical that it enables a knowledgeable reader to trace every step by which that dramatist forged personal suffering into art.

Shakespeare wrote for a much earlier age, to be sure, some four hundred years ago now, and belonged to an age that at least partly embraced a vision of the artist as a maker, a compiler, an enlightened artificer rather than one who might create imaginative stories out of his own personal experiences. Instructional pamphlets like *The Art of English Poesie*, by George Puttenham (1589), offered practical advice to would-be writers by illustrating how various figures of rhetoric could be fitted to particular moods or situations; indeed, the composing of verse and drama was thought of as a branch of rhetoric, or the art of persuasion. Dramatists worked almost anonymously. Shakespeare's name, despite his growing reputation in London, did not appear on a title page of a published play by him until 1598, when a quarto volume of *Love's Labour's Lost* advertised itself as '*By W. Shakespeare*'. *Richard III*, appearing in that same year, was not so designated, despite its immense popularity. Writers of scripts for the playhouses, like today's scriptwriters for the film industry, were generally less well known than famous actors like Richard Burbage and Edward Alleyn.

Shakespeare did achieve fame in his own time, but not because he dramatized his own life story. He rewrote old plays; he adapted romances and historical chronicles as play scripts. He collaborated at times with fellow dramatists such as Thomas Middleton and John Fletcher, as did other dramatists of the period. He was a collaborative worker too in that he shared acting responsibilities for a while at least with the members of his acting company, the Lord Chamberlain's Men, formed in 1594 and renamed the King's Men in 1603. Shakespeare was a professional writer for the theatre, not a 'creative' writer in our modern sense. He entertained hopes of being a published poet, as we shall see in Chapter 3, and indeed his sonnets have struck many biographers as intensely personal, but he chose instead to be a professional dramatist. With that he essentially closed the door on the opportunity for autobiographical writing. He appears to have accepted that his very nature would be 'subdued / To what it works in, like the dyer's hand' (Sonnet 111).

At the same time, Shakespeare presumably had some control over what old stories or plays he might choose to dramatize, no doubt with increasing authority as his reputation grew. He was a full member of his acting company, prized so highly as their leading playwright that he seems to have been relieved of at least some acting duties in his later years. Biographers have often asked whether he turned to subjects that interested him personally in such a way as to allow him as writer to reflect on such themes as personal ambition, anxiety about courtship and marriage, jealousy, pessimism, scepticism, worries about ageing, and thoughts about the approach of retirement and death. Biographers have been prompted to ask whether his choices were particularly relevant to the stages of his own life, and also to social and political developments in the world of England of which he was a part.

One purpose of the present study will be to examine ways in which Shakespeare's biographers have addressed such questions. Do the plays and poems give any hints about his religious affiliations in a time of intense sectarian conflict? Can his writings afford reliable clues as to how he personally felt about the Catholic faith, about Puritanism and Calvinism, about Jews, about blacks? In his historical plays, can we discern an authorial alignment towards the monarchy and the established order, or conversely towards popular discontent and radicalism? Are his own personal convictions discernible as to whether human beings should practise sexual restraint or some degree of freedom? Some recent biographers, such Stephen Greenblatt and René Weis, welcome the opportunity to pursue the intriguing possibility of formulating at least tentative answers to such questions.

All writers agree that caution is necessary. Shakespeare's extraordinary ability to present a subject from conflicting viewpoints through the speeches of his characters must warn the biographer that dogmatic statements about the author's own views are inherently suspect. Shakespeare's position as a popular dramatist writing for a diversified London audience suggests that he had good reason to be fair-minded and inclusive, though even here we find in critical studies of Shakespeare a lively debate as to whether that audience was truly popular (Alfred Harbage's view) or more affluent and elitist than previously supposed (the contention of Ann Jennalie Cook; see the bibliography at the end of this book). Still, we have the plays and poems as some kind of evidence, and indeed the only evidence that Shakespeare has provided us apart from what others have said about him. If biography is to achieve its goals of a just appraisal of the man and his work, it must attempt to look at the whole picture and read what Shakespeare wrote with as much circumspection and insight as possible.

How have biographers and other writers about Shakespeare approached the complex problem of characterizing an author who has left us virtually no first-hand account of his own life or artistic achievement? To begin with factual information, a number of scholarly researchers have compiled impressive archival data from parish church records, guild registers, wills, court depositions, and the like. Mark Eccles's *Shakespeare in Warwickshire* (1961) provides extensive information on Shakespeare's ancestors and parents, his schooling in Stratford, his neighbours, his wife's family, the large house called New Place that was his Stratford home from 1597 until his death in 1616, his acting colleagues, and his last years. Robert Bearman's research on the houses and streets of Stratford is equally valuable. So too are the labours of Catherine and Ronald Page, local amateur historians, whose brilliant detective work in identifying the house of

Shakespeare's grandfather Richard Shakespeare was aided and eventually edited by Bearman. Bearman's collaboration with Nathaniel Alcock in identifying Mary Arden's true house is yet another triumph of recent archival research in Stratford. The records of the Shakespeare Birthplace Trust in Stratford-upon-Avon that underpin the work of these scholars are in themselves immensely valuable. See also Roland Lewis's collation of materials in *The Shakespeare Documents* (1940). These are only some of the researchers who have added so substantially to our factual knowledge about Shakespeare's life.

T. W. Baldwin's massive study of *William Shakspere's Small Latine & Lesse Greeke* (1944) tells us everything we could hope to know about the curriculum of the free grammar school in Stratford which the young Shakespeare must surely have attended, even if the records of his attendance have perished. Charles William Wallace and his wife Hulda discovered in 1909 a deposition dated 19 June 1612 in the Court of Requests that provides an account of Shakespeare's role as character witness in the suit of *Belott* v. *Mountjoy*. Shakespeare had lived in the Mountjoy household on Silver Street as a tenant in 1604 and was thus able to testify on behalf of Stephen Belott in regard to a domestic dispute. Charles Nicholl's *The Lodger* (2007) gives further insight into what Shakespeare's life on Silver Street must have been like. Ian Wilson's *Shakespeare: The Evidence* (1993) is devoted to 'unlocking the mysteries of the man and his work'. Robert Bearman has provided solid documentation, from a sceptical point of view, on the controversial question as to whether Shakespeare and his father had Catholic leanings.

Documentary information of this sort has been assembled in several impressive volumes by Samuel Schoenbaum: *William Shakespeare: A Documentary Life* (1975), *William Shakespeare: Records and Images* (1981), and an abbreviated version in *William Shakespeare: A Compact Documentary Life* (1977). The first two volumes cited here offer handsome photographic representations of the major documents. Schoenbaum's *Shakespeare's Lives* (1991) informs us about those who have undertaken to write biographies of Shakespeare, from early collectors of anecdotes to the present day, not excluding Delia Bacon, Thomas Looney, and other so-called anti-Stratfordians who would deny the authorship of the works to Shakespeare. E. K. Chambers's

William Shakespeare (2 vols., 1930) is, as its subtitle declares, 'a study of facts and problems'. Chambers's *The Elizabethan Stage* (1923) extends the purview outward to the world of Shakespeare's theatre and his professional colleagues. C. S. Lewis's *English Literature in the Sixteenth Century Excluding Drama* provides valuable historical information.

The writing of comprehensive biographies of Shakespeare begins with Nicholas Rowe in 1709. Studies of this sort, undertaking to present all that is known biographically about Shakespeare together with an appraisal of his achievement as dramatist and poet, have been numerous. Notable undertakings in earlier years include those of Edmond Malone (1790), Edward Dowden (1875), J. O. Halliwell-Phillipps (1890), Sidney Lee (1898), Edgar J. Fripp (1938), and Peter Alexander (1939). More recently, and of particular interest to this present book, are Park Honan's *Shakespeare: A Life* (1998), Katherine Duncan-Jones's *Ungentle Shakespeare* (2001), Stephen Greenblatt's *Will in the World* (2004), and René Weis's *Shakespeare Revealed* (2007). Other 'standard' biographies include those by David Masson (1914), Georg Brandes (1916, translated 1898), John Bailey (1929), Hesketh Pearson (1942), Marchette Chute (1949), M. M. Reese (1953), Ivor Brown (1968), A. L. Rowse (1973), M. C. Bradbrook (1978), Russell Fraser (1988), Peter Levi (1988), Dennis Kay (1992), Andrew Gurr (1995), Anthony Holden (1999), and Michael Wood (2003). Many of these, especially by Pearson, Chute, Levi, Holden, and Wood, are popular studies by authors who have written on other subjects; some, such as Park Honan's biography, are monuments of carefully researched scholarship bringing the entire subject up to date.

Some recent studies of Shakespeare with important biographical dimensions choose to focus on a particular aspect of his achievement. Stanley Wells's *Shakespeare: A Dramatic Life* (1994; also published under the title *Shakespeare: A Life in Drama*, 1995) and *Shakespeare for All Time* (2003) look at Shakespeare as a writer of dramatic texts whose plays are central to the history of the English stage. John Southworth's *Shakespeare the Player: A Life in the Theatre* (2000) adopts a similar strategy. Germaine Greer's *Shakespeare's Wife*, already mentioned above, undertakes a spirited defence of Anne Hathaway and her marriage to William Shakespeare. Eric Sams, in *The Real Shakespeare* (1995), is intent on 'retrieving the early years, 1564–1594'. E. A. J. Honigmann's *Shakespeare: The 'Lost' Years* (1985) asks where

Shakespeare was and how he made a living in the seven or so years prior to 1592. James Shapiro's *1599: A Year in the Life of William Shakespeare* (2005) explores the many dimensions of Shakespeare's life and artistic achievement in the year that saw the completion of *Henry V, Julius Caesar,* and *As You Like It,* and the drafting of *Hamlet.* Joyce Rogers's *The Second Best Bed* (1993) studies Shakespeare's will 'in a new light'. Heinrich Mutschmann and Karl P. Wentersdorf explore *Shakespeare and Catholicism* (1952), as do Peter Milward in *Shakespeare's Religious Background* (1973) and Richard Wilson in *Secret Shakespeare: Studies in Theatre, Religion, and Resistance* (2004). *Region, Religion, and Patronage: Lancastrian Shakespeare,* edited by Richard Dutton, Alison Findlay, and Richard Wilson (2003), asks what the implications might be for our interpretation of Shakespeare's writings, especially *Twelfth Night, Romeo and Juliet, A Midsummer Night's Dream,* and the history plays, if we were to imagine that he began his theatrical career as 'William Shakeshafte' in Lancashire (see Chapter 5) and was thus acquainted with prosperous Catholic households and provincial touring.

A. D. Nuttall's *Shakespeare the Thinker* (2007) makes clear by its title that it traces the development of Shakespeare's ideas in the course of his writing career. Two books by Jonathan Bate pursue a similar tack. *The Genius of Shakespeare* (1997) defines that genius in terms of his value as both a national poet and a writer of timeless appeal, attractive both for his 'peculiarity' and his universality. *Soul of the Age* (2009) is 'a biography of the mind of William Shakespeare', moving through the seven ages of humankind from infancy and childhood to old age and oblivion that Shakespeare so brilliantly characterizes in *As You Like It* (II. vii). My own *Shakespeare: The Seven Ages of Human Experience* (2002, 2005) explores the same pattern in terms of romantic courtship, coming of age, misogyny, midlife crisis, and retirement as reflected in the stories that Shakespeare chooses to dramatize.

Richard Dutton's *William Shakespeare: A Literary Life* (1989) shows by its subtitle that its interest is in the writer's development more than in the personal biography. Richard Wilson's *Will Power* (1993) is subtitled 'Essays on Shakespearean Authority'. Gary Taylor's *Reinventing Shakespeare* (1989), though not a biography in the usual sense of surveying the life of the dramatist, is a cultural history of the myriad ways in which Shakespeare has been reinvented by generations of readers and audiences from the Restoration down to the present day.

Several biographers, writing around the start of the twentieth century, chose as their special subject Shakespeare's world of Stratford: J. W. Gray's *Shakespeare's Marriage, his Departure from Stratford* (1905), Charles Elton's *William Shakespeare, his Family and Friends* (1904), and Charlotte Stopes's *Shakespeare's Family* (1901) and *Shakespeare's Warwickshire Contemporaries* (1907). Kate Emery Pogue's more recent *Shakespeare's Friends* (2006) catalogues the persons Shakespeare knew in Stratford, London, and the theatre, including the wives of these persons where known.

Still another approach has been to fictionalize various aspects of Shakespeare's life, making free use of the artistic licence that fiction enjoys as distinguished from more factual biography. Anthony Burgess's *Nothing Like the Sun*, subtitled *A Story of Shakespeare's Love-Life* (1964), delves with abandon into a tale of Shakespeare's sudden amorous encounter with Anne. Robert Nye's novel entitled *Mrs. Shakespeare: The Complete Works* (2000) tells its story from the point of view of Anne as widow, recalling, among other matters, how she was greeted by Mr Shakespeare the only time she ever went to London. Garry O'Connor's *William Shakespeare: A Life* (1991) is heavily fictionalized. Christopher Rush's *Will* (2007) portrays the hot sensations of a young Shakespeare who, mad with lust, succumbs to his desire for Anne Hathaway. Another novel with the same title, *Will*, by Grace Tiffany (2004), tells of a Shakespeare who must deal with the wrathful enmity of Christopher Marlowe and a not-always-faithful wife in Stratford who tries to win him back into a shared marriage. Tiffany has also written an endearing fictional account of Judith Shakespeare in *My Father Had a Daughter* (2004), supposing that Judith is distressed to discover that her father has written a play (*Twelfth Night*) about the apparent drowning of a young male and the survival of his twin sister, Viola; Judith was herself the twin sister of Hamnet, who had died in 1596.

As this survey suggests, essays in Shakespearean biography have been both extensive and varied in method. Some concentrate on ascertainable, documented details of Shakespeare's life. Some are more concerned with particular aspects of his life and career: the

Stratford years both early and late, the so-called 'lost' years, the year 1599, his marriage, his last will and testament. Some are concerned chiefly with theatrical history, or with literary history, or social history, or literary reputation. Some focus on the mind of the author, on his ideas, his genius, his interest in religious questions, his scepticism, and his humanity. Shakespeare's personal silence about such important matters positively invites speculation.

Not surprisingly, then, we encounter a wide range of differing opinions on matters that seem so central to a study of Shakespeare's life. Was he unhappily or happily married? Greenblatt and Weis are among the many biographers who see evidence that he felt trapped in a marriage he could not escape other than by moving to London without his family after he and Anne had borne three children. Greer, conversely, argues that the story of a fleeting sexual encounter between an 18-year-old lad and a woman some seven or eight years his senior, followed by a hastily arranged marriage and then the husband's virtual desertion of his family, is a myth perpetrated largely by misogynistic male critics. Was Shakespeare's father a Catholic for at least part of his life, and was the son similarly inclined? Critics continue to argue both sides of the case, even if the theory of Shakespeare's sojourn among Catholic families in Lancaster in the late 1580s (see Chapter 5) has perhaps lost some of the impetus it enjoyed around 1999. Did he live in London without his family from the early 1590s until his retirement in 1611 or so, as is generally assumed, or (as Bate has argued in *Soul of the Age*, ch. 20) might he have moved from London to Stratford as early as 1604–5, thereafter providing his acting company with plays but no longer actively involving himself in stage productions? Did Shakespeare perhaps die of complications arising from venereal disease, as Duncan-Jones and Holden suppose (see Chapter 3), or are we to believe the Stratford vicar and physician John Ward, who noted in his diary, some half a century after the event, that 'Shakespear Drayton and Ben Jhonson had a merry meeting and it seems drank too hard for Shakespear died of a feavour there contracted' (Schoenbaum, *Documentary Life*, 241)? These are only a few of the puzzles we encounter.

The methods of the biographers are as varied as their topics. Some, like Schoenbaum, assemble verifiable data and speculate as to their meaning only with great caution. For some others, inferences are to be drawn from the known facts so long as they are plausible. Since Shakespeare lived for such a considerable time in London apart from his wife and children, can we assume or at least speculate that he had amorous encounters? The danger here is to assess the probabilities by the standards of twenty-first-century morality that may well be at variance with those of the sixteenth and early seventeenth centuries. Did he feel guilty about such purported violations of his marriage vows? Do the plays and poems, where we can certainly find expressions of guilty remorse and even revulsion about the sex act (as in Sonnet 129 and *The Rape of Lucrece*, 190 ff.), testify to personal experience on the part of the author? Did he contract syphilis? Increasingly, biographers have worked with the assumption that Shakespeare must have been fundamentally like us today, and that he wrote allusively about himself even when he was telling a story derived from sources.

We should begin with an account of what early biographers and anecdotalists have said about Shakespeare the man and the writer. Their testimonials have perhaps a special value in that they were close in time to their subject and were not influenced by the weight of tradition and reputation that has gathered around Shakespeare in more recent times. What sort of person was Shakespeare imagined to be by his contemporaries and those who came soon after him?

2

The Art of Biography

The first formal biography of Shakespeare did not appear until 1709. Nicholas Rowe included a biographical essay at the head of his six-volume edition in that year, which, not coincidentally, was also the first real 'edition' of the author's works in the sense of providing a reader's text of the whole corpus with lists of characters for each play, textual emendations, modernized spelling and pronunciation, and commentary notes. (The second, third, and fourth Folio editions of the plays in 1632, 1663–4, and 1685 had simply reprinted the text as derived successively from the first Folio of 1623, with minor corrections, some new typographical errors, and some sporadic providing of lists of characters.) Shakespeare was by 1709 an established major English author, to be edited seriously as one edited the authors of the ancient classical world. Such a major author deserved a biography.

Prior to 1709, for over a century, information about Shakespeare accumulated anecdotally and haphazardly. One early mention of him is, sad to say, vitriolic. It is attributed to the writer Robert Greene, who, in a maudlin confessional work called *Greene's Groatsworth of Wit Bought with a Million of Repentance* (1592), lashed out at 'an upstart crow, beautified with our feathers, that with his "Tiger's heart wrapped in a player's hide" supposes he is as well able to bombast out a blank verse as the best of you, and, being an absolute *Johannes Factotum*, is in his own conceit the only Shake-scene in a country'. Greene was addressing his fellow dramatists Christopher Marlowe, Thomas Nashe, and George Peele. The quotation, 'Tiger's heart wrapped in a player's hide', parodies a line from Shakespeare's *3 Henry VI*: 'Oh, tiger's heart wrapped in a woman's hide!' (I. iv. 137), a play enjoying current success on the London stage. The allusion to Shakespeare is made even more clear by the acid quip, 'the only Shake-scene in a country'. Greene's contention is that Shakespeare is flourishing as a playwright because he is only too willing to purloin ideas and language from practising writers like Marlowe and Peele, or indeed from Greene himself. Shakespeare, the 'upstart crow' or parvenu dramatist, is beautifying himself with the feathers of handsomer birds than he.

Until recently, biographers of Shakespeare (including Sidney Lee and Samuel Schoenbaum) have taken this account as truly pointing to Greene as the author of the attack; and indeed, it savours of the envying despair of a man about to die in wretched alcoholic poverty. Greene was himself an inveterate plagiarist. Yet several biographers (including Stanley Wells, *Shakespeare for All Time*, 49, and Stephen Greenblatt, *Will in the World*, 212) now suspect strongly that Henry Chettle, who saw to the publication of *A Groatsworth of Wit*, was himself a contributor to this vilification. Thomas Nashe was, and still is, suspected too of involvement, especially by Katherine Duncan-Jones (pp. 43–4); Nashe vehemently denied any part in the enterprise, but of course his denial could be a cover. Duncan-Jones's contention is that Shakespeare, a man of no university education, had aroused the indignation of several of the so-called University Wits, educated at Oxford and Cambridge and now finding themselves thrown on their talents as writers in the highly competitive world of London drama. She wonders (pp. 49–50) if Thomas Nashe's diatribe against scribblers who read 'English Seneca' by candlelight, affording them 'whole Hamlets, I should say handfuls, of tragical speeches', traditionally seen as an attack on Thomas Kyd as author of *The Spanish Tragedy*, might also be a swipe at Shakespeare. Nashe's preface to Robert Greene's *Menaphon*, containing this passage, had appeared in 1589, by which time Shakespeare could conceivably have entered the London dramatic scene and could have written, or contributed to, the lost early *Hamlet* to which Nashe seemingly alludes. All this is speculative, of course, but the whole episode does at least suggest that Shakespeare's genius as a young dramatist provoked an envious response.

Whatever the nature of Chettle's involvement in the 'upstart crow' episode, he did at least apologize for it—on behalf of the now-dead Greene, and perhaps implicitly on his own behalf, having realized that the thing had gone too far. 'I am as sorry as if the original fault had been my fault', Chettle wrote in *Kind-Heart's Dream*, 'because myself have seen his demeanor no less civil than he excellent in the quality he professes. Besides, divers of worship have reported his uprightness of dealing, which argues his honesty and his facetious grace in writing that approves his art.' The 'he' referred to here is traditionally supposed to be Shakespeare, though that interpretation has been vigorously challenged by Lukas Erne (1998). In any case, whether or not Chettle praises Shakespeare or someone else for 'the quality he professes', namely acting, and for his 'facetious grace in writing', the episode does indicate that Shakespeare was becoming well known in London's theatrical world, and was even a controversial figure.

Other early allusions to Shakespeare during his lifetime incorporated in modern biographies are generally positive as well, though they tend to praise him for his skill as a writer without discussing him as a person. These allusions illustrate how quickly Shakespeare's genius, especially as a poet, was recognized. Henry Willobie, in his *Willobie His Avisa*, 1594, describes admiringly how 'Shakespeare paints poor Lucrece' rape' in the poem *The Rape of Lucrece*, published in that year. Richard Barnfield's *Poems in Divers Humors* (1598) has warm words for the 'honey-flowing vein' of Shakespeare's *Venus and Adonis* (1593) and *The Rape of Lucrece*. John Weever, in an epigram 'Ad Gulielmum Shakespeare', in *Epigrams of the Oldest Cut and Newest Fashion* (1599), is no less rapturous about 'Rose-cheeked Adonis, with his amber tresses, / Fair fire-hot Venus, charming him to love her; / Chaste Lucretia virgin-like her tresses, / Proud lust-stung Tarquin seeking still to prove her.' The importance of *Venus and Adonis* and *The Rape of Lucrece* to Shakespeare's growing reputation is noteworthy in such tributes, suggesting how high-style poetry in the vein of Edmund Spenser and Philip Sidney was quick to win attention and approval from the literary cognoscenti.

Even Francis Meres, a clergyman whose *Palladis Tamia* (1598) gives us our first nearly comprehensive list of Shakespeare's writings up till that time, begins his encomium with the non-dramatic poems:

As the soul of Euphorbus was thought to live in Pythagoras, so the sweet, witty soul of Ovid lives in mellifluous and honey-tongued Shakespeare: witness his *Venus and Adonis*, his *Lucrece*, his sugared sonnets among his private friends, etc.

As Plautus and Seneca are accounted the best for comedy and tragedy among the Latins, so Shakespeare among the English is the most excellent in both kinds for the stage: for comedy, witness his *Gentlemen of Verona*, his *Errors*, his *Love's Labour's Lost*, his *Love's Labor's Won* [*The Taming of the Shrew?*], his *Midsummer Night's Dream*, and his *Merchant of Venice*; for tragedy, his *Richard the II*, *Richard the III*, *Henry the IV*, *King John*, *Titus Andronicus*, and his *Romeo and Juliet*.

The highest praise Meres can afford Shakespeare, given the classical education shared by Meres and his readers, is to rank Shakespeare as among the greats of ancient Rome. Shakespeare is the Ovid, the Plautus, and the Seneca for an England bursting with excitement at her own newly discovered potential for high literary achievement.

Gabriel Harvey, some time between 1598 and 1601, noted down in a copy of Speght's *Chaucer* a tribute that once again praises the poems, especially *The Rape of Lucrece*, pairing that poem (rather surprisingly, to our modern tastes) with *Hamlet*. Harvey wrote: 'The younger sort takes much delight in Shakespeare's *Venus and Adonis*, but his *Lucrece* and his tragedy of *Hamlet, Prince of Denmark* have it in them to please the wiser sort.'

To be sure, other more critical assessments of Shakespeare do emerge during these same years, lending support to Duncan-Jones's contention that the conventional image of a 'gentle' Shakespeare needs to be re-examined. When Shakespeare ventured to write *1 Henry IV* in 1596–7 about Prince Hal's escapades with an endearing old rogue called Sir John Oldcastle—a name he had borrowed from a rollicking anonymous play of about 1587–8 called *The Famous Victories of Henry the Fifth*—Puritan-leaning descendants of the historical Oldcastle cried foul. Prominent among those living descendants in 1596–7 was Sir William Brooke, Lord Cobham, who served as Lord Chamberlain (and hence nominal patron of Shakespeare's acting company) for a brief time from the death of Henry Carey, first Lord Hunsdon, in August 1596 until Cobham died and Lord Hunsdon's son, Sir George Carey, second Lord Hunsdon, became Lord Chamberlain on 17 March 1597. The Careys were supporters of the players and especially of their own acting troupe; Cobham was more inclined to be hostile. To him and his supporters, the Lollard martyr Oldcastle of the reign of Henry V, who similarly bore the title of Lord Cobham, was a noble forerunner of the Protestant Reformation who had been denounced by the Pope as Antichrist and burnt at the stake for his heresies (see Ian Wilson, *Shakespeare: The Evidence*, 224–8, Peter Ackroyd, 298–9, and Chambers, i. 64, 283). By the time of *1 Henry IV*, Oldcastle had been enshrined in John Foxe's *Book of Martyrs*, known officially as *Acts and Monuments of the Church*. The outcry produced a rival play by the Admiral's Men in 1599 called *Sir John Oldcastle*, piously declaring that it featured no 'pampered glutton' or 'aged counselor to youthful sin'. Shakespeare seemingly was obliged to backtrack by changing his Oldcastle's name to Falstaff, in recollection of a cowardly knight who had been stripped of his Order of the Garter by Lord Talbot for dishonourable conduct in the wars with France. (Shakespeare had already told that story in *1 Henry VI*, IV. i.)

Falstaff and his cronies soon became a common topic of gossip. In 1599, the Countess of Southampton wrote to her husband of having read in a letter 'that Sir John Falstaff is by his Mistress Dame Pintpot made father of a godly miller's thumb, a boy that's all head and very little body', using this as a way of alluding to some privately understood bit of news. Similarly, in a letter of 1600, Sir Charles Percy complained jocosely to a friend that he feared his prolonged stay at his country estate might earn him the reputation of 'Justice Silence or Justice Shallow'.

Another dig at Shakespeare, or at his fans, emerges in a trilogy of plays called *The Pilgrimage to Parnassus* and *The Return from Parnassus* in two parts, acted by students at St John's College, Cambridge (1598–1603). In the third of these plays, a small group of university graduates, finding themselves unemployed in London like other University Wits, laugh scornfully at foppish courtiers who seem to do nothing but plagiarize *Venus and Adonis* and *Romeo and Juliet*. When they make a desperate attempt at becoming actors, they are requested to recite some famous lines from the opening of *Richard III* ('Now is the winter of our discontent', etc.). They do so in such a way as to suggest that the speech has already become overly familiar and hackneyed in the eyes of the cognoscenti.

Another passage in the third *Parnassus* play seems to connect Shakespeare with the so-called War of the Theatres: 'Why, here's our fellow Shakespeare puts them all down, ay, and Ben Jonson, too. Oh, that Ben Jonson is a pestilent fellow! He brought up Horace giving the poets a pill, but our fellow Shakespeare hath given him a purge that made him bewray his credit' (lines 1809–13). Whether or not Shakespeare did anything of the sort, possibly in *Troilus and Cressida* (as James Bednarz argues), the story at least attests to his high visibility in the contentious literary scene of London. These stories suggest that some university graduates who had become wits about town might poke fun at Shakespeare as unsophisticated even if talented. (Shakespeare's reputation as a 'popular' writer did not, however, stop Oxford undergraduates of a later generation from reading *Romeo and Juliet* in the library copy of the 1623 Folio to such a fervent extent that the pages were worn thin, necessitating the purchase of a replacement.)

Other tributes gathered by biographers from the 1600s say virtually nothing about Shakespeare as a person, though they vividly attest to the notice he was receiving as poet and dramatist. Anthony Scoloker, in his epistle prefatory to *Diaphantus, or the Passions of Love* (1604), refers to 'friendly Shakespeare's tragedies' and wishes that all plays in that genre 'could please all, like Prince Hamlet'. William Camden, the learned antiquary with whom Ben Jonson had studied, listed Shakespeare along with Edmund Spenser, Ben Jonson, Samuel Daniel, Hugh Holland, Thomas Campion, Michael Drayton, George Chapman, and John Marston as 'the most pregnant wits of these our times, whom succeeding ages may justly admire' (*Remains of a Greater Work Concerning Britain*, 1605). The Earl of Essex's followers evidently commissioned Shakespeare's company to do a revival of *Richard II* on the eve of Essex's ill-fated rebellion attempt in early 1601. Oddly enough, the captain of the East India Company ship *Dragon*, off the coast of Sierra Leone in 1607 and 1608, encouraged his crew to perform *Richard II* and *Hamlet*, the second on two occasions, as a means of keeping the crew members 'from idleness and unlawful games or sleep'.

In the following decade, and still prior to Shakespeare's death in 1616, John Davies of Hereford toasted Shakespeare as 'our English Terence' (*The Scourge of Folly*, 1610). To Thomas Freeman, in his *Run and a Great Cast* (1614), Shakespeare provides both virtuous instruction and cautionary examples of its opposite: 'Who loves chaste life, there's *Lucrece* for a teacher; / Who list read lust, there's *Venus and Adonis*.' And no less a poet and dramatist than John Webster offered high tribute in a note to the reader accompanying his *The White Devil* (1612), ranking Shakespeare for 'right happy and copious industry' with Thomas Dekker, Thomas Heywood, Chapman, Jonson, and Beaumont and Fletcher.

Ben Jonson has given us the most considered contemporary appraisal of Shakespeare as a writer. Jonson was not reluctant to criticize Shakespeare from a rigorously neoclassical perspective for foisting 'tales, Tempests, and suchlike drolleries' on his unsophisticated audience (Induction to *Bartholomew Fair*, published 1631), for bringing on stage a Chorus that 'wafts you o'er the seas', for presuming to represent great battles in English history 'with three rusty swords, / And help of some few foot-and-half-foot words' (*Every Man in His Humour*, prologue to Jonson's 1616 Folio edition), and the like. Jonson complained to William Drummond of Hawthornden that Shakespeare 'wanted art', as illustrated by the fact that in a play (*The Winter's Tale*) he 'brought in a number of men saying they had suffered shipwreck in Bohemia, where there is no sea near by some hundred miles'. In response to claims that Shakespeare allegedly 'never blotted out [a] line', Jonson sharply replied, 'would he had blotted a thousand' (*Timber, or Discoveries*, published posthumously in 1641). Even in his commendatory poem 'To the Memory of My Beloved, the Author, Mr William Shakespeare', contributed to the Shakespeare First Folio of 1623, Jonson could not resist making the disparaging observation that Shakespeare had 'small Latin and less Greek'. (Jonson himself had plenty of both.) Still, all in all the poem is remarkably generous. It praises Shakespeare as England's greatest poet, exceeding Chaucer, Spenser, Beaumont, Kyd, and Marlowe. It compares Shakespeare favourably for tragedy with Aeschylus, Euripides, Sophocles, Seneca, and some others, and then goes on to propose that for comedy Shakespeare simply stands in a class all by himself, with no rival even 'in insolent Greece or haughty Rome', i.e. Aristophanes, Plautus, and Terence.

This is a remarkable tribute from a man who fancied himself as the literary lion of his time and the upholder of neoclassical tradition.

Jonson's estimate held sway down through the seventeenth century into the time of John Dryden, who also had some critical things to say about Shakespeare's lack of decorum and refinement, but who freely acknowledged that Shakespeare had transcended the limitations of his unrefined age (*Essay of Dramatic Poesy,* 1668).

Early biographers, then, have uncovered for us a lot of pre-eighteenth-century information about Shakespeare's reputation as poet and dramatist, but what about the man? Stories are indeed told about him, but from the very first are so anecdotal and unsupported that we cannot be sure of their veracity. Many date from succeeding generations and thus rely on word of mouth. Nicholas Rowe asserted in 1709 that John Shakespeare had enrolled his son William 'for some time at a Free-School, where 'tis probable he acquired that little Latin he was master of'. Whether this reflects a tradition that came to Rowe by word of mouth or was simply his inference, the idea seems entirely likely, since Stratford had a grammar school, the King's New School as it was known. John Shakespeare, a leading citizen of the town as assessor, Chief Alderman, and deputy bailiff, the highest offices the town had to offer, would scarcely have passed up the opportunity to educate his son in such a grammar school that was only a short walking distance from their house in Henley Street. The school records have perished with time, along with the names of the students and the curriculum they studied, but the latter is easily reconstructed by examples of similar schools (as analysed in detail by T. W. Baldwin).

Better documented are the circumstances of Shakespeare's marriage at the age of eighteen to Anne Hathaway, eight years his senior. The bishop's register for Worcester records, on 27 November 1582, the issuing of a licence for the marriage of William Shakespeare to Anne 'Whately', also referred to in the bonds of sureties issued the next day as Anne 'Hathaway'. Evidently because Anne was already three months pregnant, a licence was required to indemnify the bishop in the event of any challenge to the marriage after the reading of the banns in church only once instead of thrice. The readings of such banns or announcements of a forthcoming marriage, normally to allow for any challenge to be heard and investigated, were suspended during the season of Advent, as also in Lent. (See Eccles, 63–70.) We shall consider in the next chapter what biographers have had to say about these irregular proceedings. Documentation of the wedding itself has not survived, but a record of baptism of the couple's first child, Susanna, is recorded on 26 May 1583. Their only other children, the twins Hamnet and Judith, were baptized, also in Stratford's Holy Trinity Church, on 2 February 1585.

Thereafter, for what have become known as the seven 'lost' years, almost no official records have survived—though Jonathan Bate, in his *Soul of the Age*, 294–303, reminds us of the too-often-forgotten circumstance that Shakespeare was named as a party to a suit brought before the Queen's Bench in October, 1589. This lawsuit had been initiated earlier by his parents against John Lambert concerning property at Wilmcote, near Stratford (see Wells, 'Contemporary Allusions to Shakespeare', in *The Complete Works*, p. xxxviii; see also Schoenbaum, *Documentary Life*, 37). Shakespeare had been named, along with his parents, in a complainant's bill filed with the court in Michaelmas Term of 1588. Possibly he travelled to London to represent the family in this suit, or may have been living there by this time. Perhaps then the so-called seven 'lost' years should be reduced by half! Even so, the late 1580s provide an intriguing gap in the record.

How have biographers coped with this gap? One of the first was the late-seventeenth-century antiquary John Aubrey, who collected bits of information in an enthusiastic but desultory way that were to be published much later in his *Brief Lives* (1898). In assembling such items for his 'Minutes of Lives', Aubrey turned for help to one John Beeston, who had a reputation for knowledge of theatrical tradition; Dryden called Beeston 'the chronicle of the stage'. Aubrey made a note to himself: 'W. Shakespeare—quaere [i.e. inquire of] Mr Beesten, who knows most of him'. Aubrey goes on to cite Beeston as his authority for the following titbit: 'Though, as Ben Jonson says of him, that he had but little Latin and less Greek, he understood Latin pretty well, for he had been in his younger years a schoolmaster in the country.' Beeston, an experienced theatrical manager and son of Christopher Beeston, who had been an actor with the Lord Chamberlain's Men (Shakespeare's company) around 1598, is just the sort of authority to whom Aubrey might indeed turn for theatrical gossip. But can we rely on this assertion? Modern biographers tend to be cautious, allowing that although Shakespeare's lack of university training would have denied him the credentials for a mastership in a school like that in

Stratford, he might have 'filled the humbler post of usher or *abece-darius*' (Schoenbaum, *Documentary Life*, 88). Or he could possibly have been retained as a private tutor in some noble household. Such employment would have afforded him the opportunity to become better acquainted with the Latin works of Plautus, Ovid, Seneca, and the like which figure plentifully in citations in the early plays. But then Shakespeare had had to study many of these same texts as a pupil in school.

Aubrey himself seems to prefer an alternative to the schoolmaster hypothesis, derived again from Beeston: 'This William being inclined naturally to poetry and acting came to London I guess [at] about 18 and was an actor at one of the playhouses and did act exceedingly well.' Such a report, if true, would put Shakespeare in London quite early, in 1582 or so, before the start of the so-called 'lost years', at the time of his marriage and before the births of his three children. Such an early date seems implausible. Shakespeare did of course make his way to London at some point, but when and under what circumstances are uncertain. Alternatively, perhaps, as Edgar Fripp (*Shakespeare's Stratford*, 23) and Duncan-Jones (p. 22) argue, Shakespeare and his growing family might have crowded into the house on Henley Street for some period of time. Germaine Greer (pp. 103–4), to the contrary, cautions that such an arrangement was not practical or customary; she proposes instead that the newly married couple might have taken rooms in the Maiden Head Inn. Short on finances, Shakespeare may well have perceived few opportunities to escape from a life of grinding poverty until the lure of London and its theatrical world presented itself to him.

Aubrey asserts elsewhere that, once he had got to London, Shakespeare 'was wont to go to his native country once a year'. This claim supports the widely held view that Shakespeare saw relatively little of Stratford and of his family during the two decades or so of his working career, though Stanley Wells (*Shakespeare for All Time*, 28) observes that Stratford was no backwater town and that it enjoyed important links with the capital. Germaine Greer (p. 146) points out that desertion of a wife was a crime in early modern England, punishable in the ecclesiastical and civil courts. Nonetheless, biographers have generally accepted that Shakespeare kept his family in Stratford while he rented rooms in London.

Aubrey asserts further that when Shakespeare made his annual visits to Stratford, he 'did commonly in his journey lie' at a tavern belonging to the Davenants, presumably as a family guest. A difficulty with this assertion is that the Davenants moved to Oxford only in 1601, having lived for years just off Three Cranes Wharf across the Thames from the Bankside theatres. The circumstances have nevertheless given rise to the suggestion that William Davenant was Shakespeare's godson, or possibly even his natural son. Alexander Pope is recorded by William Oldys as having entertained the Earl of Oxford's guests at dinner in 1741 with an account of this business, quoting Thomas Betterton as his authority (reprinted in Schoenbaum, *Documentary Life*, 165–6). Davenant as actor and manager certainly had an important role in the growth of Shakespeare's reputation in the seventeenth century. He seems also to be the authority for a theatrical tradition that Shakespeare had instructed John Lowin, his fellow actor, in the performance of the role of King Henry VIII in Shakespeare's play on that subject (1613), and that Lowin had passed this instruction on to Davenant, whence it passed by line of succession to Thomas Betterton, the leading Shakespearean of the late seventeenth century (John Munro, *Shakspere Allusion-Book*, ii. 437–8). Davenant had personally seen *Hamlet* performed by Taylor of the old Blackfriars company, who had been 'instructed by the author Mr. Shakespear' (Downes, *Roscius Anglicanus*, 51 [21], 55 [24], quoted by Gary Taylor, *Reinventing Shakespeare*, 14). If so, Shakespeare's day-to-day involvement in the activities of his acting company remained vital to within three years of his death, even though he may have given up acting before then.

Aubrey reports, less convincingly, that Shakespeare's father was a butcher, and that when Shakespeare was a boy 'he exercised his father's trade'. 'When he killed a calf,' Aubrey continues, 'he would do it in a high style, and make a speech.' This legend feeds in turn on the testimonial of one John Dowdall, who, on a visit to Stratford in 1693, heard from an old parish clerk a story of how Shakespeare had been bound as an apprentice to a butcher but ran away to London, whereupon he was taken into a playhouse as 'servitor' (Schoenbaum, *Documentary Life*, 87). The business about killing a calf sounds like a tale type, especially since it resembles accounts of rural entertainments in which the slaughter of a calf was enacted at country fairs.

A particularly appealing legend, again without solid foundation, has to do with deer-stealing. According to the Revd Richard Davies, who jotted down some notes in the manuscript of a fellow antiquary, William Fulman, some time around the end of the seventeenth century, Shakespeare was 'much given to all unluckiness in stealing venison and rabbits, especially from Sir—Lucy, who had him oft whipped and sometimes imprisoned and at last made him to fly his native country, to his great advancement' (Schoenbaum, *Documentary Life*, 79). Nicholas Rowe picked up this account in his 1709 biography, along with further allegations that Shakespeare had composed a satirical ballad about Lucy, adding thereby to the urgency of his departure. Rowe proposed that this Lucy is to be equated with Sir Thomas Lucy of Charlecote Hall near Stratford, and that this person is then immortalized by Shakespeare in his satirical portrait of Justice Shallow in *2 Henry IV* and *The Merry Wives of Windsor*. Evidently the Lucys were for ever agitating in Parliament for poaching to be made a serious felony and capital offence, as indeed it was to become under the so-called Bloody Code. Although some modern biographers, notably René Weis, Stephen Greenblatt, and Michael Wood, are inclined to credit the story or at least take it seriously, others (such as Schoenbaum) are more sceptical. Charlotte Stopes (*Shakespeare's Warwickshire Contemporaries*, 23–41) and Ian Wilson (p. 92) note that Sir Thomas Lucy did not even have a deer park at Charlecote. Germaine Greer concludes (as do many biographers) that 'we need better evidence than an unsupported anecdote and a reference to deer-stealing in one of Shakespeare's plays [*The Merry Wives of Windsor*] before we can decide once for all that Shakespeare was a deer-stealer' (p. 142), or that the purported episode tells us anything about Shakespeare's reasons for leaving Stratford.

Nicholas Rowe seems not to have known Aubrey's anecdotes; they were published much later. Rowe's biography is of course imperfect; it contains inaccuracies, unverified accounts, and numerous omissions that have been supplied by later biographers. Still, it differs markedly from Aubrey and other collectors of gossip in that it presents a coherent narrative. It speaks of Shakespeare's family and of the hard times on which John Shakespeare appears to have fallen, which, together with 'the want of his [William's] assistance at home', forced his father to withdraw the lad from the King's New School. It reports that Shakespeare's wife, Anne, was 'the daughter of one Hathaway, said to have been a substantial yeoman in the neighborhood of Stratford', i.e. Richard Hathaway—an item confirmed by later investigators, including James Orchard Halliwell-Phillipps, who reported in 1848 that Richard (according to his last will and testament) had died by the time of his daughter's marriage.

Rowe supposes that Shakespeare, arriving in London without financial means or friends, made pocket money by tending the horses of gentlemen as they came to see plays, and by supervising the work of other hired boys under him with such alacrity that he was taken in by the players in a low station from which he quickly advanced. (The story was further elaborated by Samuel Shiels in *The Lives of the Poets* (1753), and then by Samuel Johnson in his edition of 1765; see Schoenbaum, *Documentary Life*, 111–12.) Rowe also reports a tradition handed down by William Davenant, who, Rowe confidently believes, 'was probably very well acquainted with his [Shakespeare's] affairs', 'that my Lord Southampton, at one time, gave him a thousand pounds to enable him to go through with a purchase which he heard he had a mind to'. (More on this in the next chapter.)

Rowe testifies that the part of Falstaff 'is said to have been written originally under the name of Oldcastle; some of that family then remaining, the Queen was pleased to command him [Shakespeare] to alter it; upon which he made use of "Falstaff" '. Rowe informs us how Queen Elizabeth gave Shakespeare 'many gracious marks of her favour', and 'was so well pleased with the admirable character of Falstaff, in the two parts of *Henry the Fourth*, that she commanded him to continue it for one play more, and to show him in love. This is said to be the occasion of his writing *The Merry Wives of Windsor*.' Rowe laments that no lists of assigned parts enable us to determine what roles Shakespeare himself undertook in his own plays, but adds his own assurance 'that the top of his performance was the Ghost in his own *Hamlet*'. Rowe records an episode in which a wealthy citizen of Stratford, John Combe, had the misfortune to become the butt of Shakespeare's biting wit in the form of an imagined extempore epitaph, ending, 'If any man ask, "Who lies in this tomb?" / "Oho!" quoth the devil, "'tis my John-a-Combe".' Of Shakespeare's latest years, Rowe writes: 'He had the good fortune to gather an estate equal to his occasion, and in that, to his wish; and is said to have spent some years before his death in his native Stratford.'

Despite some evidence of satirical sharpness, Rowe is at pains to characterize Shakespeare as an admirable person. 'Besides the advantages of his wit', writes Rowe, 'he was in himself a good-natured man, of great sweetness in his manners, and a most agreeable companion, so that it is no wonder if with so many good qualities he made himself acquainted with the best conversation of those times.' In Stratford, adds Rowe, 'his pleasurable wit and good nature engaged him in the acquaintance, and entitled him to the friendship of, the gentlemen of the neighborhood'. Aubrey similarly insists that Shakespeare 'was a handsome, well-shaped man, very good company, and of a very ready and pleasant smooth wit'. As we have seen, Shakespeare had enemies and critics too, so that, with Duncan-Jones (who notes that Shakespeare's supposedly placid last years were not infrequently marred by quarrels with family and friends), we must be wary of a gathering movement to idealize Shakespeare in the decades, and then the centuries, after his death. Still, it is comforting to realize that many people have wanted to think of him as not only a great writer but a splendid person. The persona that emerges collectively from Shakespeare's writings has no doubt contributed to this tendency to enshrine him as England's greatest writer and exemplary human being. As Rowe put it in 1709, the spirit of the man is to be found in his works.

With Rowe, Shakespeare biography was officially launched, and it retained the basic shape that Rowe had given it for a century at least, with of course added information and commentary. As we have seen, Samuel Johnson, in his 1765 edition of Shakespeare, picked up on and elaborated Rowe's account of Shakespeare supervising hired boys in assisting gentlemen with their horses at the playhouses. Edward Capell, in 1779, provided further details. Edmond Malone, though he did not live to complete the biography on which he worked so assiduously, has provided us with much new information and insight. He conjectured that Shakespeare worked for some country attorney while still living in Stratford. Malone assumed on the basis of stage tradition that Shakespeare's 'first office in the theatre was that of prompter's assistant', that 'his own lively disposition' may have made him acquainted with players like Richard Burbage when they visited Stratford, and that he might then have joined the Queen's Men or 'Lord Warwick's comedians'.

Malone tracked down and published what he understood to be the last will and testament of Shakespeare's father, though he came to doubt the authenticity of the document. (More on this in Chapter 5.) He estimated that Shakespeare earned some £200 a year from his theatrical activities. From his examination of Edward Alleyn's papers, Malone deduced that Shakespeare lived in Southwark, near the Bear Garden, from 1596 to 1608 (the latter portion of which term is unlikely; indeed, Malone may have lost some key records referring, among other matters, to Shakespeare's residency on Bankside). He concluded, from the reference in Shakespeare's will to the 'second-best bed' estated to Anne, that the bequest was symptomatic of 'how little he esteemed her'.

To the late seventeenth-century antiquary William Oldys, who was apparently the first to affix the date 23 April to Shakespeare's birth (St George's Day and three days before the officially recorded baptismal date of 26 April 1564), we are indebted for a conversation that Oldys claims to have had with one of Shakespeare's brothers who, in his ripe old age, recalled having seen William 'act a part in one of his own comedies, wherein, being to personate a decrepit old man, he wore a long beard, and appeared so weak and drooping and unable to walk that he was forced to be supported and carried by another person to a table, at which he was seated among some company, who were eating, and one of them sung a song' (reprinted in Schoenbaum, *Documentary Life*, 149). This item was published by George Steevens in his edition (1778) of the Johnson Shakespeare of 1765. The part that Shakespeare is here reported to have taken must be old Adam in *As You Like It*, in II. vii. Edward Capell, assuming the role to have been that of Adam indeed, added that the old man had been carried on stage 'upon another man's back', presumably that of Orlando (*Notes and Various Readings to Shakespeare*, 1779–83). Since then, biographers have constructed a hypothesis that Shakespeare played old men and perhaps kings (see, for example, Ackroyd, 234), since, as Rowe had claimed, Shakespeare took the part of the Ghost in *Hamlet*. A suspicious weakness to the claim, however, is that none of Shakespeare's three brothers lived on into the time of the Restoration, when the conversation with Oldys purportedly took place. Jonathan Bate suggests that 'the company joke' of having Shakespeare play Adam in *As You Like It* 'would be complete if he also doubled in the role of young William towards the end of the play' (*Genius of Shakespeare*, 7).

By the end of the eighteenth century, Shakespeare's biography had taken its basic shape and had accumulated much new material. The many biographies still to come, including those by Halliwell-Phillipps (mid-nineteenth century), Dowden (1876), Lee (1898), Stopes (1907), Eccles (1961), Schoenbaum (1977–91), Ian Wilson (1993), Wells (1994, 2002), Bate (1997, 2009), Honan (1998), Duncan-Jones (2001), Greenblatt (2004), Ackroyd (2005), Weis (2007), and Greer (2007), would of course challenge assumptions, discover new materials, and open up topics as yet unexplored. That is the subject of what follows, as we turn to particular topics that have fascinated biographers and readers ever since the early days of Shakespeare biography.

3

Sex

Many biographers of Shakespeare have looked expectantly to the plays and poems for insights as to the author's own views on courtship, premarital sex, and marriage. Some biographers detect shifting patterns over the course of Shakespeare's career as he moves from his late twenties towards retirement. Yet difficulties are manifest in attempting to determine from Shakespeare's writings his own personal feelings about erotic pleasure and guilt, about women as seen from a male perspective, and about loving relationships between men. Because this last topic is especially controversial, and because discussion of it centres particularly on the poems and sonnets, with their potential for being more autobiographically revealing than the plays, we will come to it last in this chapter.

A traditional view of Shakespeare, perhaps, is that he is 'the poet of love'. Such indeed is the title of a chapter in M. C. Bradbrook's *Shakespeare* devoted to the romantic comedies and *Romeo and Juliet*. Love, in these plays, is 'a disease—but not a serious disease' (p. 97). The plays generally side with children against their parents, notes Bradbrook, as when Hermia is finally allowed to marry the young man of her choice rather than that of her father Egeus in *A Midsummer Night's Dream*, or when Juliet marries Romeo in secret defiance of her parents' wishes that she become the bride of Count Paris in *Romeo and Juliet*. Richard Dutton speaks for many when he observes that 'most of the romantic comedies end in multiple marriages' or the prospect of such happy unions—even, by implication, *Love's Labour's Lost*. Marriage thus 'perfectly embodies the concept of personal and social concord, when divine harmony touches human lives, as the presence of Hymen suggests at the end of *As You Like It*. At the same time, if marriage is to be 'a world-without-end bargain (*Love's Labour's Lost*, V.ii.779), it must not be undertaken without a trial of the individuals concerned' (Dutton, 93–4; see also James Shapiro, *1599*, 226–9). Portia and Nerissa in *The Merchant of Venice* torment Bassanio and Gratiano with the spectre of marital infidelity; Beatrice and Benedick in *Much Ado About Nothing* spar with each other so incessantly that they have to be tricked into a reconciliation; friendship is severely put to the test by the anxieties of sexual rivalry in *A Midsummer Night's Dream*. Love in these romantic comedies is ecstatic but it is also a battlefield strewn with wounded participants. Shakespeare's comedies are thus simultaneously able to sustain flights of fantasy and to remind us insistently that time, death, and the limits of human physical existence must be acknowledged as well. A result is that these plays are open to a wide variety of interpretations; they present us with an 'inbuilt dual perspective of the fantastic and the real' (Dutton, 94–5).

This dual perspective is everywhere apparent in modern critical discourse about Shakespeare's romantic comedies. It leads to the perception, for example, that men are both the masters and the weaklings in courtship. At times, Shakespeare presents a plausible case for patriarchy and male dominance. Petruchio has his way with Kate in *The Taming of the Shrew*; whether or not she submits willingly or under intolerable duress (and modern interpretations in scholarship and in production run the full gamut from one position to the other), Petruchio is the one who seems to know what will be best for them both as a married couple. He has a plan, and he carries it through to completion, whereas Kate has to reassess who she is and what marriage can offer her. Oberon takes the changeling boy away from Titania in *A Midsummer Night's Dream*, despite her open defiance, and humiliatingly subjects her to a drug-induced love affair with the grossly human Bottom the Weaver, from which she awakens without a word of reproach to her husband. Duke Theseus is no less successful in his conquest of the Amazonian Hippolyta. At the same time, the four young lovers in this play achieve something much closer to mutuality. (See, for example, Dennis Kay, 99–102 and 154–9.)

The young women in the romantic comedies are often more emotionally mature, stable, and loyal than are their male wooers, as biographers and critics of Shakespearean romantic comedy have often observed; see, for example, Park Honan (pp. 247, 258–9). While Proteus in *The Two Gentlemen of Verona* fully lives up to his name by deserting Julia for the beloved of his best friend, Julia is constant, patient, and forgiving. Claudio, in *Much Ado*, is similarly prone to mistrust women in the affairs of the heart, so much so that he nearly destroys the happiness of the innocent and trusting Hero. The young men in *Love's Labour's Lost* are constitutionally unable to hold to their vows of abstinence from romantic engagement, and soon pass on to perjured protestations, while the young ladies they pursue are self-possessed, smart, and sure of what they want from the wooing game. Orlando, in *As You Like It*, responds to his falling in love with Rosalind by posting sonnets to her beauty on the trees of the Forest of Arden, so that to Rosalind falls the responsibility of teaching her young man, while she is disguised as a young man herself, what love should really be about. Orsino in *Twelfth Night* is in similar need of instruction from Viola; so is Bassanio in *The Merchant of Venice* as he is tormented with the spectre of male infidelity by Portia's mirthful manipulations of the ring business. Writers on Shakespeare, such as Georg Brandes (pp. 72–86) and Dennis Kay (pp. 159–63), note that in *Romeo and Juliet*, a tragedy from the time when Shakespeare was writing romantic comedies, the 13-year-old Juliet must wean her starry-eyed Romeo away from airy persiflage about his having flown over the walls of her parents' orchard garden 'With love's light wings' (II. ii. 66); she knows all too well that 'The orchard walls are high and hard to climb', and that her kinsmen will kill Romeo if they find him there.

What do modern biographers make of this paradox that patriarchal males in the romantic comedies are often such helpless fools, or else repressive cads, while the young women are often so long-suffering, wise, and charitable? One hypothesis is that we see in Shakespeare a kind of collective apology, a guilt trip if you like on behalf of males generally. Do we perceive in these plays an implicit admission that men, while they rule the roost economically and legally in domestic relationships, are in fact vulnerable, insecure emotionally, and dependent on women for approval to the vast extent that they do not really understand themselves? Or perhaps the point to be made is that such an admission of male guilt is part of a larger survey of the marriage scene by Shakespeare, a survey that embraces both successful male dominance and self-defeating male insecurity. Does Shakespeare, with his amazing gift for seeing the varying sides of an important issue like courtship and marriage, present his readers and audience with a kind of a debate on the subject, ostensibly at least without taking sides?

This is one way of searching the plays for evidence about Shakespeare himself, though of course a thesis that his approach in the comedies is multiple and even-handed leaves us with no fixed position to attach to the author. That may be the soundest approach. It does at least suggest something potentially significant in a biographical sense, that Shakespeare, writing as still a young man in his late twenties and early thirties, looks upon courtship and marriage as engrossing subjects able to provide important insights into the human psyche. Perhaps too the biographer can hazard a personal connection to what we know of Shakespeare's life. Stephen Greenblatt, for one, wonders if the deep understanding shown in *Romeo and Juliet* about 'what it feels like to be young, desperate to wed, and tormented by delay' has something to do with Shakespeare's own experience in impregnating and then marrying Anne Hathaway in 1582. That event might well have involved 'frantic haste of the rash lovers' resulting in a story of 'humor, irony, poignancy, and disapproval' (p. 122). A similar move towards autobiographical interpretation, one that is deliberately non-factual, can be seen in the film *Shakespeare in Love*, scripted by Marc Norman and Tom Stoppard, in which the young Shakespeare, blighted with writer's block, finds his inspiration for *Romeo and Juliet* in a euphoric if also doomed love affair with a young woman who longs to be an actress. The plot here is patently untrue, in that it ignores Shakespeare's extensive use of a long narrative poem by Arthur Brooke as his source, but in essence it poses an intriguing question: did the real Shakespeare have one or more love affairs in London during those long months extending into years while he lived apart from his wife and family in Stratford? Today, the answer tends to be 'Why not?' (see, for example, Bate, *Soul of the Age*, 172).

An anecdote illustrates the point. A law student, John Manningham, jotted down in his commonplace book in 1602 an account of how Richard Burbage, playing Richard III, attracted the admiration of a woman citizen in the audience. She suggested an assignation, inviting him to come by night to her 'by the name of Richard the Third. Shakespeare, overhearing their conclusion, went before, and was entertained and at his game ere Burbage came. Then message being brought that Richard the Third was at the door, Shakespeare caused return to be made that William the Conqueror was before Richard the Third. Shakespeare's name William.' The story is a tale type and unreliable as a piece of gossip, but it does at least suggest that Shakespeare may have had some reputation around town as a womanizer. Actors, then as now, are often suspected of leading bohemian lives. Bate (*Soul of the Age*, 173–4, 357) wonders if Shakespeare may have taken the part of William the Conqueror in the comedy called *Fair Em*, thus adding a piquant relevance to Manningham's story. Duncan-Jones sees in this anecdote 'a glimpse of Shakespeare as a well-loved "fellow" in the Lord Chamberlain's company, a merry man among merry men, who demonstrated strong affection for his colleagues through jocular banter and sexual competition' (p. 131).

At this point, we need more information about Shakespeare's marriage. The previous chapter has outlined briefly the documentary information: Shakespeare had to apply for a licence from the church to marry with only a single reading of the banns, evidently because Anne was three months pregnant; Susanna would be born in late May of 1583, six months after the hastily arranged marriage on 27 November 1582. Twins arrived in February 1585, some time after which Shakespeare moved to London. Biographers have generally agreed that he did not move his family to the city. The family stayed in Stratford, where Shakespeare provided well for them with handsome housing that he was soon able to afford. He visited Stratford from time to time, no doubt, invested in real estate, seems to have retired there some time around 1611–13 or perhaps earlier (see Bate, *Soul of the Age*, 335–9), and by the time of his death in 1616 had become such a leading citizen of the town that he lies buried before the altar of Holy Trinity Church, next to Anne, who died in 1623. They had no children after 1585. Shakespeare willed to her his 'second-best bed with the furniture'.

Biographers have been sharply divided, as Jonathan Bate observes (*Soul of the Age*, 179), as to whether the marriage was a success or not. To begin with the bed: a long-standing tradition has tried to explain away the seeming oddity of the bequest by supposing that Shakespeare and his family would have reserved the best bed for distinguished guests, and that (as Schoenbaum puts it) 'the less valuable bed was the one rich in matrimonial associations' (*Compact Documentary Life*, 302). Schoenbaum observes elsewhere that biographers before Edmond Malone in the late eighteenth century 'had not worried much about the poet's conjugal relations', and that as late as 1779, a biographer writing in *The Modern Universal British Traveller* confidently asserted that Shakespeare 'lived very happy' with Anne, even undertaking to fetch her to London once he had enough money to be able to do so (*Shakespeare's Lives*, 119–20). Researches into other wills of the period have found other instances of second-best beds disposed of in similar ways. Joyce Rogers has devoted an entire book to the proposition that Shakespeare's will 'was conventional as possible' and that 'even the phrase "second best" was in accordance with the law and custom of his time' (p. xiv). Jonathan Bate reminds us that 'under common law Anne Shakespeare would have been entitled to a third of her husband's estate and to residence in his house for the remainder of her life' (*Genius of Shakespeare*, 4), even if the will should fail (as in this case) to bequeath her anything more material than a bed. J. W. Gray defends the marriage against 'The long series of adverse comments upon Shakespeare and his wife' (p. 2) that began in the late seventeenth century. In A. L. Rowse's view, Shakespeare 'showed exceptional care for the comfort of his widow' (letter to the *TLS*, 25 November 1994, quoted by Duncan-Jones, 272).

Germaine Greer, conceding that Shakespeare's last will and testament is 'lop-sided' and unusual in not appointing Anne (or Ann, as Greer prefers) as executor, wonders if Shakespeare might have considered Anne, at 60 years of age, too old to handle the responsibility well, or might have disagreed with her over his 'meanness' towards their daughter Judith for having 'thrown herself away on Thomas Quiney much as Ann Hathaway had on young Will Shakespeare'. More plausibly, in Greer's view, Shakespeare had written up a settlement at the time of Susanna's marriage to John Hall in such a way that he 'was not free to split his estate or devise any of it to Judith, or, indeed, to Ann'. Anne may have been financially independent by this time. Other 'second-best beds' turn up in wills without any implication of slighting the recipient. Beds were valuable objects. Other properties, such as Shakespeare's books, not mentioned in the will, could easily have been transferred by other deeds. (An inventory presumably did exist, but is now lost.) The will is surprisingly ungenerous in its provisions for the relief of Stratford's poor, and Shakespeare's gifts to colleagues in the King's company were comparatively meagre. Perhaps then the lack of a more substantial bequest in the will for Anne is not a legitimate cause for concern (pp. 242, 314–25).

On the other hand, a more disparaging interpretation, going back at least to Malone (see Schoenbaum, *Documentary Life*, 247–8), sees the bequest as churlish and the marriage as beset by difficulties. Malone quoted an observation by William Oldys in 1691 that Sonnets 92 and 93 'seem to have been addressed by Shakespeare to his beautiful wife on some suspicion of her infidelity' (Schoenbaum, *Shakespeare's Lives*, 119, citing Malone's *Supplement* to the 1778 Johnson/Steevens edition of Shakespeare's plays (1780), 1. 653). Ernst Honigmann, in his essay on 'The Second-Best Bed', concludes that Shakespeare's will is indeed uncharitable towards his wife when it is compared with similar documents of the period. Katherine Duncan-Jones joins with Honigmann in finding other evidence in the will of anger or disappointment, as seen in the large number of names struck out or omitted. She speculates as well that Shakespeare was suffering from syphilis in his last illness, and that he may have been depressed and dependent on alcohol as a pain-reliever (pp. 266, 272–5).

Anthony Holden (*William Shakespeare: His Life and Work*, 128–9) is equally convinced that Shakespeare must have experienced 'a bout or two of the clap (gonorrhoea)', and that the fear of syphilis hung over him in his later years, inspiring outbursts against 'Consumptions' that 'sow / In hollow bones of man' (*Timon of Athens*, IV. iii. 153 ff.) and against the 'sulfurous pit' of consumption that the mad King Lear imagines to inhabit the sexual anatomy of women (*Lear*, IV. vi. 128–9). Shakespeare's last two sonnets, 153 and 154, with their talk of 'a seething bath' employed as a 'sovereign cure' for 'strange maladies', may suggest that he took the mercury-bath cure for syphilis (Bate, *Soul of the Age*, 47, 175–7). Germaine Greer wonders if a bout with a sexually transmitted disease in Shakespeare's early years, a succumbing to 'a momentary urge', might have cost him the 'connubial comforts of his marriage to Ann', lest he infect his wife with this dread illness (pp. 296–7). Perhaps too, Greer speculates, we can see signs of mental confusion in his declining years that could have been the unhappy result of illness and of debilitating treatment with mercury chloride, leading to a shortening of his writing career and his early death (p. 305). The presumably happy picture of Shakespeare's retirement has been called into question, and with it the issue as to whether he was reconciled to spending his last years with Anne.

The circumstance of the hastily arranged marriage in 1582 has prompted a number of biographers to conclude that the marriage was a mistake. Whether or not the pregnancy was brought on by a passionate encounter, as imagined somewhat luridly by Anthony Burgess in his *Nothing Like the Sun* (p. 28 ff.), one can suppose, with Greenblatt, that an 18-year-old lad might not have been eager to tie himself down in marriage, especially with a woman eight years his senior and at a time in his life when financial resources and employment opportunities must have been scarce. Many writers on Shakespeare (e.g. Ackroyd, 90 and Rees, 22) have wondered if the portrayal in *Measure for Measure* of an unwanted pregnancy and ensuing difficulties with the law might not be Shakespeare's way of revisiting, via his art and after an interval of some twenty-one years, the scene of his own costly youthful indiscretion.

The whole subject of marriage *de presenti*, a favourite topic of recent feminist criticism, has depicted Shakespeare as fascinated with the way in which an engagement could, in principle at least, become binding for ever if a man and a women exchanged vows in the presence of a witness (or not), quite apart from any church ceremony. Germaine Greer, to be sure, asserts that 'premarital pregnancy was no disgrace at all' for 'an honest woman who was not free with her favours' (p. 122). Jonathan Bate (*Soul of the Age*, 252) concurs that 'it was not necessarily scandalous for the bride to be pregnant'. Greer insists that even if the impregnation were accidental rather than deliberate, Shakespeare 'could have evaded marriage with her if he so chose, just as Lucio evaded marriage with Kate Keepdown in *Measure for Measure*', promises of marriage, prolonged cohabitation, and pregnancy to the contrary notwithstanding (pp. 77–8); but Greer allows that the exchanging of vows while holding right hands was indeed binding. The words—'I take thee Anne to be my wife' and 'I take thee William to be my husband'—'were what constituted the sacrament' (p. 87).

The fact that William and Anne had no more children after the twins in 1585 has been interpreted as a sign that they did not cohabit after that date, though divorce would have been impossible (see Ackroyd, 99–100 and ff.). Germaine Greer is of course right that the reasons for their having no more children could have been medical, given the traumas and risks of infection associated with giving birth in an age of rudimentary health care, and she is also right that many gentlemen preferred to leave their wives in the country for months or even years on end without any implication of marital difference (pp. 143–4). Even so, the combined circumstances have seemed, for many biographers, to hang together: a romantic encounter, an unplanned pregnancy and hasty marriage, and children within the first three years of that union followed by the evident decision of the husband to live and work in London for two decades or more while supporting his family in Stratford and retiring there only when he needed to retire, perhaps for reasons of health. The fact that he continued to write for his company, collaborating with John Fletcher on *Henry VIII* in 1613 and *The Two Noble Kinsmen* and perhaps *Cardenio* soon after that, after some earlier collaborating as well on *Timon of Athens* among other plays (*Macbeth* was revised by Thomas Middleton), has also suggested to biographers (e.g. Greenblatt, 378–9, and Holden, *Life and Work*, 305–6) that Shakespeare remained a part of the London theatrical scene, even if part-time, as long as he was able.

Some of the late romances, notably *The Winter's Tale* and *The Tempest*, have struck writers like Stephen Greenblatt and Richard Wheeler as filled with autobiographical resonance. *The Winter's Tale*, with its saga of a man who apparently sacrifices his loyal wife and son to his irrationally jealous rage, abandons his newborn daughter to seeming death, and then at last is given the almost miraculous chance to recover his wife and daughter and to discover that he still loves the woman he abandoned a whole generation ago, fits so well the imagined pattern of Shakespeare's own long separation and reunion that writers have wondered if the dramatist is using the theatre as a space of personal fantasy to sort out his own life. Perhaps too he is settling scores with Robert Greene, as Duncan-Jones suggests (p. 229); Greene too had lived apart from his wife and then supposedly wrote a penitent letter to her the day before he died. *The Tempest*, as Stephen Orgel notes, writes the wife almost completely out of the story, leaving a widower father with a single daughter and a son-in-law to his immense liking—a gesture, it might seem, in the direction of Dr John Hall, whom Susanna had married in 1607. Does the disappearance in *The Tempest* of the happily recovered wife of *The Winter's Tale* point to a disappointment of hopes that retirement could bring with it a genuine reconciliation? The subject is much debated; see, among others, Bevington, *Shakespeare* (2005), and *Shakespeare's Ideas* (2008). More on this in Chapter 6.

What potential hints do we find in the plays and poems about Shakespeare's own sexuality? The topic is of course risky and specu-lative, but is one that has inevitably engrossed some biographers. Are the situations that Shakespeare chooses to dramatize a possible key to his own fantasies? Orsino, in *Twelfth Night*, is visibly attracted to a seeming young man of indeterminate sexual characteristics. 'Diana's lip / Is not more smooth and rubious', he says to Viola/Cesario. 'Thy small pipe / Is as the maiden's organ, shrill and sound, / And all is semblative a woman's part' (I. iv. 31–4). Modern stage productions sometimes make comic capital out of an Orsino who in the finale is not quite sure whether he would prefer to couple with Sebastian or Viola, since they look so much alike. Greenblatt wonders if part of Shakespeare's early fascination with theatre was that, with boy actors in women's parts, 'theatrical performance and sexual arousal were braided together' (p. 28).

The early poem *Venus and Adonis* (1593) revels in the portrait of a young man who 'burns with bashful shame' at the prospect of be-coming the lover of the goddess Venus. He and the reader are invited to inspect her ample body in an extended erotic blazon of her sexual anatomy, and yet his preference is for manly hunting. The poem is as much interested in caressing the physical charms of Adonis as it is those of Venus, dwelling for example on the dimples in his cheeks, 'lovely caves' and 'round enchanting pits' where Love might wish to be swallowed up and buried (ll. 49–50, 229–48; see Greenblatt, 243, and Honan, 173–4). René Weis is sympathetic to the idea 'that a latent homosexuality attracted Shakespeare to boy-girl transvestism', noting that he uses the motif in no fewer than five plays spanning his artistic career from *The Two Gentlemen of Verona* to *Cymbeline* (p. 256).

Revulsion at the physicality of heterosexual lovemaking is a strik-ingly recurrent theme in Shakespeare, even if it is by no means his invariable response to erotic desire for the opposite sex. When Posthumus Leonatus is led to believe, in *Cymbeline*, that his wife Imogen has betrayed him with other men, what offends him most is that she seemed so reluctant even in the intimate embraces of their marriage. 'Me of my lawful pleasure she restrained / And prayed me oft forbearance; did it with / A pudency so rosy the sweet view on't / Might well have warmed old Saturn, that I thought her / As chaste as unsunnèd show' (II. v. 9–13), he laments. This young man has cherished what we might call frigidity in his wife because it has seemed to betoken a lack of desire for sexual ecstasy that ought to safeguard her against desire for other men. And yet, he fantasizes, at the first such opportunity the hated sexual rival, without so much as a word, 'Cried "Oh!" and mounted' (l. 17). The language is, as A. D. Nuttall observes, 'relishingly gross' (p. 344). Hamlet's fervent lecture to his mother on the need for sexual restraint is laden with images of her bestial coupling with Claudius 'In the rank corruption of an enseamèd bed, / Stewed in corruption, honeying and making love / Over the nasty sty' (*Hamlet*, III. iv. 94–6). In Hamlet's tortured imagination, she has allowed Claudius to savour 'a pair of reechy kisses' and to paddle in her neck 'with his damned fingers' (ll. 191–2). 'The heyday in the blood' should be 'tame' at Gertrude's time of life (l. 70), he insists, in a woman past menopause and with a grown son.

King Lear's mad ranting about women's 'riotous appetite', demonstrating to him how 'Down from the waist they're centaurs, / Though women all above', is all the more devastating in that Lear, though he has been grossly mistreated by his two elder daughters, has not been subjected himself, so far as we know, to the torments of cuckoldry. He has wondered fleetingly if his dead wife's tomb might be 'Sepulch'ring an adultress' (II. iv. 130–1), but that was in his hyperbolic rage at the thought that his wife could have presented him with such a daughter as Regan. Lear comes to recognize, as Janet Adelman observes, 'not only his terrifying dependence on female forces outside himself but also an equally terrifying femaleness within himself' (*Suffocating Mothers*, 104). These are of course dramatizations on Shakespeare's part, not personal confessions, but they have prompted biographers like Greenblatt and Weis to speculate that they are fantastical reworkings of a life in which Shakespeare, choosing to dwell apart from his wife, then found himself desperately in need of some other emotional attachment but also revulsed by his own carnality (see, for example, Greenblatt, 143, 254).

At the same time we must not forget the extent to which Shakespeare's romantic comedies, early in his career, do seem to celebrate the coupling of young men and women. A London newspaper reported some years ago that the headmistress of a girls' school had decided not to take her charges to a performance of *Romeo and Juliet* because, as she said, 'the play is so relentlessly heterosexual'. (She must have been unaware of a recent theatrical trend to explore the potentially homoerotic dimensions of Mercutio's fondness for Romeo, but let that pass.) The plays of the early years especially are alive with portrayals of male desire and fascination with the female body, however awkwardly the young men put these longings to use in the rituals of courtship. One endearing example is in *Love's Labour's Lost*, when the infatuated Dumaine imagines what it would be like to have a street paved with his eyeballs; if his beloved Katharine were to walk on such a street, what then would the eyes behold? 'Oh, vile!' he exclaims. 'Then, as she goes, what upward lies / The street should see as she walked overhead' (IV. iii. 276–7). The imagined prospect is both repellent and irresistible to Dumaine in his voyeuristic curiosity to see what lies hidden beneath her skirt. Germaine Greer, intent on defending Shakespeare's marriage to Anne as a loving one, wonders if Shakespeare's wife Anne might not have recognized in the oddly matched coupling of Venus and Adonis a portrait of 'the desirous older woman and her boy husband', that is, Anne herself and Shakespeare (p. 190). In Sonnet 145 too, argues Greer, Anne 'would have encountered herself as Will's relenting mistress' (p. 257), and perhaps in other sonnets as well, such as Sonnets 25, 27, 28, 29, 110, 111, 116, and 117, along with 'A Lover's Complaint' (p. 260).

The young men of the early plays are often more eager for sex than are the young women. Lysander, in *A Midsummer Night's Dream*, loses his way in the forest, perhaps by design, so that he can propose to Hermia that they bed down together for the night on the forest floor. 'One turf shall serve as pillow for us both; / One heart, one bed, two bosoms, and one troth', he hopefully suggests (II. ii 47–8). She demurs, amiably enough, but with a chaste firmness of purpose that may add some psychological dimension to Lysander's deserting her when, under the influence of the love juice, he awakens and finds himself in love with Helena instead. Romeo's suggestive plea to Juliet on the night of their first extended conversation, 'Oh, wilt thou leave me so unsatisfied?' similarly elicits from Juliet a response that is impeccably chaste though still loving: 'What satisfaction canst thou have tonight?', she asks, leaving Romeo to come up with a comically lame excuse: 'Th'exchange of thy love's faithful vow for mine' (*Romeo and Juliet*, II. ii. 125–7). Elsewhere, too, as M. C. Bradbrook argues, this is 'an exceptionally bawdy play' (p. 100), albeit with a kind of heartily heterosexual joking that presumably endeared itself to popular London audiences and, more recently, to historical critics like Alfred Harbage.

Harbage's insistence, in *As They Liked It* and *Shakespeare and the Rival Traditions*, on the wholesomeness of the sexuality in Shakespeare's romantic comedies attempts to position the dramatist as a centrist, a truly popular writer, unlike trendy avant-garde writers like John Marston who, in Harbage's view, exploited the boys' theatre for its salacious and transgressive potential. Such a view must do battle today with an increasing acknowledgement by Shakespeare's biographers that his sexual orientation may have been bisexual and even homosexual, perhaps latently so. The Sonnets have of course been the text most avidly analysed for clues.

The topic has caused considerable distress. As early as the late eighteenth century, George Steevens remarked (in the so-called Johnson–Steevens edition of 1773) that he found it impossible to read Shakespeare's sonnets 'without an equal mixture of disgust and indignation'. Steevens wrote this as Romanticism was coming into fashion in Great Britain. With that movement came a strong urge to read Shakespeare as a Romantic poet before his time, chronicling the most profound feelings of the human heart and soul in a movingly autobiographical testimonial. Wordsworth and Keats were to urge the point in the early nineteenth century. Wordsworth wrote: 'With these poems Shakespeare unlocked his heart.' Samuel Taylor Coleridge, caught up in that spirit of Romanticism and thus wanting to read the Sonnets as a psycho-biography of England's greatest writer, was sufficiently alarmed by the spectre of homoeroticism that he preferred to see the Sonnets (all but two) as having been written to a woman (see Stallybrass). Better this, in Coleridge's view, than to allow that the jewel of England's literary heritage was gay! Coleridge insisted (inaccurately) to his son Hartley that the entire Shakespeare canon contains not even one allusion 'to that very worst of all possible vices'; Shakespeare's love for his friend was 'pure' (see Hyder Rollins's Variorum edition of *The Sonnets* (1944), ii. 232 ff.). Even earlier, the first reprint of the Sonnets in 1640 had altered some pronouns from male to female 'as if in deference to the requirements of decorum' (Wells, *Shakespeare for All Time*, 89, 361).

Coleridge's argument that nearly all the sonnets were written to a woman was too implausible to win many adherents, but it at least pinpointed the problem. A major tactic in the early twentieth century and even earlier has been to historicize the issue by demonstrating how sonnet sequences in the late sixteenth century were very often formal exercises, conforming to the dimensions of a popular genre with no distinguishable autobiographical content. And indeed, the confections of sonneteers like Thomas Watson, Samuel Daniel, Henry Constable, Thomas Lodge, William Percy, Michael Drayton, and others during the height of the sonnet craze in the 1590s, in which poet-personas bewailed in Petrarchan fashion their unrequited loves for Delia, or Diana, or Licia, or Celia, amply showed how artifice frequently carried the day. Conversely, to be sure, Spenser's *Amoretti* and Sidney's *Astrophel and Stella* provided substantive material for autobiographical interpretation. Still, the historical perspective offers the valuable caveat that sonnets need not be autobiographical in any detailed sense, and that Shakespeare, with his mastery of dramatic voices in his plays, was certainly capable of narrating a sonnet sequence without having lived through a comparable experience, just as he was capable of dramatizing a murder without having, so far as we know, killed anyone. John Donne said of himself, late in life, in a letter to his friend Sir Robert Ker: 'I did best when I had least truth for my subjects.' As Alexander Dyce drily put the matter, in his 1857 edition of Shakespeare's works: 'I have yet to learn that the fancy of Shakespeare could not luxuriate in rural images even amid the fogs of Southwark and the Blackfriars.' (See 'The Sonnets: Divers Theories' in Schoenbaum, *Shakespeare's Lives*, 314–20.)

Today, this cautionary historical argument has lost favour. Whereas formerly scholars and biographers were inclined to be sceptical about the ordering of the sonnets, especially in view of the seeming fact that Shakespeare was not involved in their publication in 1609, today the ordering of the sonnets is accepted as not only the best solution we have but a meaningful one. Caution in identifying the Earl of Southampton as the love-object behind Shakespeare's outpourings of emotional attachment and the patron who enabled Shakespeare to buy a share in the Chamberlain's Men in 1594 has given way in many instances to an argument that the relationship was indeed a love affair and perhaps consummated physically. Weis speculates that Southampton and Marlowe may have enjoyed 'ganymedic relations' on more than one occasion, thus fueling the anxiety that the poet-persona of Shakespeare's sonnets feels for the rival poet (p. 138). Shoreditch, says Weis, was a place to which homosexuals gravitated, Southampton among them (p. 259). Southampton's connection with the Earl of Essex, who was sometimes lauded (by George Chapman among others) as the Achilles of his generation, might seem to have inspired Shakespeare's portrayal of homosexuality in his *Troilus and Cressida*; Weis is confident that Southampton is to be seen in the character of Achilles's 'male whore', Patroclus (pp. 262, 331), and is no less sure that 'at its most daring', the loving relationship of Southampton and Shakespeare was 'a full-blown homoerotic affair which stopped just short of physical consummation' (p. 116). Perhaps Marlowe introduced them to each other (p. 129).

Weis (pp. 114–15) is also inclined to credit the assertion of Rowe, offered back in 1709, that 'Southampton at one time gave him [Shakespeare] a thousand pounds', whereas Schoenbaum among others is doubtful that the earl, who was under some financial pressure at the time, would have offered such an astonishingly large gift (*Compact Documentary Life*, 179); Duncan-Jones too concludes that 'the sum reportedly named really is incredible' (p. 85).

Greenblatt too considers Southampton to be the likeliest candidate as the young man to whom the early sonnets are addressed, but adds that William Herbert, the Earl of Pembroke, who was also to show favour to Shakespeare, is a more likely recipient of the sonnets of the late 1590s (p. 232). Jonathan Bate (*Soul of the Age*, 205–16) adds that the later sonnets, written around 1603–5, may have been intended both for Pembroke and for his brother Philip. Greenblatt sees Shakespeare as having been profoundly shaken in 1601 by the execution of the Earl of Essex, after his failed uprising, putting in immediate jeopardy of a similar fate 'Shakespeare's patron, friend, and possible lover, the Earl of Southampton' (p. 308). Peter Ackroyd (p. 210) and Bate (*Soul of the Age*, 6) think it quite possible that Shakespeare became secretary to Southampton for a time in 1593.

Duncan-Jones, on the other hand, introduces a note of caution: 'Perhaps Shakespeare's "love" for his young patron was distant and formal', she suggests, adding, 'Perhaps, on the other hand, it was not' (p. 81). Artists and writers of the period not uncommonly eroticized their proclamations of devotion to a patron, and thus their effusions need not be taken too seriously in any given case. Schoenbaum argues that the tone of Shakespeare's dedication to Southampton of *Venus and Adonis* (1593) 'argues no great intimacy between poet and patron'; and, although (*pace* E. K. Chambers) he does concede a greater warmth in the 1594 dedication to *The Rape of Lucrece* than in *Venus and Adonis*, Schoenbaum stops short of suspecting anything amorous (*Compact Documentary Life*, 173–8). Dutton notes the total lack of evidence of Shakespeare's having sought patronage after 1594, from Southampton or anyone else (p. 39). Dutton stresses too the formal nature of Petrarchan love poetry as discouraging autobiographical speculation. Ackroyd argues that the Sonnets 'are perhaps best seen as a performance' (p. 307). John Bailey is similarly sceptical: 'Poetry is imagination, not fact' (p. 60). Ian Wilson is convinced that Southampton is indeed the young man addressed in the sonnets, but argues for a 'marriage of true minds' based more on a shared and secret Catholic sympathy than on erotic attraction; Shakespeare, in Wilson's view, was (unlike Marlowe) 'genuinely God-fearing, at a time when sodomy was a capital offence and religious people of all persuasions regarded it as an instant passport to hell' (p. 146).

Chambers was the first to suggest that Southampton's gift (of whatever size) was an act of patronage in response to the two dedications, and that the money might have secured for Shakespeare a coveted membership as actor-sharer in the Chamberlain's company that year. Andrew Gurr, on the other hand, has proposed (in a personal communication to Duncan-Jones, 85, agreed with by Greer, 202) that Shakespeare might have paid for his share by the play-manuscripts that he brought with him from his previous labours for other acting companies. Biographers generally agree that Southampton had a reputation for a kind of feminine beauty, as borne out in contemporary portraits of him by Nicholas Hilliard and others.

Southampton is thus a strongly plausible candidate to have served as patron, since Shakespeare did address two dedications to him. His age and family situation make him a plausible candidate too for the fair youth of the Sonnets (as Eric Sams argues, 103–13), since his family were anxious that he marry and would no doubt have welcomed a poetic endorsement by Shakespeare of that idea in the early sonnets of the sequence. The theory of a deeply emotional relationship depends on one's assessment of the Sonnets themselves, and on other possible hints of homoerotic or bisexual leanings in other of Shakespeare's writings.

What then of the Sonnets as a purported source of insight into Shakespeare's own personal life? As Stanley Wells puts the matter, much 'direct information about Shakespeare's intimate life can be derived from his Sonnets—provided, that is, that we take them to be autobiographical' (*Shakespeare for All Time*, 84). As Touchstone in *As You Like It* famously exclaims, 'Much virtue in if!' (V. iv. 101–2). Wells, fully aware of the hazards of such speculation, admits that in his own view the Sonnets, especially 'those that seem most revelatory of sexual infatuation and self-disgust, are private poems, personal and almost confessional in nature' (pp. 87–8). Here is where Shakespeare's Sonnets differ from the sequences of his contemporaries. Without laying any great stress on a particular historical connection, Wells persuasively views the Sonnets as a testimonial to the inner and imaginative life of their author. Park Honan too insists that, whatever may or may not have been the historical 'facts' behind the Sonnets, Shakespeare unquestionably 'delights in sexual ambiguity' in these poems, giving to his narrative a 'homoerotic or, at times, bisexual aspect' (p. 186). Peter Levi entertains 'no doubt at all' from his writings that Shakespeare 'was imaginatively bisexual' (p. 33). Germaine Greer, on the other hand, finds the idea preposterous. 'If the sonnets had been interpreted as any such thing', she writes, 'they would have been suppressed, and all known copies burnt. Thorpe would never have dared openly publish them. Sodomy, if proven, was a hanging matter' (p. 255).

The Sonnets centre primarily on a deep emotional attachment of the poet-speaker to a 'a man right fair' (Sonnet 144, line 3), a 'lovely boy' (126. 1), a 'fair friend' (104. 1) who is so much above the poet-speaker in social station that the poet reckons himself unworthy of reciprocated affection. Nonetheless the poet-speaker revels in his happier moments in this love. The loving relationship offers him consolation against the ravages of time, human ingratitude, and his own failings. The poet eagerly offers to his friend advice on marrying, so that the friend's beauty may be eternized through procreation. Physical absence from his friend is a torment, compensated only by the all-important realization that true friendship can hope to transcend distance and separation. Many of Shakespeare's best-known sonnets are read today at wedding ceremonies and anniversaries and such because they celebrate a love that is strong, eternal, and proof against the vicissitudes of human suffering.

Yet the Sonnets also explore jealousy, betrayal, self-loathing, and bitter disappointment. A rival poet claims the friend's attention and personal loyalty. Sleepless and heartbroken, the poet finds himself rejected where most he seeks comfort. He finds that he cannot blame the friend for leaving him, for the poet is only too aware of his own shortcomings. Self-pityingly, he bids the friend not to mourn the poet when he dies, lest the world mock him for caring for a person of such small significance. The poet doubts his ability as a writer. He confesses in Sonnets 110–11 that he has made himself 'a motley to the view' and deplores his career of 'public means which public manners breeds'—something that an actor might say of himself (see Nicholl, 23, and Bate, *Genius of Shakespeare*, 19).

These are the expressions of deep and painful emotional involvement, felt by a male speaker towards a handsome man. Beyond question, the speaker feels a strong and infatuated love for the man he addresses. To be sure, he is at pains, in Sonnet 20, to insist that physical consummation is out of the question. Nature has 'pricked' the friend out 'for women's pleasure' by providing him with 'one thing to my purpose nothing', namely, the phallus; the poet speaks as though physical union between two males is impossible, or at least contrary to 'Nature'. The important point for the speaker is that he has what really matters, the friend's love; women may enjoy the friend's sexuality and enable him to procreate children, but to the poet such erotic and biological processes are peripheral to true love and indeed are likely to be distracting and harmful. (Possibly, of course, the speaker here 'doth protest too much'; Joseph Pequigney has devoted a book-length study to arguing that the Sonnets do portray a consummated homosexual love affair.)

Heterosexual love in the Sonnets, at least as embodied in the poet's compulsive desire for a dark-complexioned lady whom the friend then takes away from him, is an unhappy and even disgusting experience for the poet-speaker. 'Lust in action', he says, is 'perjured, murd'rous, bloody, full of blame, / Savage, extreme, rude, cruel, not to trust'. Such lust is 'Past reason hunted', and then, 'no sooner had / Past reason hated'. The sad truth of this observation is universally acknowledged, and yet no one knows how 'To shun the heaven that leads men to this hell' (Sonnet 129). As in the passage quoted above from *Cymbeline* in which Posthumus Leonatus expresses mistrust of women and a deep longing for surcease from the self-loathing of male sexual desire, these painful ruminations are suggestively autobiographical to Wells and others (Greenblatt, Weis) because they originate in Shakespeare's imagination. He may not have done all the things chronicled in his Sonnet sequence, but he lived at least a vicarious existence in these remarkable poems. Bate deems it highly probable that Sonnet 129 is premised on distasteful personal experience, and that 'it is hard to imagine a Shakespeare who had no sexual life during his long residence in London' (*Soul of the Age*, 172). Other passages in Shakespeare's writings testify to an absorbed interest in the question, as when, in *Love's Labour's Lost*, Berowne castigates himself for his enslavement to a dark-haired beauty 'With two pitch-balls stuck in her face for eyes' (III. i. 195), or when Angelo, in *Measure for Measure*, finds himself unable to control his desire to ravish the novitiate Isabella when his whole life up to this point has been anchored in self-control and punishment of sexual laxness in others.

Biographers and other critics have had to deal with the question of male-to-male emotional attachment elsewhere in the Shakespeare canon. Is Antonio, in *The Merchant of Venice*, what we would call gay? He certainly is fond, even doting, in his affection for Bassanio, to the extent of risking his very life for the young friend. He speaks explicitly of his love for Bassanio, who replies in kind (I. i. 131–2, 154). At the play's end, Antonio remains unattached amidst a heterosexual parade to the altar. Ask any actor today if Antonio is gay, and the answer is likely to be, 'Yes, of course, why do you ask?' René Weis wonders if, in the 'homoerotic subtext' that 'may linger beneath the surface', we are to read Shakespeare himself in Antonio, with

Southampton as the Bassanio who marries and thus leaves his friend behind (p. 236). Thus to Weis the play is 'the final salvo in a contest between homosexual and straight sex that involved Shakespeare, Southampton, Marlowe, and Emilia Bassano' (p. 238)—the so-called 'Dark Lady' of the Sonnets identified as such to his own satisfaction and to almost no one else's (other than Michael Wood) by A. L. Rowse, the ironic consequence of which has been to establish Emilia Lanier Bassano not as the 'Dark Lady' but as today a much-appreciated woman writer of the English Renaissance. (Bate, *Genius of Shakespeare*, 54–8, makes a more intriguing case for the wife of John Florio, who was also the sister of the poet Samuel Daniel, as the Dark Lady.) The 'silent stoicism of homosexual men in ordinary heterosexual cultures' is something that Antonio shares with Iago, Weis suggests (p. 288). Greenblatt concurs that Antonio 'is hopelessly in love with the young man' (p. 257). Jeremy Irons, in Michael Radford's 2004 film, sensitively portrays Antonio as a man who perhaps does not understand his own unexplored feelings for Bassanio. In Bill Alexander's production at Stratford-upon-Avon in 1987, as Wells writes, 'there was no doubt that Antonio's melancholy stemmed from frustrated desire for Bassanio: he reeled as Bassanio spoke in praise of Portia, and kissed him with despairing passion but little response as they parted' (*Shakespeare: A Dramatic Life*, 162). More sceptical observers point out that Antonio does everything in his power to encourage Bassanio's marriage to Portia, and joins with them in the finale as a happy avuncular witness to their marital bliss. The question remains very much in debate.

Another Antonio, in *Twelfth Night*, speaks movingly of his love for Sebastian after they have landed ashore in Illyria and must decide what to do next. 'If you will not murder me for my love, let me be your servant', pleads Antonio, asking that he be allowed to accompany Sebastian in whatever happens (II. i. 1.33–4). As Wells observes, 'That is strong language' (*Shakespeare for All Time*, 89). Again, actors today opt almost without exception for a gay interpretation, as when, in Andrei Serban's 1989 production at the American Repertory Theatre in Cambridge, Massachusetts, this scene was set in a dimly lit singles bar with men in their undershirts.

Biography has also explored the question of whether Iago is motivated in his evil plotting by 'a subconscious affection for the

Moor, the homosexual foundation of which he did not understand' (Ernest Jones, quoted in Marvin Rosenberg, *The Masks of Othello* (1961), 158, and Wells, *Shakespeare for All Time*, 361–2), and whether Coriolanus's feelings of love and hate for Aufidius need to be explained in similar terms. More traditional interpreters point out that the language of love was used more freely among men in the Early Modern period than we encounter today, and argue that recent gay interpretations are anachronistic in their definitions of terms. Still, we are left with Shakespeare's world of imagination in which fantasies of bisexual or homoerotic longings are an enduring and perhaps deeply personal part of his artistic vision, along with a no less keen interest in womanly beauty as seen from a male perspective.

We will come back to issues of sexuality in Chapters 6 and 7, when we look at jealousy, misogyny, fears of ageing, and similar questions that come into special prominence in the second half of Shakespeare's career.

4

Politics

Ever since the early nineteenth century, if not before, the divisive issue among biographers and other writers on Shakespeare as a political thinker is whether, in the words of W. S. Gilbert, he should be considered as having been born into this world 'either a little Liberal / Or else a little Conservative'. Or perhaps something of both, or else unknowable in personal terms since he is so adept as a dramatist at portraying multiple sides of any given issue. The terms 'liberal' and 'conservative' are of course in need of definition. In an Early Modern context they tend to posit on the one hand a faith in the popular voice and change towards some degree of participatory government, and on the other a belief in monarchical divine right and hierarchy in the state and family as a surest defence against anarchy. In these terms, does Shakespeare offer critique or support for official policies, both country-wide and local, on such issues as the waging of war, national security at home, protection of civil liberties, censorship, immigration, poor laws, and distribution of wealth?

Such topics are inviting to biographers because they often involve specific historical circumstances, including war with Spain in 1588 and afterwards in which England sided with the Protestant Netherlands, rebellion in Ireland in 1597, the abortive rebellion of the Earl of Essex in 1601, the passing of an Elizabethan Poor Law in that same year charging parishes with providing for the needy, King James's troubles with the Puritan wing of the English church at the Hampton Court Conference of 1604, and the attempt by Guy Fawkes and other conspirators in 1605 to blow up the houses of Parliament. Can Shakespeare's positions on such developments be adduced from his plays and poems, and do those positions and developments then form a part of his evolving biography?

A related question for biographers is whether we should fault Shakespeare for failing to live up to what we might hope or expect of England's greatest writer, or whether we should be tolerant of attitudes that perhaps differ from ours in view of his having lived some 400 years ago. A more revisionist tactic, as signalled in the title of Jan Kott's *Shakespeare Our Contemporary*, published first in Polish and then in English in 1964 after the Second World War and in the era of growing opposition to the war in Vietnam, is to argue that Shakespeare's nominal acceptance of the status quo in his own day was a necessary cover for unacceptably radical ideas and that he really is, today, our contemporary. Productions on stage and on screen have participated in this lively debate. Then, too, the biographer may wish to consider whether Shakespeare's positions on political matters shifted as he gained in age and experience and as England went through a change of dynasties from the Tudor Queen Elizabeth I to the Stuart James VI of Scotland and I of England.

Over the centuries, investigation of this topic in Shakespeare has started from a prima facie assumption that he was a conservative. After all, he wrote plays for the acting company that became, in 1603, the King's Men. Would it have been prudent, or even possible, for him to bite the royal hand that fed him and his colleagues? He belonged to a society that was, by and large, patriarchal. He was baptized in the Anglican faith in 1564 and was buried in front of the altar of Holy Trinity Church in Stratford in 1616. He and his fellow communicants heard in church, at regular intervals, readings of an official homily against disobedience and wilful rebellion. In his plays he dramatizes the lives of many kings and aristocrats, sometimes admiringly. Crowds in his plays can be unpredictable and even violent. William Hazlitt, in the early nineteenth century, deplored what he took to be Shakespeare's warmongering approach to battle, as in *Henry V*. So did George Bernard Shaw, a century or so later. Shakespeare has loomed for many biographers and other critics as an Establishment figure. England's greatest poet is, for better or worse in the varied opinions of such critics, a defender of the status quo.

Recently, biographical investigation has tended to question these assumptions and ask if Shakespeare has been misunderstood in these terms. That proposition, at the very least, makes the question more interesting. We might begin with the Roman plays, since they do not posit a monarchical system of government and are free of providential ideas about England as a chosen people of God. They seem to have enabled Shakespeare, and can enable us, to explore political dilemmas and impasses with a kind of historical distance and objectivity that were harder for Shakespeare and his contemporaries to achieve in the context of their own country's recent history.

As Andrew Gurr (101–3), S. Schoenbaum (*Documentary Life*, 106), and others have pointed out, the first recorded performance of *Julius Caesar* was at the newly erected Globe Theatre on the Bankside in 1599. Thomas Platter, a visitor from Basle, noted that on 21 September he and his luncheon partners went 'across the water' at two o'clock, where, 'in the straw-thatched house we saw the tragedy of the first Emperor, Julius Caesar, very pleasingly performed, with approximately fifteen characters' and a graceful dance at the end. The event coincided with a significant shift in Shakespeare's career as a writer: he was at the point of setting aside, for more than a decade, the English history play as a favourite genre, along with romantic comedy. *Julius Caesar*, both history play and tragedy, opened the door for him into the world of *Hamlet*, *Othello*, and the rest that were to follow.

Despite the nominal distance of Rome from England in time and cultural practices, *Julius Caesar* points repeatedly in the direction of Shakespeare's own contemporary world. The famous anachronisms at which Ben Jonson jeered—the 'walls and battlements', the 'towers and windows', yea, the 'chimney tops' described by Marullus in scene i (38–9), the striking clock (II. i. 193) in defiance of the fact that mechanical clocks had not been invented until about 1300, the 'sweaty nightcaps' thrown in the air by the jubilant crowd when Mark Antony offers Caesar a crown (I. ii. 245–6)—attest to the impression that, in Richard Dutton's words, Shakespeare's audience was watching not only 'timeless history' but also 'very specifically English history' (p. 10).

Katherine Duncan-Jones reinforces the point with several suggestive parallels. Though Shakespeare's dramatization in 1599 of the assassination of Caesar preceded the attempted Essex rebellion of 1601, audiences would have had no trouble remembering other earlier plots to overthrow the government of Elizabeth I, such as the Babington conspiracy of 1586 on behalf of Mary Queen of Scots.

(See also James Shapiro, *1599*, 150.) Nor could they have missed the point that Essex was already, in 1599, an icon of disaffection and a darling of some restive elements in the London populace, including many theatregoers (see Holden, *Life and Work*, 77–8). *Henry V*, also performed in 1599 at the Globe, alludes in celebratory terms to the expected and hoped-for return of Essex from his Irish campaign (Chorus to Act V)—'the boldest, most specific topical allusion in [Shakespeare's] entire work' (Bate, *Soul of the Age*, 254). The prominence of large crowds in *Julius Caesar* might seem to comment implicitly 'on the Globe Theatre's own "full house", a mixed and wavering mob moved this way and that by powerful speeches' (Duncan-Jones, 113). Indeed, Casca explicitly compares the malleability of the Roman crowd with that of a theatre audience: 'If the rag-tag people did not clap him and hiss him, according as he pleased and displeased them, as they use to do the players in the theatre, I am no true man' (I. ii. 258–61, quoted in Duncan-Jones, 116). Shakespeare's portrayal of Caesar, argues Duncan-Jones, might well put his audiences in mind of Elizabeth's penchant for public or semi-public appearances calculated to dramatize her love for the people and theirs for her as a semi-divine figure (p. 117). Later, in the reign of Charles I and its bloody aftermath, *Julius Caesar* was to prove immensely popular (second only to *Hamlet*) for its 'depiction of an overweening ruler who is assassinated by his own friends and advisers' (p. 282). At Oxford, in the seventeenth century, *Julius Caesar* ranked second to *Romeo and Juliet* as best known among Shakespeare's plays.

Is *Julius Caesar* to be viewed, in such a heady topical environment, as endorsing or deploring rebellion against strong-man single rule? Biographers and other critics have predictably split on this issue; so have stage productions. To Duncan-Jones, the play 'in no way' endorses the conspiracy against Caesar (p. 108). The power vacuum created by the assassination of Caesar is filled ultimately not by the would-be defenders of republican liberty but by other strong men, Antony and then Octavius Caesar, who use the emergency to strengthen their repression of civil liberties. 'In its first, 1599, context', writes Duncan-Jones, '*Julius Caesar* could be viewed by civil authority as an awful warning to any hot-blooded young courtiers who might be wearying of Elizabeth's long reign.' Elizabeth was widely viewed, like Caesar, as 'uniquely valuable and irreplaceable' (p. 117). René

Weis, on the other hand, is more attuned to Cassius's exultant cry as he and the conspirators bathe their hands in Caesar's blood: 'How many ages hence / Shall this our lofty scene be acted over / In states unborn and accents yet unknown! . . . So shall the knot of us be called / The men that gave their country liberty' (III. i. 112–20). 'A more resounding endorsement of republicanism is hard to imagine', Weis concludes (pp. 253–4).

The mob in *Julius Caesar* is of course too easily swayed and violent. It is also vital and fascinating, no doubt like the jostling crowds that Shakespeare must have encountered in the narrow streets of London. 'The sight of all those people—along with their noise, the smell of their breath, their rowdiness and potential for violence—seems to have been Shakespeare's first and most enduring impression of the great city', writes Stephen Greenblatt (p. 169). Perhaps the cobbler in scene 1 who is so intent on leading men about the streets, as he jocosely says, 'to wear out their shoes, to get myself into more work' (lines 29–30) is a recollection of Shakespeare's early days in the house of his leather-working father (p. 56). At any rate, the crowd is only partly to blame for civil disorder. The play explores the contributions to such violence by the conspirators, by Antony and Octavius Caesar in their cynical readiness to use civil unrest as an occasion for clamping down on civil freedoms, and by Julius Caesar himself in his arrogant unwillingness to temporize with ordinary mortals. A spirit of sardonic irony suffuses the play. Brutus is as blind to his own hubris as is the would-be tyrant he kills. The rebellion achieves nothing so much as the destruction of those values for which the most well-meaning of the conspirators proceeded to do what they did. Human beings at some times are their own worst enemies. Many writers on *Julius Caesar*, such as Norman Rabkin and John Velz, have sought a balance of this sort in assessing the play's political thrust. Whether such a balance represents Shakespeare's own political view is harder to argue, but it does at least illuminate the way in which he may have wished the play to be understood by his London audience in 1599.

Stage productions have fought both sides of the issue. Moderate and balanced views sometimes prevail, to be sure, as in Joseph Mankiewicz's 1953 black-and-white film with a host of stars in the major roles: Marlon Brando as Antony, James Mason as Brutus, John Gielgud as Cassius, Louis Calhern as Caesar, Deborah Kerr as Portia; casting of this sort encouraged multiple sympathies. More outspokenly, Orson Welles's *Death of a Dictator*, at the Mercury Theatre in New York in 1937, invited its audiences to see Caesar as the Italian dictator Benito Mussolini, complete with the trademark thrust-out chin and Fascist uniform. Brutus was a thoughtful idealist overwhelmed by the forces of repression. In John Barton's production for the Royal Shakespeare Company in 1968, Caesar bore a striking resemblance to Charles de Gaulle. Conversely, in the early nineteenth century Antony was the big heroic role for the likes of William Charles Macready, and later too for Herbert Beerbohm Tree (1898, at Her Majesty's Theatre). When the Duke of Saxe-Meiningen brought his German-speaking actors to London in 1881, the elaborately staged crowd scenes played up the instability of mob violence (see Wells, *Shakespeare for All Time*, 307–8).

Coriolanus has been no less a battleground among biographers and others (including theatre directors) curious to deduce what Shakespeare's own political views might have been. Again, parallels to contemporary England have been urged by biographers. Menenius Agrippa's way of disarming the potential violence of the plebeians in Scene i bears a striking resemblance, in the view of Schoenbaum (*Documentary Life*, 157) and Dutton (pp. 31–4), to the authorities' handling of the so-called 'Ill May-Day' London riots of Henry VIII's reign, which had recently been dramatized in the play about *Sir Thomas More* and to which Shakespeare may have provided a rewritten scene when the treatment of civil unrest had proved too controversial for the authorities. Park Honan points out that when an emboldened Parliament in 1607–8 failed to ratify some of King James's expenses, he retaliated by calling his critics 'Tribunes of the people, whose mouths could not be stopped' (p. 346). Leah Marcus argues plausibly that although Coriolanus cannot be equated with James in any simplistic fashion, Coriolanus 'is associated with abuses of local authority like those which the City of London was contesting in the early Stuart period' (*Puzzling Shakespeare*, 203). Dearth and famine 'were acute problems' for London in the famine of 1608, resulting in some rioting (p. 204).

Duncan-Jones argues that *Coriolanus*, 'with its treatment of food riots, civil rebellion and a war hero turned invader', was, at the time it was written (*c.*1608), 'far too explosive for performance, despite its ancient Roman setting' (p. 204). Indeed, food riots had become a major worry for the authorities in those years, especially in the summer of 1607, when scarcity of grain prompted civil disobedience in Northamptonshire, Warwickshire, and Leicestershire. All London theatres had been closed down for some days in the wake of a play by George Chapman (*The Tragedy of Charles Duke of Byron*) that had offended the French ambassador. Coriolanus, as a 'war hero turned invader', uncomfortably brought to mind the ill-fated rebellion of the charismatic but mercurial Earl of Essex. Weis ventures that Shakespeare wrote *Coriolanus*, as well as a few other late plays, 'with never a chance of putting them on' (p. 331).

The mob certainly turns ugly in *Coriolanus*, although, to some recent critics (e.g. Marcus, 204–7), the citizens' motivation for unrest is more understandable than in *Julius Caesar*. Hunger to the point of threatening starvation is a serious business. Moreover, the common-ers in *Coriolanus* seem remarkably patient and willing to put up with Coriolanus's taunting of them until they are worked over by their tribunes, Junius Brutus and Sicinius Velutus. The people are ready to vote for Coriolanus in Act II, Scene ii, even though they sensibly perceive that he is no friend to their interests. The derogatory lang-uage used in the play to excoriate the plebeians for their 'stinking breaths' (II. i. 235) and the like is deployed chiefly by Coriolanus; he hates their breath 'As reek o'th' rotten fens' (III. iii. 131) with such vehemence that the accusation amounts to an indictment of Coriolanus himself for irrational intolerance.

As a result, some evaluations have argued for a balance of forces and of sympathies in *Coriolanus* not unlike that in *Julius Caesar*. Brutus and Sicinius are well-meaning from their own point of view; they are genuinely concerned that the people's rights are being threa-tened by Coriolanus. They are also self-interestedly concerned about their own powers and privileges, and they manipulate the plebeians quite cynically to achieve their ends. Coriolanus, for his part, also acts as he does out of passionately sincere conviction; he worries that if the tribunes are allowed to have their way, Rome will know no end to popular incursions on aristocratic privilege, and with this decay of traditional conservative authority will come anarchy. Both sides op-erate out of principle, and both sides are prepared to use force or intimidation to achieve what they view as necessary ends.

Consequently, a case can be made for both conservative and liberal readings today of Shakespeare's own presumed position. Dutton speaks plausibly enough when he insists that 'Shakespeare shows no signs of having been at heart a democrat' (p. 31). On the other hand, we can understand why the political leadership in Nazi Germany, having long regarded *Coriolanus* as critical of militarism, exiled the scriptwriter of a liberal radio adaptation in 1932, and then adopted their own more reactionary version of the play 'as a schoolbook to demonstrate to Hitler Youth the unsoundness of democracy and to idealize Martius [Coriolanus] as an heroic *führer* trying to lead his people to a heathier society, "as Adolf Hitler in our days wishes to lead our beloved German father-land"' (M. Brunkhorst, cited by Wells, *Shakespeare for All Time*, 366).

A more tempered view, as expressed for example by Norman Rabkin in '*Coriolanus:* The Tragedy of Politics', is that the play is not unlike *Julius Caesar* in its ironic and even sympathetic perceptions. William Hazlitt once quipped that 'a viewing of *Coriolanus* would save one the trouble of reading both Burke attacking the French Revolution and Paine defending it because Shakespeare gave both sides of the argument' (cited in Bate, *Genius of Shakespeare*, 202–3). Bate's own view is that Shakespeare's extraordinary ability to present two or more sides to an argument, his Keatsian 'negative capability', bears an uncanny resemblance to Werner Heisenberg's 'uncertainty principle' and the puzzling self-contradictions of quantum mechanics. Undecidability, as posited too in William Empson's *Seven Types of Ambiguity*, is 'a condition of nature, not a fallibility or predilection of the interpreting mind' (p. 331).

Viewed in this dispassionate way, the various parties to the political debate on Rome's future in *Coriolanus* are more or less equally misguided, self-blinded, and doomed to be participants in a process by which their own best interests are sacrificed to ideological extremism and polarization. Compromise and pragmatism eventually prevail, but at the expense of a national hero and of many shattered ideals. Rome muddles through, but ingloriously so. Is this perhaps close to Shakespeare's own view, and if so, what circumstances in the England of his own day may have helped drive him to this conclusion? Does this represent Shakespeare's opinion, for example, of the growing conflict between King James and his vociferous opponents in the

Parliament and in the reformed wing of the Anglican church? That would at least help explain why Shakespeare wrote this play some time around 1608. These are questions on which biographers and other writers on Shakespeare will continue to disagree.

Antony and Cleopatra is primarily about other matters, and will be considered in more detail when we get to late Shakespeare in Chapter 7, but insofar as the play does tell its great love story against a backdrop of political conflict, several critics (e.g. Jan Kott, 169–77, and Janet Adelman, *The Common Liar*, 40–9) have pointed out ways in which it conforms to the pattern already described in *Julius Caesar* and *Coriolanus*. Octavius Caesar is deeply cynical about the Roman mob, and knows how to use its vacillations to his own advantage. 'This common body', he lectures Lepidus, 'Like to a vagabond flag upon the stream, / Goes to and back, lackeying the varying tide / To rot itself with motion' (I. iv. 44–6). Weakness of this sort requires single rule and ruthlessness. The Octavius who as a younger man in *Julius Caesar* unceremoniously agreed with Antony to the proscribing of their political enemies, including Cicero and some seventy other senators (IV. iii. 176–9), is now prepared, in *Antony and Cleopatra*, to cashier the triumvir Lepidus when he is no longer useful (III. vi. 29–31). Octavius Caesar never takes unnecessary chances. Antony, conversely, wins the loyalty of his followers through charisma and sharing with them the dangers and rewards of battle. He is recklessly generous even to those who ultimately desert him, like Enobarbus. History is impartial, even sardonic, in the face of such contrasting styles of leadership. Antony, having been a partner with Octavius Caesar at Philippi, is ultimately no match for the relentless and dehumanizing efficiency of Octavius's war machine. Success belongs to those who know how to win. Whether the play celebrates this victory is another matter. The triumph of Caesarism is of world-shaking importance, but it happens without any moral sanction. It just happens.

When we travel back to the 1590s and to the decade in which Shakespeare wrote most of his English history plays, we move from the Jacobean period to the Elizabethan, and in fact to the end of Queen Elizabeth's reign when anxieties about the threat of Spain were at their height. We also enter a world in which Christian and providential ideas about history are constantly on the minds of the chief participants as they are not in the Roman tragedies. History has a substantially different use in these plays from that which pertains to the Roman tragedies. Pressed by the danger of Spanish invasion and several conspiracies on behalf of Mary Queen of Scots in the 1580s, then vastly relieved by the great victory over Philip's Armada in 1588, England in the 1590s needed to reflect on her own troubled birth of a nation. Civil war had ravaged the country throughout most of the fifteenth century, until Henry Tudor's victory over Richard III at the battle of Bosworth Field in 1485 provided a chance for stability. The Tudor dynasty, culminating in the long reign of Elizabeth I (1558–1603), might well seem to call for celebration. Shakespeare, born during the reign of Elizabeth and having known no other monarch when he wrote all of his history plays except the late *Henry VIII*, must have had his own personal views about what the story of England meant to him and his fellow citizens. He certainly knew how to address those citizens with what they wanted to hear; the plays were enormously popular from the start.

A place to begin is not with the earliest plays that Shakespeare wrote on English history but with the play that starts off the whole sequence of political conflicts leading ultimately to the Tudors' rise to power: *Richard II* (*c*.1595). Shakespeare presents us with two radically opposite ways of reading the story of the deposition of Richard II: as a violation of divine will calculated to bring down God's wrath on a wayward people, or as a complex struggle between two contenders for the English throne that results in a usurpation and takeover by the man whose son turns out to be the great Henry V. The Bishop of Carlisle expresses the first view when, on behalf of the church, he defines Richard as 'the figure of God's deputy, / His captain, steward, deputy elect, / Anointed, crownèd, planted many years'. To Carlisle, the usurpation of Richard's crown is a 'heinous, black', and 'obscene' deed for which 'The blood of English shall manure the ground / And future ages groan for this foul act' (IV. i. 126–39). The converse view is expressed by the man who supplants Richard as king, Henry Bolingbroke. He protests to his uncle York and then to Richard that he has returned from exile solely for the purpose of claiming his rightful inheritance to the dukedom of Lancaster willed to him by his father but taken away from him by Richard. 'My gracious lord, I come but for mine own', he insists to Richard even as he is in the process of enforcing that non-negotiable demand by the threat of military force (III. iii. 196). Where does Shakespeare appear to stand on this question, if that can be determined, and how have his biographers handled the matter as an important episode in Shakespeare's development as a dramatist, especially in view of the often-noted parallel between Richard and Queen Elizabeth?

As Wells observes, 'When Shakespeare wrote *Richard II*, around 1595, the question of who would succeed Elizabeth as sovereign was already much in the air', so much so that 'the spectacle of a sovereign of England giving up his crown to a usurper was considered too politically sensitive to be presented on stage as long as the Queen was alive' (*Shakespeare for All Time*, 72). Hence the deposition scene was removed from the text as first printed in 1597 and was not allowed into print until a fourth quarto edition in 1608. The official position of Elizabeth's government could easily be inferred from the homily against wilful disobedience and rebellion and from other pronouncements declaring that, in Dutton's words, 'it was the subjects' duty to serve whomever God had placed in sovereignty over them'. 'If God sends us a weak or evil monarch, it is punishment for our sins and to be suffered with patience.' Such a monarch 'will find retribution in heaven and should not be resisted on earth' (p. 83). The fact that the Tudors themselves had come to the English throne by way of violent overthrow of a sitting monarch was an inconvenient truth to be explained away as deftly as possible, but the rule still had official endorsement since any other exception might justify armed resistance to Elizabeth and her ministers.

The principles underlying this self-justifying position, known widely as the doctrines of divine right of kings and of passive obedience to monarchical rule, are eloquently expressed by important characters in *Richard II*, notably the Dukes of Lancaster and York— the father and uncle, respectively, of the young Bolingbroke who eventually seizes power from Richard. They were also uncles of King Richard himself. 'God's is the quarrel', insists John of Gaunt, Duke of Lancaster, to his widowed sister, in response to her pleas that Gaunt avenge the death of her husband and Gaunt's younger brother. 'God's substitute, / His deputy anointed in His sight, / Hath caused his death'—that is Richard has ordered the death of Thomas of Woodstock, Duke of Gloucester—'the which if wrongfully / Let heaven revenge, for I may never lift / An angry arm against His minister' (I. ii. 37–41). The Duke of York implicitly agrees when he berates his nephew Bolingbroke for having dared to return from exile 'In gross rebellion and detested treason' (II. iii. 109). To bear arms against his sovereign is to disobey the will of God, however grievous the provocation under which Bolingbroke is suffering. York protests he would 'attach you all and make you stoop / Unto the sovereign mercy of the King' if he were militarily able to do so (ll. 156–7). Both dukes, then, anticipate the ominous prediction of the Bishop of Carlisle that 'if you raise this house against this house, / It will the woefullest division prove / That ever fell upon this cursèd earth' (IV. i. 146–8). Shakespeare's audience knew only too well that the prediction would fulfil itself in the bloody internecine wars of the fifteenth century. Ackroyd (p. 282) wonders if Shakespeare himself may have taken the role of King Richard in performance, with Burbage as Bolingbroke.

In biographical terms, then, Shakespeare had every reason to endorse the wisdom of this conservative defence of monarchy. His very livelihood depended upon it, as did the welfare of his audience. In view of that fact, critics and biographers have found it all the more striking that *Richard II* gives such eloquent play to the opposing point of view embodied in the Bolingbroke who becomes Henry IV. Perhaps, Holden speculates, 'the touchy theme of a nation labouring under weak leadership, so weak as to justify the intervention of a heroic usurper', was suggested to Shakespeare by Southampton or even by the Earl of Essex (*Life and Work*, 147).

A major problem is that King Richard is so cavalier in regarding himself above the law. He appears to be directly implicated in the assassination at Calais of his youngest uncle, Thomas of Woodstock, Duke of Gloucester. He attempts to cover the matter up by scheduling and then breaking off a trial by combat between Bolingbroke and Thomas Mowbray, Duke of Norfolk, who is accused of the actual murder of Woodstock since not even Bolingbroke dare implicate the King openly of the crime. Richard then banishes both men in a desperate attempt to get them out of the way. He does so with the reluctant consent of his Privy Council (including Gaunt and York), but then goes on to seize 'The plate, coin, revenues, and movables / Whereof our uncle Gaunt did stand possessed' (II. i. 161–2)—in other words, Bolingbroke's rightful inheritance. This action is illegal in the deepest sense, as York angrily points out; it violates the very 'charters' and 'customary rights' of 'fair sequence and succession' by which Richard himself inherited the kingship (ll. 196–9). No less outrageously, the King has licensed his agents to 'farm the royal realm' with 'blank charters' and other oppressive weapons of arbitrary taxation (I. v. 43–8).

Accordingly, Bolingbroke's return to England from exile to claim his own wins the support of disaffected nobles like Northumberland and even the reluctant acquiescence of York. Yet insofar as that return is the illegal violation of a royal order of banishment approved in council, it too strains at the fabric of the English constitution. York goes along because he cannot effectively resist Bolingbroke's advances on English soil. Shakespeare invites sympathy for Bolingbroke up to the point of armed intervention and deposition of a reigning monarch—an event for which England's unwritten constitution has no guidelines. Like the violent political changes in *Julius Caesar* and *Coriolanus*, revolution just happens. Whether Providence exacts a price is not clear, since the *coup d'état* does lead, in the course of time, to the successful reign of Henry V. Still, another consequence, arguably, is prolonged and devastating civil war in the time of Henry VI. Shakespeare is clearly fascinated by the struggle, and expects his audience to be, since that conflict is the cauldron out of which Tudor England is to emerge in the sixteenth century, but whether Providence directs all this eventful history is left open to interpretation.

Whether or not Shakespeare intended *Richard II* as a pointed comment on current affairs in 1595 is open to question also, though he must have known that the topic was controversial. At any rate, all biographers (e.g. Schoenbaum, *Documentary Life*, 158–60; Wells, *Dramatic Life*, 133–40; Honan, 216–19; Bate, *Soul of the Age*, 233–67) see topicality in the events of 1601, when the Earl of Essex, Queen Elizabeth's troublesome favourite, mounted an abortive rebellion against the government. Augustine Phillips and other members of the Lord Chamberlain's company were commissioned by some of Essex's followers to perform, on 7 February, at the Globe Theatre on the very eve of the rebellion, 'the play of the deposing and killing of Richard II'. Phillips pleaded afterwards that the play (surely Shakespeare's) was an old one and not likely to draw a large crowd, and that the acting company had been offered a payment of 40 shillings 'more than their ordinary' for the performance, but the authorities at his examination were no doubt sceptical of this excuse. Did not the Queen later say (on 4 August 1601), 'I am Richard II, know ye not that?' by way of making clear what she thought of the business? Had not her government imprisoned the historian John Hayward simply for having published his 'First Part of the Life and Reign of Henry the IV' in 1599–1601 with a dedication to Essex? As James Shapiro notes, the dedication troubled Archbishop Whitgift so greatly that he 'instructed the Stationers' Company to tear out the dedication to Essex from all unsold copies', with the result that 'the rest of the print run quickly sold out' (*1599*, 118–21). The Lord Chamberlain's company was let off, but only after two of the key conspirators were questioned about the performance and its role in the insurrection (Greenblatt, 309–10; Weis, 260).

If Shakespeare was known to have connections still with Southampton, as in 1593–4, the suspicion of complicity must have been all the stronger, since Southampton was a close associate of Essex and was put on trial for his involvement in the rebellion (Duncan-Jones, 127–8). Southampton got off with his life but was imprisoned in the Tower for the rest of Elizabeth's reign, as was Hayward. Shakespeare and his company surely understood that they had run a serious risk and needed to be careful. Their decision to stage a play (*1 Henry IV*) with a fat knight named Sir John Oldcastle as its chief comic character ran them into further difficulties, though this time with the Puritan wing of the reform movement, as we have seen in Chapter 2.

The final three plays in Shakespeare's four-play historical sequence written in 1595–9 (*1* and *2 Henry IV* and *Henry V*) centre on Prince Hal, his ebullient but politically unwise friendship with Falstaff, and his uncertain advancement to the throne. Many circumstances in Shakespeare's life have been proposed by biographers as grist for Shakespeare's mill. Duncan-Jones reads the story of the ultimate rejection of Falstaff as an imaginative reworking of Shakespeare's having been abandoned by Southampton, thus casting Shakespeare in the role of Falstaff. Southampton, like Hal, had been a madcap in his youth. Just as Shakespeare was eventually rejected, or at least 'forgotten or marginalized', by Southampton, Duncan-Jones proposes, 'the prodigal jesting knight Sir John Falstaff had been crushingly repudiated by his "sweet boy" ' at the end of *2 Henry IV*, leaving the newly crowned King free to embrace 'a calling far higher than fooling around with his social inferiors' (p. 104). Ackroyd similarly interprets the story of Falstaff and Hal as 'a comic version of the relationship between Shakespeare and the "young man" of the sonnets in which infatuation is succeeded by betrayal' (pp. 301–2).

Perhaps this feeling of betrayal prompted Shakespeare to apply in 1596 for a coat of arms for his father. His motives for doing so may have been exacerbated in part by the death on 23 July 1596 of Henry Carey, the old Lord Hunsdon and Lord Chamberlain (as noted in Chapter 2, above), with the result that Shakespeare's acting company had lost for a time its protector and patron; and by the death of Shakespeare's only son, Hamnet, in August of 1596, at the age of 11. Germaine Greer argues that Shakespeare's motives may also have included a wish to affirm his belief 'in his mother's descent from a gentle family' (p. 203).

The application for a coat of arms bore unmistakable signs of social ambition, and was a shabby affair in some ways. The motto chosen for this new coat of arms, 'Non sanz droict', seemed to say, as Duncan-Jones expresses it, 'We are of ancient military lineage, with legitimate claims to bear arms' (p. 96). Yet Shakespeare and his father had no inherited claim to be gentlemen, and the grant was deplored, as were others of a similar nature, by those who wished to preserve the presumed integrity of armorial honours. The official who approved the grant, William Dethick, Garter king-of-arms, was challenged by Ralph Brooke, York Herald, for having wrongfully granted armiger-ous status to some twenty-three applicants of whom Shakespeare was one (see Schoenbaum, *Documentary Life*, 171–3). Dethick was notori-ously unfit for his office and had to be dismissed. Shakespeare appears to have been sensitive to the allegation that the patent he acquired in 1596 was highly questionable (Duncan-Jones, 89–102).

At about this same time, in the spring of 1597, Shakespeare bought New Place, the second biggest house in Stratford, a residence that had about it the aura of dignity and substance even if it was perhaps not as handsome or as well maintained as has often been supposed (see Greer, 207, and Bate, *Soul of the Age*, 154). This purchase was yet another move that savoured of *nouveau riche* aspirations. *The Merry Wives of Windsor*, written also about this time, perhaps with the cachet of Shakespeare's having been commanded by Queen Elizabeth to write a play about Falstaff in love, is notably bourgeois in its Windsor setting, its poking fun at Robert Shallow (with a dig, possibly, at a litigious Justice of the Peace, William Gardiner; see Hotson, *Shakespeare Versus Shallow*, and Schoenbaum, *Documentary Life*, 146–7), its admiring portrayal of the comfortable wealth of the Pages and the Fords, and at the same time its caring gestures towards Windsor Castle and the revered ceremonies honouring the Order of the Garter (V. v. 60–1). Do these circumstances suggest something about the dramatist who, in 1596–8, devoted much of his imaginative life to the story of a scapegrace reveller and an ambitious young prince? Might part of Shakespeare's own psyche have been involved in the portraiture of Hal, the once and future king? Might the *agon* between Falstaff and Hal betoken an inner debate about friendship and ambition, social tolerance and social advancement? The fact that readers of the *Henry IV* plays are so divided in their appraisal of Falstaff as a quintessential life-force or as a threat to stability might leave us uncertain as to Shakespeare's own political alignment, but by the same token the debate may encourage a reading in which the issues at stake were of vital importance to the author.

To the extent that Falstaff may have reminded Shakespeare of Robert Greene and his drunken demise in 1592, as Greenblatt suggests, the question of what to do about Falstaff becomes all the more intriguing and problematic. In the theatrical games that Hal and Falstaff play in the tavern, 'kingship is a theatrical performance by a gifted scoundrel', while the real King Henry IV 'has no more legitimacy than Falstaff'. Greene may have represented for Shakespeare not simply a 'sleazy parasite' of 'seedy charm' given at times to 'noisy, short-lived fits of repentance'; he was also 'a grotesque Titan, a real-life version of the drunken Silenus of Greek mythology or of Rabelais' irrepressible trickster, Panurge' (pp. 216–19). Falstaff was much more than this, of course; he was, as Greenblatt says, an 'exceptionally amusing, exceptionally dangerous friend', the rejection of whom by King Hal could not happen without a huge tug at the heartstrings. 'It is difficult to register the overwhelming power and pathos of the relationship between Hal and Falstaff without sensing some unusually intimate and personal energy' (p. 71). To Jonathan Bate, similarly, Falstaff is 'a true Epicurean', like Cleopatra, in the positive sense of one who dispenses with belief in the immortality of the soul or divine intervention in human affairs, embracing instead friendship and bodily experience as essential to the good life, with the result that Shakespeare, something of an Epicurean himself, cannot help falling in love with both Falstaff and Cleopatra (*Soul of the Age*, 390–3; see also Bloom, *Shakespeare and the Invention of the Human*, chaps. 17 and 27).

The remarkable energy of Hal's companionship with Falstaff emerges, in Greenblatt's view, from Shakespeare's struggle to rise from the status of a Stratford glover's son to that of chief playwright for London's leading theatrical troupe and wealthy burgher of the town of his artisanal origins. Then, too, the *Henry IV* plays are ceaselessly fascinated with the tense relationships between sons and fathers, not just in Hal's case but also in that of Hotspur, the plays having been written at a time in Shakespeare's life when he lost his only son and more or less simultaneously applied for a coat of arms for his father.

On a political level, the *Henry IV* plays may have seemed timely to Shakespeare's audiences in the context of the Elizabethan government's difficulties with Catholic opposition, both external and internal. The leaders of the so-called Northern Rebellion of 1569 on behalf of Mary Queen of Scots had included Thomas Percy, seventh Earl of Northumberland, and Charles Neville, sixth Earl of Westmorland; these names surface meaningfully in *1 Henry IV*'s account of rebellion against the new king by disaffected nobles in the north and west. (See Shapiro, *1599*, 255.) Queen Elizabeth had been excommunicated by Pope Pius V in 1570. Plots against her life were uncovered nearly every year from 1570 until the execution of Mary Queen of Scots in 1587. War with Spain began in 1588. The very first lines of *1 Henry IV*, 'So shaken as we are, so wan with care, / Find we a time for frighted peace to pant', must have seemed painfully appropriate still in 1596–7. In these and many other ways, biographers have found suggestive parallels to Shakespeare's life in those years.

The parallels offer tantalizing potential hints as to Shakespeare's own political alignment, and yet his penchant for evenhandedness leaves central issues in doubt. Does he sympathize with Henry IV as a pragmatist dealing with political opposition as efficiently as he can, or does Shakespeare leave room for the view that Henry IV is a usurper burdened with the guilt of having been responsible for the murder of his first cousin, and plagued now with a seeming insurrection in his own family that could perhaps be attributable to God's anger at Henry? Even in *Henry V*, ostensibly a celebration of one of the great heroes of English monarchy, is the tribute qualified by an implication that England in 1599 is no longer under the governance of a young king who can lead his country against her enemies? Is the paean of praise offered to Essex in the Chorus of Act V a slap at a Queen who lacked the charisma of the dashing Robert Devereux? The debate, aptly characterized by James Shapiro (*1599*, 88–91), continues.

When we work backwards into the first years of Shakespeare's career as a dramatist, in the early 1590s, the issues are in some ways more clear. The portrait of Richard III as hunchbacked, malicious, divisive, and guilty of the murder of his two nephews owes a great deal to Tudor-inspired propaganda directed against the Yorkist monarch whom Henry VII, Queen Elizabeth's grandfather, had overthrown at Bosworth Field in 1485. We can understand why Henry Tudor commissioned Polydore Vergil to blacken the name of Richard III in his history of England begun as early as 1505 and published in 1534. We can perhaps understand why Thomas More gave credence to many of the same defamatory stories in his *History of Richard III*, published imperfectly in Richard Grafton's version (1543) of John Hardyng's *Chronicle* and then picked up by Edward Hall in his *Union of the Noble and Illustre Famelies of Lancastre and York*; though More was not always on the best of terms with Henry VII, he had lived through the tense years of 1483–5 and had a story to tell. Shakespeare's own willingness to go along with the official Tudor line does not sit well with our image of him as fairmindedly above the fray, but it makes sense in terms of the overall design of his first tetralogy, *Henry VI Parts I, II*, and *III* and *Richard III*.

That epic saga has as one of its underlying purposes a demonstration of the evils of civil war and the deliverance of England from that terrifying spectre through the agency of Henry VII. Hence, in the concluding action of *Richard III* (c.1592–4), the portraiture of Henry Tudor is, for most modern readers and critics (see James Siemon, 361–78), an unconvincing whitewash. The name of God is constantly in his mouth. As a general he is calm, reassuring, decisive, and eloquent, while his opposite number can only appeal to fear and hatred. The real Henry Tudor, once he was king, got rid of his political enemies with as ruthless dispatch as the historical Richard had used in his ascent to the throne, but Shakespeare, for artistic reasons as well as political ones, could not afford to say that. His audience, in the wake of the Spanish Armada triumph of 1588, expected patriotic fervour on behalf of the Tudor monarchy, and Shakespeare knew how to please his audience. For all we know, he may have agreed. The more significant point is that artistically his four-play saga needed a triumphant conclusion.

A quotation from Thomas Nashe in 1592 gives evidence of what Stanley Wells (*Shakespeare for All Time*, 155) calls 'an uninhibited degree of emotionalism in the reactions of Elizabethan theatre-goers' during these years. 'How it would have joyed brave Talbot, the terror of the French, to think that after he had lien two hundred years in his tomb he should triumph again upon the stage, and have his bones new enbalmed with the tears of ten thousand spectators at least (at several times)', wrote Nashe in his *Pierce Penniless* of the hero of *1 Henry VI*, Lord Talbot. The description attests to patriotic veneration of an English general who had done well against the French and against Joan of Arc. At the same time, the *Henry VI* plays are filled with anxieties about failed leadership and deeply divisive factionalism at home in the English court. Shakespeare does not choose Marlowe's path, in his highly successful *Tamburlaine* plays (1587–8), of astonishing London audiences with superheroes daring all political structures and the gods alike in his overreaching quest for dominance. Some of Shakespeare's characters, like Jack Cade or Richard of Gloucester (later Richard III), rant and boast in Marlovian cadences, but, says Greenblatt, Shakespeare's audiences are invited into his theatre not 'to fantasize about possessing absolute power', but, on the contrary, 'to shudder at the horrors of popular uprising and civil war' (pp. 196–7). A conservatism of viewpoint seems to reaffirm 'the traditional cautionary precepts that Marlowe in *Tamburlaine* had boldly called into question', as though in conformity with Shakespeare's own 'refusal to throw himself fully into a chaotic, disorderly life' (p. 209). François Laroque, similarly, cannot be persuaded 'that Shakespeare may be fairly presented as a pre-Marxist playwright or even as a radical upholder of popular sedition' (p. 76).

2 Henry VI is notable for its vivid depiction of the Jack Cade rebellion of 1450, when as many as 30,000 men of Kent and Sussex marched on London to demand governmental reforms and the restoration to power of the Duke of York. Shakespeare, as Richard Wilson (*Will Power*, 26–7) and other critics have observed, darkens the episode to frightening proportions, partly by incorporating aspects of the earlier Peasants' Revolt of 1381. The behaviour of the mob in this early play is as unsettling as is that of the crowds in *Julius Caesar* and *Coriolanus*, with the added dimension that Shakespeare is here writing about his own country and the capital city in which he lived for many years. Wilson points out that urban rioting had been rare in England ever since the Ill May-Day of 1517; Shakespeare's crowd scenes written in the 1590s belong 'to the period of the emergence of the city mob as a force to be reckoned with in English politics' (pp. 25–6). Perhaps, as Jonathan Bate suggests, we can detect here 'a genuine fear of anarchy on the dramatist's part', despite the sensible caveat that in general terms Shakespeare's 'own political position cannot be inferred from the drama' (*Genius of Shakespeare*, 109). Anxieties about the Elizabethan succession intensified fears of internecine strife, as Leah Marcus observes (p. 91). Shakespeare himself had lived both in an English country town and in the metropolis, and might well approach the Cade event with a divided sensibility. It is as though 'he could split apart elements of himself and his background', suggests Greenblatt. The nightmare presented in the play is a personal one for Shakespeare, with London controlled 'by a mad, belligerently illiterate rabble from the country' (p. 167).

Yet, as in the later Roman tragedies, the urban crowd in Shakespeare's early history plays is far from solely responsible for social unrest. Factious nobles begin the trouble between the houses of Lancaster and York. Ambitious aristocrats such as Richard Plantagenet are ready, like Antony in *Julius Caesar*, to foment popular unrest in order to further their own self-interested schemes. 'This devil here shall be my substitute' (*2 Henry VI*, III. i. 371), says Plantagenet (now Duke of York) in soliloquy, pointing to Cade as the rabble-rouser whose machinations will pave the way for Plantagenet's drive for the throne. Long-time enemies cynically form short-term alliances of expedience in order to destroy the good Duke Humphrey of Gloucester, uncle of King Henry VI, because his very integrity and willingness to listen to popular complaints hinder the unleashing of anarchy that Gloucester's enemies seek as their way to personal advancement. In *Richard III*, as in the *Henry VI* plays, the commoners are patiently and wisely aware of troubles at court in which they desire to have no part. 'Leave it all to God', they conclude (II. iii. 46), unconsciously echoing the principle of passive obedience to corrupt authority to which Gaunt and York subscribe in *Richard II*. The blame for England's civil chaos rests far more squarely on the shoulders of England's ruling class than on the overburdened and oppressed citizenry. At the same time, Shakespeare does appear to dislike mob violence, however it may have been set in motion, and never more so than when a crowd of jeering and violent hooligans attack the institutions and workplaces of his beloved city.

King John is an anomalous play in that it takes up a period of history far separated from the fifteenth century in which Shakespeare's two four-play sequences from *Richard II* to *Henry V* and from *1 Henry VI* to *Richard III* are situated. Even so, Shakespeare's dramatization of English history in the early thirteenth century turns out to share to a significant degree the viewpoint of those other history plays. As pointed out for example by Dutton (p. 8) and Virginia Mason Vaughan (pp. 380–1), Shakespeare's treatment of King John is studiously ambivalent. Shakespeare knew the virulently anti-Catholic interpretation of John's regime as represented in John Bale's earlier play of *King Johan* (1538, later revised) and in the more recent anonymous *The Troublesome Reign of King John* (*c.*1587–91), in which that monarch, for all his failings, was portrayed as a heroic pre-Reformation martyr in his attempt to stand up to the papacy. Shakespeare dramatizes John's defiance of the papal legate, Cardinal Pandolph, and introduces a fictitious supporter of the king, Philip the bastard son of Richard Lionheart, to play up sentiments of national pride and hatred of foreign interference in England's affairs. As in Shakespeare's sources, we are told that John is poisoned by a monk. Still, the tone is notably impartial. John is a usurper of the throne that rightfully belongs to his older brother's son, Arthur. He is implicated in the death of that admirable lad, even if the circumstances of the death are complex. John is his own worst enemy, but then so are his nobles when they are misguidedly drawn into an alliance with the French Dauphin Lewis, whose motives are unmistakably predatory. The church too overplays its hand by encouraging Lewis only to realize too late that Lewis's concerns are for himself and not for

Rome. Through it all, we are led to conclude that civil faction in England serves only the purposes of her enemies on the Continent. As the Bastard declares, in the play's final moments: 'Naught shall make us rue, / If England to itself do rest but true.'

Shakespeare's views on politics, then, insofar as biographers have been able to discern them, may be 'conservative' in the sense of preferring public order and an end to anarchy, and in not pleading 'liberal' causes of retraining monarchical authority, but he is even-handed in presenting issues to his London public and quite ready (implicitly) to criticize royal or autocratic meddling and incompetence when they manifest themselves in English history. The evidence suggests that his audience agreed on the whole, for these plays were as popular as they were timely.

5

Religion

No topic has proved more controversial for biographers and other writers on Shakespeare than his religion. Was he Anglican, or covertly a Catholic, or a sceptic? The question is more complex than it might at first appear, since one possible answer is that he was a member of the English church, like the vast majority of English subjects, but with significant Catholic sympathies and connections. And he could have been both of these things while harbouring increasing uncertainties about the extent, if any, of divine providential intercession in human affairs. Sceptical possibilities of this sort will be explored in the next two chapters.

The question is also complex because Anglicanism and Catholicism, despite the battle lines that were drawn during the Reformation, could in fact shade imperceptibly into one another in individual practice. Queen Elizabeth herself, though staunchly Protestant in her insistence that she was the head of the English church without any obligations to Rome, had a predilection for what we would call 'high church' worship: incense, a sung service, rich ecclesiastical garb, and all the rest. She supported and evidently enjoyed the music (much of it in settings of the Mass and other Latin texts) of William Byrd, joint-organist of the Chapel Royal in 1569 and then beneficiary of a monopoly on issuing printed music and music paper in 1575, even though he became a Roman Catholic recusant.

Elizabeth's church was 'episcopal' in the sense of retaining the ecclesiastical structure of bishops and archbishops that Catholicism had long practised, with the crucial difference that the hierarchy terminated at the top with the Archbishops of Canterbury and

York, both of whom acknowledged the supremacy of the Tudor state. Elizabeth's subjects were generally free to follow their consciences in such matters so long as they acknowledged her as supreme head of church and state and so long as they attended the services of the Established Church. (A fine of 1 shilling could be imposed for failure to attend.) Such latitude could have afforded Shakespeare the right to be privately sympathetic to the Catholic faith if he so chose, so long as he toed the line in outward conformity to what was officially required and did not countenance subversion or conspiracy against the established order.

The issue was inflamed throughout Shakespeare's lifetime. The papacy, which in 1570 had excommunicated Queen Elizabeth, proclaimed in 1580 that anyone assassinating the queen would be absolved of mortal sin. She was thus in effect proscribed, marked for violent death. The celebration of Catholic Mass was forbidden as illegal in England. King Philip II of Spain prepared a mammoth invasion of England in which he and his generals fully expected to gain the active support of English Catholics once the landings had taken place in 1588. Everyone knew that the invasion was coming; it was far too large an operation to be kept secret, and indeed Philip wished English Catholics to prepare for the day of their 'liberation'. Earlier, in 1554, he had married Mary, Elizabeth's older half-sister, as part of an ongoing campaign to bring England back into the Catholic fold.

Under these alarming circumstances, Catholics in England were under intense suspicion. A sequence of conspiracies throughout the 1580s on behalf of Mary Queen of Scots, culminating in the Babington conspiracy of 1586 and then the execution of Mary in 1587, added to the mounting tension and anxiety. To be a Catholic in England in these difficult times was to place oneself in danger. Yet the Protestant authorities knew only too well that the Protestantizing of the church was very unpopular in some parts of the country, especially to the west and the north in regions generally distant from London and the royal court. Many recusants in Warwickshire, writes Wells (*Shakespeare for All Time*, 24), paid the monthly fine rather than attend Anglican services.

Some biographers suspect Shakespeare's father, John Shakespeare, of having harboured Catholic sympathies. The proposition is plausible enough, since, after all, John (born some time in the 1520s) had lived through the early years of the English Reformation and England's return to Catholicism under Mary in 1553–8 and thus could remember, or at least idealize in his thoughts, a world in which there was but one catholic and universal church. He had, moreover, married into a family with significant Catholic loyalties (though Germaine Greer, pp. 29, 32, is dubious about this; see below). Mary Arden's prosperous farmer father died in 1556, as Greenblatt reports, 'commending his soul, like a good Catholic, "to Almighty God, and to our blessed Lady Saint Mary, and to all the holy company of heaven"' (p. 59; the will is quoted at length in Charlotte Stopes, *Shakespeare's Family*, 37–8). He chose as first witness to his will a curate 'so stubbornly Catholic', Honan tells us, 'as to be dismissed later from Snitterfield vicarage for adhering to the old faith' (p. 15). The Arden clan to which they belonged could trace their lineage back to the Domesday Book and were important property holders in Warwickshire.

John Shakespeare may or may not have subscribed to a 'spiritual testament' of a formulary sort, printed with blank spaces for names and smuggled into England by the Jesuits to enable those wishing to die in the Catholic faith to do so by placing their names in a copy of the document. The authenticity of this so-called Borromeo testament, first published as a fragment by Edmond Malone in the late eighteenth century and then doubted by him, has been bolstered in more recent years by the discovery of its Italian original, though John's signature is still in question. In one of its provisions, paragraph XII, John Shakespeare purportedly beseeches his parents and kinsfolk to pray that his soul be delivered from the torments of Purgatory (Schoenbaum, *Documentary Life*, 41–6). The fact that John's parents were both dead when the document was executed reinforces some scholars' conviction that it was formulaic rather than individually fashioned. It could nonetheless have been an instrument by means of which Shakespeare's father wished to reconcile himself to the faith of his fathers. John Shakespeare, concludes Honan, 'seems to have been brought up as a Catholic', and was married to a Catholic-raised wife, so that 'their son William was raised in the shadow of the old faith' (p. 15).

Yet John Shakespeare, as a civic official in Stratford, acted more than once on behalf of the Protestant Reformation. During the period when he was one of two chamberlains charged with keeping the borough's financial accounts, in 1564, a Last Judgement mural over the chancel arch of the Guild chapel was whitewashed and defaced, not to be rediscovered until centuries later. A mural depiction of St George and the Dragon was similarly plastered over by order of John Shakespeare 'as too papist to be tolerated' (Anthony Burgess, *Shakespeare*, 33). As chief alderman in 1571, John Shakespeare may have taken part in a council session ordering that all Catholic vestments in the inventory of the Guild Chapel were to be sold off (Corporation Minutes, 4.149, quoted by Fripp, i. 48–9), though Heinrich Mutschmann and K. Wentersdorf see no direct proof of John Shakespeare's involvement, and point out that the very existence of these vestments in the Guild Chapel inventory a dozen years after the Anglican Church settlement would seem to suggest that Stratfordians were not especially zealous in adopting Protestantism (pp. 41–2). To be sure, John Shakespeare would not have been acting alone, and would presumably have kept any private dissenting opinion to himself.

Schoenbaum (*Documentary Life*, 36–9), Wells (*Shakespeare for All Time*, 25), and Honan (p. 39) argue that the fines imposed on John Shakespeare for lack of church attendance cited financial, not religious reasons; his name appears among those of whom it is said that they 'come not to church for fear of process of debt', not in another list of those who are recusants for reasons of religious conviction (p. 25). John had twice been accused of illegal wool-dealing. His financial situation was weak by 1576 and in succeeding years. He was exonerated from paying certain fines owing to his inability to pay. He missed council meetings. He sold off land for ready money. He ceased giving for the relief of the poor. The Midlands were experiencing economic hard times in these years, and the government was cracking down on wool traders in view of a shortage of wool. These circumstances appear sufficient to most biographers to justify the absences and fines without resorting to sectarian explanation. The very fact that the Corporation retained John as alderman despite his financial troubles until he was finally replaced in 1586 is, to Germaine Greer, 'proof, if proof were needed, that John Shakespeare was not a Catholic but a full member of the reformist brotherhood. No tolerance whatever was extended by the Corporation to papists who defaulted' (p. 40). (See also Bearman, 'John Shakespeare'.)

Was John Shakespeare, then, Catholic or Protestant? Greenblatt concludes that he was both, caught up in a divided sensibility not unlike that perhaps of other English people who saw that England might again change allegiance in the see-sawing battle of Catholic vs. Protestant and that the best thing to do was to conform outwardly to the established church while keeping one's head down. John Shakespeare, wanting 'to keep both his options open', lived a double life, says Greenblatt, one as an official of the Protestant religious settlement, another as a secret worshipper of the faith of his ancestors. Did his son come to acquire a double consciousness like that of his father? Greenblatt's view is that William 'was on his way to being neither' Catholic or Protestant, 'deeply skeptical of both' (pp. 102–3, 113).

Wells represents a more cautious position on John Shakespeare's religion. The only positive evidence of Catholic allegiance for Wells is the 'Borromeo spiritual testament', the authenticity of which is weakened in Wells's estimation because the story of its having been found by a master-bricklayer in the roof of the Henley Street house in Stratford was the invention in 1770 of one John Jordan, the person who sent a manuscript copy of the will to Edmond Malone. Perhaps Wells gives too little credit to John Jordan, the purported discoverer of the Borromeo will; Jordan did commit the foolish act of forging the missing first leaf of the will he sent to Malone, but we nonetheless owe him a debt of gratitude as an antiquarian for a precious eighteenth-century drawing of New Place before it was destroyed and for his efforts in preserving what he thought to be Mary Arden's house. Moreover, Jordan may not have been as guilty of deception as Wells suggests; the will may have migrated from the rafters of the Shakespeare house to ownership by a direct descendant (Thomas Hart) of one of Shakespeare's sisters and thence to a town councillor from Shottery before eventually finding its way circuitously into Malone's possession, at which point Jordan became involved. Cumulatively, the evidence in favour of the authenticity of the Borromeo will is uncertain. At all events, Wells's scepticism on the larger question of John Shakespeare's religious affiliation is generally well placed. We do have positive evidence of John Shakespeare's actions on behalf of the Protestant cause. Both John and his son conformed throughout their lives to the Established Church. The theory of William Shakespeare's having had a Catholic upbringing is, in Wells's view, tenuous (*Shakespeare for All Time*, 25).

The verdict on John Shakespeare's purported Catholicism remains divided. Schoenbaum has no doubt that 'The religious training provided for Shakespeare by his community was orthodox and Protestant' (*Compact Documentary Life*, 55). Germaine Greer, who dismisses all the speculation about Shakespeare's purported Catholicism as 'modish brouhaha', points out that 'John and Mary Shakespeare baptized all their children in Holy Trinity Church and all of them, bar one, were buried there' (p. 29). Edgar Fripp sets forth the documentary evidence for regarding John Shakespeare as a Puritan-leaning reformer (i. 34 ff.). Peter Levi, on the other hand, has 'no doubt that John Shakespeare was inclined toward Catholicism', perhaps not obstinately so but troubled by the deep divisions of the nation that 'in 1580 the shades were darkening for him personally'; 'his Catholic identity was at least at that time important to him' (p. 17). Recent biographers are thus not agreed on this significant point.

Shakespeare's mother Mary was the daughter of the devoutly Catholic Robert Arden. That, at least, is the opinion of most biographers, though Germaine Greer observes sceptically that the argument in favour of Robert Arden's Catholicism rests chiefly on the wording of the preamble to his will in 1556—a wording that was 'the formula in use in the third year of the reign of Bloody Mary' (p. 29). The Ardens proudly connected their lineage to the socially important Ardens of Park Hall (though Greer insists that no direct relationship can be traced; p. 32). Edward Arden, the head of that family, seems to have secretly harboured a Catholic priest, Hugh Hall, in the guise of a gardener. Sir Thomas Lucy of Charlecote, an energetic supporter of the Reformation and chief figure in a commission empowered to detect signs of Catholic conspiracy, held the Ardens in suspicion. Greenblatt speculates on the basis of this slender connection (Mary was the youngest daughter of an obscure branch of the Arden family) that the Shakespeares on Henley Street, living in fear of detection, were driven to the expedient of hiding rosaries, crucifixes, and other incriminating religious tokens (pp. 100–1, 159–60). Once again, Greer is sceptical: Stratford and vicinity, she insists, had been systematically protestantized by the Reformation authorities, leaving the Stratford Corporation in the hands of 'a closed oligarchy of sturdy protestants, into which no papist could dream of intruding' (pp. 28–9). Richard Wilson, while arguing the case for connections between the Shakespeares and dangerous Catholics in both Stratford and Lancashire, concedes that Shakespeare's plays manifest a persistent hostility towards Jesuits and other extremists (pp. 44–70). At all events, the evidence is inconclusive as to whether Mary wished to bring up her son as a Catholic.

To be sure, Edward Arden of Park Hall was implicated in a Catholic conspiracy of the utmost seriousness. His son-in-law, John Somerville, head of an ancient Catholic family and evidently having been drawn into conversations with the priest Hugh Hall in his father-in-law's household, was arrested in 1583 on suspicion of plotting against the life of Queen Elizabeth and was saved from being hanged, drawn, and quartered only by having been strangled in his cell in the Tower of London. Edward Arden himself was hanged, drawn, and quartered. Both their heads were displayed on London bridge as a warning to would-be traitors (Mark Eccles, 79; Ian Wilson, 52–3). Still, this tells us nothing conclusive about Mary's role as mother in her own immediate family.

What then of William? We have the unsubstantiated claim made more than half a century after Shakespeare's death by Richard Davies, a clergyman, that the dramatist 'died a papist' (quoted in Schoenbaum, *Documentary Life*, 47). Some recent biographers have sought to bolster this assertion with hints of Shakespeare's possible whereabouts shortly before his marriage in 1582; as we have seen, he has been imagined to have taught school, or to have apprenticed himself to some trade, or to have betaken himself to London in the company of travelling actors. Alternatively, might he have encountered at first hand the Catholic culture that was so widespread in his native Midlands? One possibility that especially intrigues some biographers is to ask whether he is to be identified with a certain 'William Shakshafte' or 'Shakeshafte' whose name is mentioned in the 1581 will of Alexander Hoghton (or Houghton), a wealthy Catholic landowner of Lea Hall in Lancashire (as first proposed in 1937 and discussed by Mark Eccles, 74; Sams, 36–8; Holden, *Illustrated Biography*, 68–74; and Dutton et al., *Region, Religion, and Patronage*). An international conference at the University of Lancaster in 1999 devoted its attention to this question and to the desirability of establishing a centre at Houghton Towers to encourage further study. The issue has become intensely partisan, as Wells notes (*Shakespeare for All Time*, 21).

'William Shakshafte' is named in the will as having dwelt with Hoghton, and is recommended to Hoghton's half-brother Thomas, or to a friend, Thomas Hesketh, for future employment—possibly as an actor or musician. The form of the name is not 'Shakespeare' or any of its many variant spellings ('Shaxberd' for example). 'Shakshafte' or 'Shakeshafte' does not turn up in Warwickshire records of the sixteenth century (Wells, *Shakespeare for All Time*, 22; see also Bearman, 'Was William Shakespeare . . . Revisited'). It is, on the other hand, a common name in Lancashire, so that its appearance in a Lancashire testament need not occasion surprise.

At the same time, biographers and other researchers have uncovered links that, however circumstantial, are at least numerous. John Cottam, a man of strong Catholic connections, had taken the post of schoolmaster in Stratford from 1579 to 1581, whereupon he returned to his family home in Lancashire, an area where Catholicism flourished. His two predecessors as schoolmasters in Stratford appear to have been Catholics also: Simon Hunt, who occupied the position from 1571 (when Shakespeare was 7) to 1575, and who subsequently went to the Catholic seminary at Douai and became a Jesuit, ultimately succeeding Robert Parsons (or Persons) as English Penitentiary at St Peter's in Rome (Weis, 26; Ian Wilson, 54, 111); and Thomas Jenkins, of St John's College, Oxford, who held the post of schoolmaster from 1575 to 1579.

Cottam's younger brother Thomas, a Jesuit priest, had been arrested in 1580 as he attempted to travel from the Continent to Stratford's neighbouring village of Shottery, and was tortured and executed in 1582. A leader of this secret mission, the Jesuit Edmund Campion, was tortured and executed in late 1581; another leader, Robert Parsons, managed to survive until 1610. Prior to their joining the Jesuit order, all three had studied at Oxford, where St John's College in particular had a reputation for countenancing Catholics so long as they professed loyalty to the crown (Greenblatt, 96–8). Weis speculates that Stratford was being targeted by Catholic recusants as a fertile ground for indoctrination of the young (p. 26). Ian Wilson proposes that Warwickshire was of particular interest to the Campion–Parsons Jesuit mission 'because Shakespearean Stratford was ringed not only by Ardens, Throckmortons and Catesbys, but several more Catholic families of prominence', including the Grants, Sommervilles, Underhills, Smiths, Reynoldses, and Cloptons (p. 48).

The late-seventeenth-century antiquary John Aubrey is, as we saw in Chapter 2, the uncertain authority for a tradition or rumour that Shakespeare 'had been in his younger years a schoolmaster in the country'. We saw too that some biographers have speculated that Shakespeare could have served for a time as a tutor in a private household. 'In the country'—but where? Those who are devoted to the Lancastrian claim have proposed that Shakespeare followed Cottam to Lancashire as a tutor. Since John Cottam's estate was only ten miles or so from that of Alexander Hoghton, might Cottam have been asked by Hoghton's distinguished family to recommend a young man, preferably of Catholic leanings even if outwardly Protestant, to serve as tutor in their household? Such is the proposition of Ernst Honigmann, and seconded by Peter Milward, Richard Wilson, and others.

Another purported link is that the Hoghtons and Heskeths were on good terms with the Earl of Derby and his family. *Titus Andronicus*, Shakespeare's early tragedy, was published in 1594 'as it was played by the Right Honorable the Earl of Derby, Earl of Pembroke, and Earl of Sussex Their Servants'. As the acting company sponsored by Lord Strange (Ferdinando Stanley's title before he became earl), they had performed a '*Harey the vj*'. Might Thomas Hesketh, having taken 'Shakshafte' under his wing in 1581, then find a spot for him in the Strange/Derby acting company, the principal players of whom were to figure subsequently in the 1594 roster of the Lord Chamberlain's Men? Might the young Shakespeare, employed as a tutor in the Hoghton household, have had the opportunity to meet Campion? Can we perhaps even imagine what they would have talked about? (Greenblatt, 108–9).

All of this depends, however, on the slender and much-debated clue about the name of 'Shakshafte' in Hoghton's will, and on the uncertain supposition that the 'Shakshafte' so named had any interest or ability in the theatre. Honan, trusting in Aubrey's memorandum, inclines to the view that the Hoghton will 'leaves open the possibility that Shakespeare spent some months in the north of England' (p. 62). Duncan-Jones, on the other hand, insists that she is 'yet to be convinced that these documents [including the Hoghton will] have anything to tell us about Shakespeare. "Shakeshafte" was a common name in Lancashire, and the possible means by which William Shakespeare of Stratford, aged seventeen, might have been recruited into the household of Alexander Hoghton of Lancashire as a player, tutor or musician have never been explained to my satisfaction' (p. xii). Dutton finds the whole business, though fascinating in its possibilities, 'a tottering edifice of speculations' (p. 7). Weis proposes that, even if Shakespeare harboured Catholic sentiments that he would have liked to share with English recusants, he need hardly have travelled to Lancashire in search of such company; near at hand were two Catholic Stratford lads close to his age, George Cawdrey, who later joined the English Seminary in Rheims to became a priest, and Robert Debdale, who was to come over to England from the Continent with Campion in 1580–1 and be executed some five years later at the age of 26 (pp. 21, 48–9). Other Catholic families in Stratford, with names such as Clopton, Greenway, Ainges, and Reeves, were near neighbours (p. 69; see also Pogue, 19). Weis finds Hoghton not worth mentioning. Thus the battle lines have been drawn.

Even if the 'Shakeshafte' case has not won anything like universal acceptance, the idea that Shakespeare was closely familiar with Catholic doctrine and worship remains entirely plausible for most biographers. Catholicism impinged on his life, and turns up in his plays and poems in ways that seem to reflect a personal fascination. Stephen Greenblatt has devoted a book-length study, *Hamlet in Purgatory*, to the question of how Shakespeare seems to have responded to Protestant denunciation of Purgatory as a pernicious Catholic fable. The Protestant attack cut off what was for many (possibly including Shakespeare's father, as we have seen) an essential way of staying in touch with the dead, but without quelling the essential need to maintain such contact. This important perception suggests other ways in which Shakespeare's writings can be plumbed for evidence of his involvement with Catholicism on an artistic level at least. Biographers need to be careful not to cross the line into assuming that what a character says in a play represents what Shakespeare himself may have thought, but that has not deterred and should not deter writers on his works from exploring the choices he makes about subject matter and approach.

Hamlet, as Greenblatt and others have observed, shows a familiarity on Shakespeare's part not only with the doctrine of Purgatory but with Catholic ritual practices for warding off its threatening effects. 'I am thy father's spirit', the Ghost of Hamlet's father tells his son when they are alone on the battlements of Elsinor Castle, 'Doomed for a certain term to walk the night, / And for the day confined to fast in fires, / Till the foul crimes done in my days of nature / Are burnt and purged away' (I. v. 10–14). Although the term 'Purgatory' is not used in this play (it does turn up twice elsewhere, in *Romeo and Juliet*, III. iii. 18, and *Othello*, IV. iii. 80), 'purged' here conveys the meaning rather precisely. In the Ghost's place of confinement, he must render up himself 'to sulf'rous and tormenting flames'. If he were to describe the torment he suffers there, the Ghost tells Hamlet, its 'lightest word / Would harrow up thy soul, freeze thy young blood, / Make thy two eyes like stars start from their spheres, / Thy knotted and combinèd locks to part, / And each particular hair to stand on end / Like quills upon the fretful porcupine' (I. v. 3–4, 16–21).

The reason that the Ghost is in Purgatory 'for a certain term' is that Hamlet's father has died sleeping, having been dispatched by a brother's hand without warning. He was thus 'Cut off even in the blossom of my sin, / Unhousled, disappointed, unaneled, / No reck'ning made, but sent to my account / With all my imperfections on my head' (ll. 77–80). These are technical terms from Catholic ritual. To die 'Unhousled, disappointed, unaneled' is to die without having receiving the Holy Sacrament and other last rites including confession, absolution, and the holy oil of extreme unction. This is entirely in accord with teachings of the Catholic Church, and indeed provides insight into why the doctrine of Purgatory (which remains today on the list of official doctrine of the Church, unlike Limbo) evolved as it did in the Middle Ages. The doctrine of Purgatory provided an answer to the question of what was to become of souls of persons who had died without receiving the sacrament of extreme unction or last rites. Doctrine held that salvation was impossible without this sacrament.

Protestants in the sixteenth century had reduced the list of seven sacraments (baptism, confirmation, the Eucharist, penance, holy orders, marriage, and last rites) to two: baptism and the Lord's Supper or Eucharist. They regarded the concept of Purgatory, among others, as a superstition to be cleared away in the interests of reform. Yet for Catholics the doctrine resolved a perfectly logical dilemma: if the sacrament of extreme unction was absolutely necessary for salvation, a person having died without receiving such blessed comfort could not go at once to his or her heavenly reward. The concept of Purgatory evolved as a place of temporary confinement, to use the Ghost's terms, where 'for a certain term' a person's 'foul crimes' done in his 'days of nature' are 'burnt and purged away'. Because the torment is not eternal, it differs crucially in that aspect from Hell. It also differs from Limbo, a doctrine designed to address a related question: what is to happen to the souls of infants who died in childbirth before they could be baptized, or to souls of persons who lived exemplary lives but before the Incarnation of Christ, so that they too were unable to be baptized? Since that Incarnation was also essential for salvation, the ancient patriarchs like Noah and Abraham or the ancient philosophers and poets like Aristotle and Virgil were necessarily excluded, if only to await the Incarnation.

What are the 'foul crimes' that Hamlet's father evidently committed in his 'days of nature', that is, while he lived on earth? In what sense was he 'Cut off even in the blossoms of my sin' (I. v. 77)? Some readers of *Hamlet* have argued that the Ghost's sin was the violent taking of human life; and, to be sure, he indeed 'smote the sledded Polacks on the ice' and slew old Fortinbras of Norway (I. i. 67, 90). Yet these are characterized by Horatio as deeds of chivalry, and are viewed as such in the play by a society that prizes manly courage. Catholic doctrine offers a simpler and more orthodox explanation of Hamlet Senior's 'foul crimes': being a frail and sinful mortal, Hamlet Senior committed the seven Deadly Sins daily as a result of his fallen nature derived from the disobedience of Adam and Eve. 'We are arrant knaves all', the son Hamlet lectures Ophelia; 'believe none of us' (III. i. 131). To be human is to be prone to temptation. Protestant doctrine too, as expounded by Luther and Calvin among others, preached the inherent depravity of the human race, necessitating the infinite grace and mercy of the Almighty. Thus Hamlet's understanding of human sinfulness is broadly medieval Christian. At the same time, *Hamlet* interweaves Catholic practices of Purgatory with popular lore about ghosts, demons, and otherwordly apparitions as found in Shakespeare's sources: the Ghost returns to earth to ask not for prayers on his behalf but for pagan revenge. This blend suits the purposes of a story about an ancient world of Denmark that also is a part of sixteenth-century Europe. The portraiture of Purgatory is at once sympathetic and knowledgeable. It makes no attempt to refute the doctrine of Purgatory as Catholic superstition.

Biographers and critics have amassed numerous other instances in which Shakespeare's presentation of Catholic doctrine and practice is open-minded and inclusive. Schoenbaum (*Compact Documentary Life*, 93–6), Ian Wilson (pp. 93–6), Dutton (p. 8), and Knapp (pp. 96–9) make the point, touched upon in the previous chapter, that Shakespeare's *King John* is markedly less anti-Catholic than are other treatments of the subject; Cardinal Pandulph, the Pope's legate, is a meddler in England's affairs to whom King John and the Bastard offer a suitably patriotic comeuppance, but other meddlers like the French ambassador Chatillon or the French Dauphin Lewis are driven by the same worldly motives, and John himself is hardly free from blame.

As writers on Shakespeare have often noticed, Catholic clerics in Shakespeare's plays are a mixed lot. Many, like Friar Laurence in *Romeo and Juliet*, are portrayed as well-meaning counselors to those who are in spiritual need. Laurence is, to be sure, as Richard Wilson points out (*Secret Shakespeare*, 61), Romeo's 'sin-absolver' and 'ghostly confessor' (III. iii. 49–50); still, he has no interest in promulgating church doctrine. He is there to help the young lovers as well as he can, and to lament his own bumbling when their story results in death. Friar Francis in *Much Ado About Nothing* is similarly a man of decency and concern about the spiritual welfare of those to whom he minis-ters. He is the first to perceive, when young Claudio angrily repudi-ates his bride-to-be Hero at the altar, that the accusation against her of wantonness even on the night before her intended wedding just does not seem even remotely plausible. 'Trust not my reading or my observations, / Which with experimental seal doth warrant / The tenor of my book', he says to Hero's father and the other distressed witnesses to the abortive wedding ceremony. 'Trust not my age, / My reverence, calling, nor divinity', he insists, 'If this sweet lady lie not guiltless here / Under some biting error' (IV. i. 165–70). His only 'evidence' for such an assertion is his knowledge of the young woman through his contacts with her as her spiritual adviser. He has noted 'a thousand blushing apparitions' and 'a thousand innocent shames' to manifest themselves in her countenance, and he has concluded from them that she must be innocent. Hero's father, her intended husband Claudio, and the Prince Don Pedro have all been misled by appearances; the friar is guided to the truth by his calling and by his goodness as a man of the cloth. Benedick, immensely to his credit, is also sceptical of the slanders directed against Hero, and Beatrice is outraged, but the men are mostly guilty of insufficient faith.

In *Measure for Measure*, one seeming friar is in fact the Duke in disguise, but he is ably assisted by Friar Thomas, whose first holy duty is to inquire carefully into the Duke's motives for donning a friar's robes and who is not afraid to lecture the Duke on his responsibilities as ruler (I. iii. 31–3). As A. D. Nuttall observes, 'Neither the Reformation nor the shock waves it produced in the counter-culture of Catholicism—the Council of Trent—make any palpable impression on the plays' (p. 17).

Nuns in Shakespeare are presented with no less generosity. Isabella, not yet a nun in *Measure for Measure*, is ultimately wooed back into a commitment to marriage (at least in traditional readings of her role), but the play seems careful not to question the seriousness of her intended devotion to a life of chastity and obedience. As she tells Francisca, a votarist of the order of Saint Clare which Isabella is about to enter, she desires not liberties but rather 'a more strict restraint / Upon the sisterhood' (I. iv. 3–5). Her choice of restraint is an understandable response to the fallen and depraved world of Vienna. Francisca herself is gracious and supportive of Isabella. To be sure, the life of a nun is represented to Hermia in *A Midsummer Night's Dream* in negative terms: if she chooses the convent, she must be prepared 'For aye to be in shady cloister mewed, / To live a barren sister all your life, / Chanting faint hymns to the cold fruitless moon' (I. i. 72–4). Hamlet caustically offers to Ophelia the choice of a nunnery rather than to be 'a breeder of sinners' (III. i. 122–3). Shakespeare even glances briefly at the sorts of alleged scandals involving nuns and friars that were trumpeted by zealous reformers, as when the fool Lavatch in *All's Well That Ends Well* quips to the Countess that his answer to her question will be as fit 'as the nun's lip to the friar's mouth' (II. ii. 25–6). Still, scholars have persuasively contrasted Shakespeare with fellow dramatists like Marlowe, for example, whose *The Jew of Malta* revels in anti-Catholic humour about the secret sexual lives of nuns and priests.

The Abbess in *The Comedy of Errors* is an upstanding person, even if, like Isabella, she too is destined in comedy to give over the religious life for one of marital devotion. Her abbey is a place of refuge and charitable tending to those in need, as also in *King John*. The 'holy privilege / Of blessèd sanctuary' is presented as a refuge for those like Queen Elizabeth and her children in *Richard III* (III. i. 27–56) who fear for their safety, all the more so when its protections are cynically vitiated by the Duke of Buckingham on behalf of Richard of Gloucester.

Some Catholic clerics are machiavels, of course, like Cardinal Pandulph in *King John*. The Bishop of Winchester, then Cardinal Beaufort, in *1* and *2 Henry VI* is a continual troublemaker as great-uncle of the King intent on furthering his own ambitions, but he is no more dangerous than Richard Plantagenet or Somerset or Suffolk, and to identify him as Catholic is only to say that he is a pre-Reformation figure at court for whom the church has offered a ready means of advancement. The Bishop of Carlisle and the Abbot of Westminster are on the losing side in *Richard II* as supporters of the King, but they are so as a matter of conscience. The Archbishop of York in *1 Henry IV* is similarly a rebel from the King's point of view, but is so because he fears the power of the regime as it threatens the nobility and the church in the north of England. In *2 Henry IV*, he innocently and ill-advisedly trusts the word of Prince John of Lancaster in their negotiations at Gaultree Forest in Yorkshire, orders his troops to disband, and then is arrested as a traitor. 'Will you break your faith?' (IV. ii. 112), he protests to Prince John, only to be answered with the shabby quibble that the Prince has promised redress of grievances but not to spare the lives of the rebel leaders. York is led off to his execution.

The Archbishop of Canterbury in *Henry V*, assisted by the Bishop of Ely, is canny in his manoeuvres to minimize the threat of taxation about to be imposed on the church, but he emerges from this negotiation as a loyal supporter of King Henry in his French wars. One would never know, from his pronouncements, both private and public, that he is a Catholic prelate, were it not that a narrative told of the early fifteenth century presupposes a pre-Reformation setting.

Shakespeare's treatment of Catholicism in *Henry V* (1599) demonstrates to many biographers and critics the suppleness with which he is able to reconcile that faith with the presumably Protestant leanings of much of his London audience. Henry V is a heroic king of the early fifteenth century whose necessarily Catholic upbringing is for the most part conveniently forgotten. He is a son of the church, to be sure, asking its blessing before he embarks on a popular war with the French, but it is not a church that manoeuvres on behalf of Rome. The papacy is never mentioned in the play. Instead, the church becomes an arm of Henry's government, loyal only to him, as it ought to be in Protestant eyes. In another way, too, Henry's style of monarchy is aptly suited to a land that will one day be Protestant: he governs firmly, but with an uncanny ability to know what his countrymen want him to do. He orchestrates the war against France by inviting his nobles, his prelates, and his commoners to voice their approval in advance and to dedicate themselves to serve the cause. The estates of the realm practically beg him in I. ii to lead them into battle, not because he is at all unwilling but because he wants this to be a consensus decision. (See Nuttall, 159–60.) That manner of proceeding is political, to be sure, but it accords well with a view of the church as also a national institution led by a popular leader who listens to his subjects. In Jeffrey Knapp's estimate, Shakespeare 'appears to believe that his audience can draw spiritual strength from their experience of the theater, and *Henry V* shows that this belief has strong affinities with orthodox English Protestant conceptions of the eucharist' (*Shakespeare's Tribe*, 119).

And yet, on the eve of the battle of Agincourt, perhaps England's greatest victory (1415) against a foreign power up to the time of the Spanish Armada (1588), Shakespeare is not afraid to depict Henry as a good Catholic. (See Peter Milward, *Shakespeare the Papist*, 136–9, and Dutton et al., *Region, Religion, and Patronage*, 91–2.) As he prays to God for forgiveness of the 'fault' that his father Henry IV 'made in compassing the crown', Henry describes how he has sought atonement. 'Five hundred poor I have in yearly pay / Who twice a day their withered hands hold up / Toward heaven, to pardon blood', he says, thereby reckoning up the very sorts of good deeds that a Catholic priest might assign as a requirement for absolution. Such reliance on works rather than divine grace was virulently denounced by Luther and other Reformers, in the English church as on the Continent. In a similar vein, Henry confides in soliloquy that he has 'built / Two chantries, where the sad and solemn priests / Still sing for Richard's soul' (IV. i. 296–300). Such chantries, or chapels endowed for the singing of Masses and offering of prayers on behalf of important persons lying buried in their tombs or vaults, were a special target of zealous Reformers, often with sledgehammers in hand to deface 'blasphemous' statuary. Henry V, in the view of many observers, is Shakespeare's perfect blend of good Catholic and proto-Protestant hero.

Shakespeare's most avowed endorsement of Protestantism is perhaps to be found in the late history play *Henry VIII* (1613, written in collaboration with John Fletcher), celebrating ultimately the triumphant birth of Elizabeth in 1533. At the play's end, Archbishop Cranmer, having escaped through Henry VIII's last-minute intervention the machinations of the Protestant-hunting Bishop Gardiner, prophesies a reign of heaven-sent prosperity under Elizabeth once she becomes queen. She will be 'A pattern to all princes', 'loved and feared'. Her foes will 'shake like a field of beaten corn'. When she dies, as a 'maiden phoenix', she will leave her blessed wisdom and strength as a legacy to her successor, namely, James I, in whose reign the play was first produced. (This passage was evidently written by Fletcher, but presumably with the blessing of his co-author, Shakespeare.) Earlier in the play, Cardinal Wolsey is as cunning and manipulative a Catholic prelate as one could hope to find. He treats the King as his subject and sends 'innumerable substance', all of it presumably gotten by underhanded means, 'To furnish Rome, and to prepare the ways... for dignities, to the mere undoing / Of all the kingdom' (III. ii. 314–31). His ambition is nothing less than 'to gain the popedom' (l. 213).

Yet *Henry VIII*'s portrayal of the Catholic Queen Katharine is notably sympathetic. She suffers nobly through a trumped-up trial aimed at removing her from the royal bed so that Henry, whose roving eye has been caught by a foxy young lady named Anne Bullen (or Boleyn), may attempt to sire a male heir. As she dies Katharine is visited by an angelic heavenly host, not simply in her imagination but in a staged vision of '*six personages, clad in white robes, wearing on their heads garlands of bays*', and still more (IV. ii. SD). She is charitable and submissive in the last message she sends to her ungrateful husband. In some mysterious way, the vexed story of England's struggles over the Reformation of the Christian church produces a providential blessing in the coming to the throne of Elizabeth and then James. The participants in the struggle, both Catholic and Protestant, are an essential part of the story of England's ascent to greatness. *Henry VIII*, in Knapp's view (*Shakespeare's Tribe*, 51), embodies a plea for religious reconciliation, in which the words of the Protestant Archbishop Cranmer resound with topical urgency: 'Win straying souls with modesty again; / Cast none away' (V. iii. 64–5). As Richard Wilson notes (*Secret Shakespeare*, 5), Shakespeare chose to frame this argument in collaboration with a co-dramatist, John Fletcher, who was identifiably Protestant.

Overall, Shakespeare's presentation of Catholicism in his plays accords well with the picture biographers have given of him as conversant with Catholic religious practice and sympathetic to many of its rituals even while acknowledging the supremacy of the Tudor state and the Established Church. As we have seen, some biographers regard as overblown the quest for evidence of a Catholic childhood and a period of service in Lancaster in a Catholic household. To be sure, René Weis's characterization of Shakespeare's writings as 'blandly ecumenical' (p. 49) is misleading; Erasmian ecumenical theology was held in suspicion. More convincing is Katherine Duncan-Jones: 'To what extent Shakespeare or his family had indeed been attached to the old religion is extremely hard to determine, since virtually all of the evidence, including most of the literary evidence, can be read in contradictory ways' (p. 193).

If Shakespeare's family perhaps leaned towards Catholicism, Anne Hathaway perhaps did not (Greenblatt, 118). Though her father had significant Catholic associations, Anne's brother Bartholomew embraced Anglicanism with fervour, and Anne herself appears to have been regular in attending service (Honan, 79). The name that Anne and William chose for their first child, Susanna, was, according to Weis, 'favoured by Puritans and derives from the Apocrypha and Susanna, the virtuous wife of Joacim' (p. 62; see also Greenblatt, 90). On the other hand, the Stratford couple Hamnet and Judith Sadler, who may have provided models for the names of Anne and William's twins born in 1585, were later (in 1606) called into church court for not taking the Eucharist (Honan, 79; Pogue, 17–18). The man whom Susanna married in 1607, Dr John Hall, is characterized by Schoenbaum as 'impeccably Protestant' (*Documentary Life*, 235; see also Pogue, 34–8), though even this can be interpreted as having provided cover for a family that needed Protestant credentials (Duncan-Jones, 193). Susanna herself was cited in the spring of 1606 for failing to take communion during the Easter season, but the marking of her name as 'dismissa' may indicate that she avoided having to pay a heavy fine by taking communion after all (Kay, 277). The question of her affiliation thus remains uncertain.

What, in the view of biographers, was Shakespeare's attitude towards Puritanism? The term itself can cover a number of possible meanings, of course, but as it surfaces in its various forms in Shakespeare's plays it tends to focus not so much on separatism or nonconformity as on self-righteous priggishness and a wish to control the moral conduct of others. In the plays, 'Puritan' is an abusive epithet inviting satirical treatment, as is the case also in contemporary plays by Ben Jonson and Thomas Dekker, among others. This animus against Puritanism is sharply aggravated by the implicit view of these dramatists (including Shakespeare) that Puritanism in its extreme form was an enemy of theatre.

The dramatists had good reason to worry. Thomas White preached a sermon at Paul's Cross in 1577 applauding the London authorities for closing down the theatres in time of plague, because, as he said, 'the cause of plagues is sin, if you look to it well, and the cause of sin are plays. Therefore the cause of plagues are plays' (see Honan, 100). Stephen Gosson's *The School of Abuses, Containing a Pleasant Invective Against Poets, Players, Jesters, and Suchlike Caterpillars of a Commonwealth* (1579), fulminated against plays as 'the invention of the devil, the offerings of idolatry, the pomp of worldlings, the blossoms of vanity, the root of apostasy, food of iniquity, riot and adultery'. Philip Stubbes's *The Anatomy of Abuses* (1583) was no less shrill. Still to come was William Prynne's *Histrio-Mastix: The Players' Scourge or Actors' Tragedy* (1633), and the closing of all theatres by reforming extremists in 1642 for the duration of the civil wars. The landowner Giles Allen, who refused in 1599 to renew the lease for the Theatre where Shakespeare's company performed, was a man of Puritan sympathies, who wished, as he said, 'to pull down the same, and to convert the wood and timber thereof to some better use' (Schoenbaum, *Compact Documentary Life*, 207; Greenblatt, 266). More moderate reforming Protestants in London in the 1580s and 1590s often flocked to the theatre, but even they were to become increasingly alienated in the 1600s and later as many plays, especially in the so-called 'private' theatres featuring boy actors and a select clientele, satirized what the dramatists perceived to be Puritan mannerisms and attitudes.

Shakespeare's *Twelfth Night*, *c*.1600–2, thus was staged at a critical time. In it, Shakespeare takes up the matter of Puritanism with what Greenblatt (pp. 82–3) and others have seen as an unusually topical edge. 'Marry, sir, sometimes he's a kind of Puritan', says Maria to Sir Toby of Malvolio as she prepares to devise a plot to be revenged on Malvolio for his humourless attempts to quash their merrymaking and his ridiculous aspirations to be a gentleman. What does she mean, that Malvolio is 'a kind of Puritan'? 'Oh, if I thought that, I'd beat him like a dog', chimes in Sir Andrew, though he is then unable to explain what he means. 'I have reason enough', he lamely concludes. Maria then redefines the issue. 'The devil a Puritan that he is', she tells her friends, 'or anything else constantly, but a time-pleaser, an affectioned ass, that cons state without book and utters it by great swaths; the best persuaded of himself, so crammed, as he thinks, with excellencies, that it is his grounds of faith that all that look on him love him' (II. iii. 139–51). She is careful not to condemn all Puritans with a blanket denunciation. If some Puritans behave officiously like Malvolio, she implies, so much the worse for them. The issue is not Puritanism as such but the behaviour of some people who evidently feel called upon to act the role of moral policeman. Theatre has no tolerance for such, and critics have wondered if Shakespeare did not entirely agree. Conceivably, Shakespeare aimed his satiric portrait of Malvolio at some officious person at court, such as Sir William Knollys, the Comptroller of the Royal Household (see Chambers, *Shakespeare*, i. 407, and Ackroyd, 407–8). At the same time, Shakespeare analyses the phenomenon with a moderating tact and precise definition.

Malvolio does behave in ways that many critics have seen as Puritan-like, for all Maria's sensible caution about applying the label too hastily. His preference for dressing in 'sad and civil' garb (III. iv. 5) makes all the funnier the way he is tricked into outfitting himself with cross-garters and yellow stockings. Maria speaks of his 'grounds of faith' in his own self-satisfaction, using a favourite metaphor of the reformers. When he finds the letter that Maria has put in his way, purportedly written by the Countess Olivia, Malvolio is fascinated by the riddling 'M.O.A.I.' and seeks to unlock it: 'If I could make that resemble something in me!' (II. v. 118–19), he says to himself, in the manner of torturing the text to yield up a predetermined meaning. Puritans were infamous for doing just that. Most of all, Malvolio is arguably Puritan-like in his hostility towards festive revelry and in his implacable determination at the end to 'be revenged on the whole pack of you' (V. i. 378). C. L. Barber (pp. 240–61), among others, interprets this as an ominous shot across the bow by Puritan forces that, in 1642, would indeed gain their revenge by closing down all theatrical activity in England.

In his few uses of the term elsewhere, Shakespeare shows that he is aware of its defamatory nature. Lavatch, the witty fool in *All's Well That Ends Well*, pairs 'young Charbon the Puritan' and 'old Paysam the papist' as opposite stereotypes, who, though 'their hearts are severed in religion, their heads are both one' (I. iii. 51–4). 'Young' and 'old' stress the contrast between the new reformed religion and the ancient faith of Catholicism. Later in the same scene, Lavatch offers his wry opinion that 'Though honesty be no Puritan, yet it will do no hurt; it will wear the surplice of humility over the black gown of a big heart' (ll. 92–4). Puritans were widely accused of hypocritically concealing pride and avarice beneath the outward appearance of simple humble dress. The Clown in *The Winter's Tale*, at the sheep-shearing, reckons that there is 'but one Puritan' amongst the singers present, 'and he sings psalms to hornpipes' (IV. iii. 43–5). Puritan weavers from the Netherlands were noted as psalm singers, and were often laughed at for their plainspoken piety. In a brothel scene in *Pericles*, the Bawd deplores the invincible virtuousness of Marina by averring that 'she would make a Puritan of the devil if he should cheapen a kiss of her' (IV. vi. 9–10). Falstaff apes Puritan mannerisms when he protests, with mock piety, 'now am I, if a man should speak truly, little better than one of the wicked. I must give over this life, and I will give it over' (*1 Henry IV*, I. ii. 92–5; see Greenblatt, 220–1).

If biographers have seen Shakespeare then as perhaps no friend of Puritanism, though cautiously avoiding any wholesale denunciation, what biographical conclusions can be ventured about his attitude towards the Jews? Offhand references provide what may be a clue to a prejudice of which the author is not particularly conscious. Greenblatt observes a number of these (pp. 259–60). 'If I do not love her, I am a Jew', says Benedick of Beatrice in *Much Ado About Nothing* (II. iii. 257–8). Benedick is not talking about the Jews; he is using a defamatory analogy in which Jews are assumed to be duplicitous. 'Jew' is a kind of swear word. 'I am a Jew else, an Ebrew Jew', is Falstaff's comically outlandish way of asserting that he is telling the truth when everyone knows that he is lying (*1 Henry IV*, II. iv. 177). 'A Jew would have wept longer at our parting', says Lance in his comic soliloquy about parting from home with his dog, Crab (*The Two Gentlemen of Verona*, II. iii. 11–12). 'Jew' is here a derogatory standard for hard-heartedness. The 'Liver of blaspheming Jew' in the Weird Sisters' cauldron in *Macbeth* (IV. i. 26) is an ingredient associated with all that is obscenely diabolical. In Costard's characterization of Mote in *Love's Labour's Lost* as 'my incony Jew' (III. i. 133), any idea of Jewishness seems to have disappeared entirely. These telltale remarks are apparently symptomatic of the pervasively and at times mindlessly anti-Semitic culture in which Shakespeare lived. Though they are the pronouncements of his dramatic characters, not his own, they are word choices and patterns that came to him as he wrote.

In his portrayal of Shylock in *The Merchant of Venice*, Shakespeare is notably and admirably more sympathetic than are his contemporary playwrights, including Marlowe in *The Jew of Malta*, to which Shakespeare's play would appear to be a reply of sorts. (Harold Bloom proposes that 'we regard the Jew of Venice as a reaction formation or ironic swerve away from Marlowe's Jew of Malta', 172–3.) Shylock is given an eloquent speech, 'Hath not a Jew eyes', etc. (III. i. 55–69), pleading his human vulnerability to the warped examples of vindictiveness provided by his Christian tormentors. The Christians in the play are sybaritic, complacent, and determined to exclude Jews from their power-wielding society except on terms they specify of renouncing the practice of usury and, finally, of conversion (forced, if necessary) to the Christian faith. Modern productions regularly play up the selfishness and hypocrisy of the Christian community in this play, and present Shylock as a victim of persecution even if also embittered and hardened by the treatment he has received (see, for example, Wells, *Shakespeare for All Time*, 308–9).

Yet even the famous 'Hath not a Jew eyes' speech translates into a justification of revenge by Christian precedent. 'If a Christian wrong a Jew, what should his sufferance be by Christian example?' asks Shylock. 'Why, revenge' (III. i. 65–7). This eye-for-an-eye ethic is characteristic of Shylock from the start, in the view of many inter-preters, even before he has been wronged by Lorenzo's stealing of his daughter and a considerable amount of wealth. 'I hate him for he is a Christian', Shylock confides in soliloquy, speaking of Antonio, 'But more for that in low simplicity / He lends out money gratis and brings down / The rate of usance here with us in Venice'. To catch Antonio 'on the hip' will serve to 'feed fat the ancient grudge I bear him' (I. iii. 39–44). Antonio has, to be sure, spat on Shylock's Jewish gaberdine, but he has done so out of hatred for what Antonio views as the anti-Christian lending of money as usury. Antonio indicates his willing-ness to accept Shylock as a good person if he will give up usury. 'The Hebrew will turn Christian; he grows kind', Antonio declares to Bassanio when Shylock has agreed to lend money without interest 'in a merry sport' with a pound of flesh as security (ll. 144–77).

For all Shakespeare's evenhandedness when compared with Marlowe, many analysts detect an ineradicable strain of anti-Semitism at the heart of the play. It takes the form of privileging Christian ideals of forgiveness and personal self-sacrifice over a Jew-ish ethic of avoiding risk and driving a hard bargain. When Shylock concedes to Bassanio that Antonio is 'a good man', he hastens to explain his meaning: Antonio is a safe credit risk. The loan that Bassanio and Antonio are seeking from Shylock is one that Shylock can prudently agree to, so long as the terms are adequately beneficial to him. When Bassanio says, of Shylock's thinking he may safely take Antonio's bond, 'Be assured you may', Shylock has a quick and witty answer: 'I will be assured I may' (I. iii. 12–28), i.e. I will make sure that the terms are to my advantage. Shylock's illustrative example of thrift from the Old Testament is a story of what Christian readers might call shystering: Jacob outwits his master, Laban, by contracting that all the parti-coloured sheep of the breeding season are to fall to Jacob's share, whereupon Jacob sets up variegated stakes before the ewes as they are copulating with the rams. All the lambs become Jacob's, to the delight of Shylock, who insists that 'This was a way to thrive, and he was blest; / And thrift is blessing, if men steal it not' (ll. 76–88).

Shylock never takes chances if he can possibly avoid them. Bassanio, conversely, embraces the highly risky adventure of a quest for the hand of Portia, mistress of Belmont. He compares this adventure to that of Jason in his voyage for the golden fleece, and to that of the schoolboy who shoots an arrow in order to find one that he has just lost (I. i. 140–72). Antonio, a merchant who prides himself on his venture-capitalist enterprise of taking huge risks for potentially huge profits that are also of commercial benefit to society at large, is also ready to risk his own life in support of his dear friend Bassanio's search for a wealthy and beautiful wife. *The Merchant of Venice* at times is notably sympathetic to Shylock, but it also sees a deficiency in the Old Testament ethic of revenge and quest for security that Christianity can potentially transform into an ethic of generosity and forgiveness. Forced conversion, in these terms, offers a blessing in disguise to those benighted souls who, however understandably, adhere to an older dispensation. Willing conversion, as delineated in the play, erases the essence of Jewishness in those who choose the better path. 'This house is hell', says Jessica of her father's home. 'I shall be saved by my husband. He hath made me a Christian' (II. iii. 2; III. v. 17–18). Lancelot, the clownish servant who also transfers his allegiance to a Christian master, agrees. 'You have the grace of God, sir', he declares to Bassanio, 'and he [Shylock] hath enough' (II. ii. 141–2).

The Christians in this play are all too apt to fail to live up to the high standards of moral behaviour their religion teaches them, as many critics and theatre directors have shown, but the vision of *caritas* remains. It is expressed in Lorenzo's musings to Jessica, on a moonlit night, of what the stars above their heads appear to signify about the harmony of the spheres: 'There's not the smallest orb which thou behold'st / But in his motion like an angel sings, / Still choiring to the young-eyed cherubins.' Mortals, closed in by their 'muddy vesture of decay', can only dimly perceive the 'harmony that is in immortal souls', but that harmony is nonetheless there (V. i. 58–65). However disappointing the actual behaviour of Christians may be, in vindictive name-calling and legal quibbling during the trial scene, the play's vision of a better world does seem postulated on the New Dispensation of Christianity rather than the Old. To that significant extent, the anti-Semitic premiss of *The Merchant of Venice* refuses to go away. Shakespeare may have known some Jews (and other 'strangers') in cosmopolitan London, some of whom had come as musicians in the time of Henry VIII and some of whom outwardly conformed to Anglicanism while being observant of their own faith in private, and such acquaintance might well have broadened his outlook as well as providing dramatic material (Honan, 99–100, and Shapiro, *Shakespeare and the Jews*). Certainly we can justly say that Shakespeare does better than his contemporaries, but the play still leaves its audience and readers with a deficiency that today seems parochial.

We have not yet explored the biographical quest for Shakespeare's attitudes, insofar as they can be ascertained, towards the Calvinism that was so prominent a feature of Anglican theology in his day, and towards more sceptical approaches to religious dogma that were also in the air. These topics are better reserved for the two chapters that follow.

6

Out of the Depths

A mood of sceptical pessimism hovers over Shakespeare's work at the turn of the century and in the decade that followed, when he focused intently on the writing of his great tragedies. Biographers have often characterized this as the third phase of Shakespeare's creativity, in a four-part pattern that owes its original inspiration to Edward Dowden's influential biography, *Shakspere: A Critical Study of His Mind and Art*, written in 1876 in the years after Charles Darwin's *Origin of Species*.

Dowden's proposed four-part structure for Shakespearean biography was based to a significant extent on nineteenth-century philological work (much of it German) on the dating of the plays. Aided with a clearer sense than before had been possible of the chronological ordering of the canon, Dowden outlined four phases in Shakespeare's development. A period of learning his trade (*The Comedy of Errors*, *Richard III*, etc., roughly 1589–94) was quickly followed by a phase of brilliant success and public recognition of his genius owing to his sublime achievements in romantic comedy (*Much Ado About Nothing*, *As You Like It*, *Twelfth Night*) and the English history play (*Richard II* to *Henry V* in 1599). Then, in about 1599–1600, more or less halfway through the journey of his professional life, Shakespeare moved in a remarkably new direction. *Hamlet*, written at about this time, was a 'point of departure in Shakspere's immense and final sweep of mind', one in which he was 'reached and touched by the shadow of some of the deep mysteries of human existence' (Dowden, 198). Shakespeare undertook to explore with ever-increasing intensity the tragic world to which he had previously devoted less attention. A final fourth period of 'contemplative serenity' was to follow, one that would provide, in Ted Hughes's phrase (p. 1), 'the redemption of the tragic action'. This fourth phase will be the subject of the next chapter.

Dowden is at pains to insist that Shakespeare's tragic phase was not necessarily for him 'a period of depression and gloom'. Nevertheless, says Dowden, Shakespeare 'was now sounding the depths of evil as he had never sounded them before' (p. 204). His whole spiritual being seemed to cry 'Out of the depths', as though echoing Psalm 130: 'Out of the depths have I cried unto thee, O Lord.' The human dilemmas he now pondered included the death of a father and a deep puzzlement about human (especially female) frailty in *Hamlet*, the contradictions of Stoical philosophy and political stalemate in *Julius Caesar*, disillusionment about war and heroism in *Troilus and Cressida*, obsessive and self-destructive human carnality in *Measure for Measure*, male inconstancy in *All's Well That Ends Well*, the nightmare of sexual jealousy in *Othello*, filial ingratitude and the prospect of a godless universe in *King Lear*, and the seemingly irresistible pull of determinism towards the killing of a king in *Macbeth*. The profound misanthropy of *Timon of Athens* and *Coriolanus*, in the late years of what Dowden calls the 'tragic' period, will be considered in the next chapter.

The present chapter takes up the phase, then, of what Dowden identifies as the dark night of the soul. The shift in direction and emphasis away from the earlier romantic comedies and English history plays seems unmistakable. Shakespeare set aside the English history play in 1599 with *Henry V* and did not return to the genre until the much later and uncharacteristic *Henry VIII* in 1613. Romantic comedy came to an end in about 1600 with *Twelfth Night*, even if comedies of a more puzzling sort continued to appear for a time in what F. S. Boas has labelled (in 1896) as the problem plays: *All's Well That Ends Well* and *Measure for Measure* (c.1601–4), and the almost unclassifiable *Troilus and Cressida* in 1601. Thereafter, comedy of any sort ceased for a time. What had happened? How have biographers since Dowden coped with the phenomenon?

The explanations have been essentially these. Perhaps Shakespeare was giving dramatic form to a series of deep personal losses. Or perhaps the shift of emphasis in his plays was a response to the alterations in England's political climate resulting from the death of

Queen Elizabeth and the coming to the throne of her cousin, James VI of Scotland and I of England, in 1603. Or perhaps the shift was something culturally larger, not simply from Elizabethan to Jacobean but from a late medieval world of religious faith to one of increasing scepticism, scientific rationalism and discovery, overseas exploration, and all the rest. Perhaps the bitterly cold weather in the winter of 1600–1, and the hostile rivalry that erupted between the adult acting companies and the newly reactivated Children of Paul's in late 1599, fostered a mood of pessimism and helpless anxiety (Honan, 274–5 ff.; Dutton, 117–18). Or perhaps Shakespeare's shift of focus was an artistic one, enabling him to set aside his by now well-practised genres of romantic comedy and English history play in favour of what was for him the relatively new and untested genre of tragedy. He had, to be sure, written two earlier tragedies, *Titus Andronicus* some time around 1590 and *Romeo and Juliet* in 1594–6, along with some English history plays like *Richard III* and *Richard II* that were identified as tragedies on their original title pages, but biographers have generally agreed that he did not really find his métier in tragedy until *Julius Caesar* in 1599 and *Hamlet* in the following year or so.

A combination of one or more of these hypotheses is another possibility explored by biographers.

Shakespeare did experience personal loss during these years, and the events have struck some biographers as having a relevance to *Hamlet*. Shakespeare's only son Hamnet, bearing a name that is uncannily close to that of the play, died in August 1596 at the age of 11. Shakespeare's father died in 1601, his younger brother Edmund (perhaps, according to Duncan-Jones, 199, his favourite brother) in 1607, and his mother in 1608. The death of Hamnet must have been a terrible blow. In that same year (1596), as we have seen, Shakespeare instituted proceedings that would enable his father—and himself—to be styled 'gentleman'. Patriarchy laid great stress on the need for a son to inherit from and continue the line of the father, and is visibly a theme of *Hamlet*. As Ackroyd argues, 'it cannot be wholly coincidental that Shakespeare was drawn ... to the tragedy of Hamlet, Prince of Denmark, who is haunted by the spectre of his dead father' (p. 288).

Shakespeare may well have been in London when the death of Hamnet occurred, perhaps suddenly. We have no way of knowing if he reached Stratford in time to bid his son farewell, but quite possibly not. The cause of death is not known, but could easily have been a swiftly fatal infectious disease. Duncan-Jones (90–1) and Greer (195–7) note that fraternal twins were (and are) apt to be premature, sometimes leaving one of the pair—perhaps Hamnet in this case—less fitted out for survival than his twin.

Yet the writing of *Hamlet* was not to come for some three or four years after the death of the son. Why did Shakespeare seemingly not pour forth his soul in some fashion, after this presumably cataclysmic event, into *Hamlet* and other plays he wrote between 1596 and 1600? These are the years of his most successful romantic comedies, *Much Ado About Nothing*, *The Merry Wives of Windsor*, and *As You Like It*, and of his most successfully 'comic' English history plays celebrating the rise to royal power of Prince Hal. Biographers (such as Kay, 169) have puzzled over Shakespeare's silence on the death of a son in these plays.

One son in these plays does die, to be sure: Hotspur, whose untimely death at the Battle of Shrewsbury in Act V of *1 Henry IV* is then mourned by his widow Kate in *2 Henry IV*. As Richard P. Wheeler observes in 'Deaths in the Family', Kate's bitter upbraiding of Hotspur's father, Northumberland, for having failed to show up at Shrewsbury in time to rescue his son bears a suggestive resemblance to the way Shakespeare could have felt if he had been unable to reach in time the bedside of his dying son, Hamnet. 'Who then persuaded you to stay at home?' Kate chides her father-in-law. 'There were two honors lost, yours and your son's. . . . / Him did you leave, / Second to none, unseconded by you, / To look upon the hideous god of war / In disadvantage' (II. iii. 17–36). Yet even if a personal note of grief is discernible here, the years 1596–1600 have otherwise struck most biographers as strangely silent on the loss of a son and heir.

The puzzle is compounded by the fact that Shakespeare shows himself fully capable of mourning the loss of a son in plays written before the death of Hamnet in 1596. Lord Talbot, in *1 Henry VI* (*c*.1589–92), grieves eloquently for the loss of his son John, whom the father has urged to flee the impending disaster of a French victory near Bordeaux, but to no avail; John stays in the name of honour and dies, darting 'Into the clust'ring battle of the French, / And in that sea of blood my boy did drench / His overmounting spirit; and there died / My Icarus, my blossom, in his pride' (IV. vii. 13–16). In *3 Henry VI*, at a battle in the civil war in Yorkshire, King Henry beholds the piteous spectacle of a father who has mistakenly killed his own son and a son who has mistakenly killed his own father. 'Bloody Clifford', in the same play, stabs Rutland, youngest son of the Duke of York, because 'Thy father slew my father', i.e. York slew old Clifford (I. iii. 47; see *2 Henry VI*, V. ii for that death). The deaths of the young princes Edward and Richard are played to full emotional effect in *Richard III* (*c*.1592–4), too late for their father, Edward IV, to have grieved for them. All these moving sequences pre-date the death of Hamnet.

Holden (*Life and Work*, 150–2) and Greenblatt would like to date *King John* in 1596, 'just after the boy was laid to rest' (p. 290), but the argument is potentially a circular one: the moving depiction of Constance's sorrow over the absence and much-feared death of her son Arthur ('Grief fills the room up of my absent child', etc., III. iv. 93–7) offers an instance in which Shakespeare could have chosen to mourn the loss of Hamnet if he wrote this passage after Hamnet had died, but the jury is still out on that dating. Dutton (22, 177) prefers a date around 1594, and Honigmann (*Shakespeare: The 'Lost Years'*, 76) a date still earlier than that. Weis proposes that the passage is 'grimly premonitory' (p. 183). Stephen Dedalus, in James Joyce's *Ulysses*, has a similar view: 'His [Shakespeare's] boyson's death is the death-scene of young Arthur in *King John*. Hamlet, the black prince, is Hamnet Shakespeare' ('Scylla and Charybdis', 208). Germaine Greer would like to see personal expression in Shakespeare's response to the death of young Arthur, because, as Greer nicely puts it, the passage so poignantly explores 'what a bereaved mother's anguish is like' (p. 200), not just what a father might feel as in *1 Henry VI*, but the dating of *King John* remains uncertain.

A more persuasive suggestion, made by Richard Wheeler ('Deaths in the Family'), is that the death of Hamnet does emerge, by way of analogy, in *Twelfth Night* in about 1600, roughly four years after the death had occurred. Four years or so might seem long, but mourning for such an event can take time and patience until the idea can be confronted and transformed into an endurable artistic fantasy. The play features boy–girl twins (compare Hamnet and Judith) who are separated by the seeming death of the boy. Viola thereupon assumes the role of her 'lost' brother until an unexpected happy ending restores the brother to her and allows her to resume her role as young woman on the verge of marriage.

Lost children do of course come back in the dreams of bereaved parents and relatives, often in seemingly miraculous circumstances like those experienced by Viola and her brother. Grace Tiffany has written a charming novel called *My Father Had a Daughter* in which Judith is imagined as outraged to discover how her famous father has had the effrontery to parade their private family loss in *Twelfth Night*, but then eventually comes around to seeing how wise and compassionate her father has really been. Weis similarly views *Twelfth Night* as 'a play about twins miraculously reunited by means of dramatic orchestration', thereby creating an artistic 'counter-reality' in which the dramatist 'is king of all he surveys' (p. 392).

Weis argues that Hamnet is also commemorated in *Hamlet*, especially since the names are essentially interchangeable, and speculates that if Hamnet had happened to drown in the Avon we would have a neat parallel to Ophelia's drowning as well as to the supposed drowning of Sebastian in *Twelfth Night* (pp. 3, 268). A Katherine Hamlet had in fact drowned just outside Stratford in 1579 in such a way that, as Duncan-Jones writes, 'an inquest had to be held to determine the exact cause of her death, so that she might have lawful burial' (p. 152). Russell Fraser wonders if this unfortunate event, occurring when Shakespeare was 15, might have stuck in his memory (p. 192). These are biographical speculations, but they do offer opportunities to biographers to think of ways in which factual circumstances can perhaps provide materials for dramatization even in an author who does not talk directly about himself.

Did the death of Shakespeare's father in 1601 perhaps provoke an emotional crisis that led to the writing of *Hamlet*? Is that play Shakespeare's way (as Weis puts it, p. 272) of 'coming to terms with his own spiritual betrayal of his father'? Greenblatt's *Hamlet in Purgatory* dwells on the Ghost's parting command to his son, 'Remember me!' (I. v. 5.92), and argues that we may see in this moment the portraiture of Shakespeare as a conforming Anglican haunted in 1601 'by the spirit of his Catholic father pleading for suffrages to relieve his soul from the pains of Purgatory' (p. 249). Weis (p. 272) similarly posits that John Shakespeare's Catholicism was a continual source of unhappy disagreement between him and his Protestant son: witness Hamlet's studying in Wittenberg, the cradle of Protestantism, where Martin Luther had nailed his theses to the door of the

Schlosskirche in 1517. Both writers presuppose that *Hamlet* was written after 8 September 1601, when John Shakespeare was buried—a preciseness of date that is hard to demonstrate, though conceivably an earlier anticipation of that death could have weighed on the son, if he knew that his father was in failing health. Equally uncertain, as we have seen, is the proposition that John Shakespeare was Catholic and his son Protestant, or (still more uncertain) that the purported difference was a source of friction and guilty feelings.

To go still further afield, the anti-Stratfordians Dorothy and Charlton Ogburn suggest that 'Remember me!' is surely the cry from the grave of the seventeenth Earl of Oxford, putative author of the works of 'Shakespeare', pleading to some future researcher like the Ogburns to rescue Oxford from an undeserved anonymity. 'Remember me!' can mean many things to many readers.

More reliably, perhaps, *Hamlet* can be read as an imaginative representation of new and challenging doubts and questions to which Shakespeare turned at this point in his artistic career. *Hamlet* is full of debates and uncertainties on questions of the utmost seriousness. Is Hamlet right to interpret his own story, finally, as one in which 'There's a divinity that shapes our ends, / Rough-hew them how we will' (V. ii. 10–11) and in which 'There is special providence in the fall of a sparrow' (ll. 217–18)? His resolution to 'Let be' (l. 222) shows a courageous and self-assured calm that all will turn out as it pleases God, and indeed the denouement of the play's final scene does deliver into his hands the slaying of Claudius and the cessation of his own troubled life. Yet Horatio interprets Hamlet's story very differently, as the consequence of chance encounters, of 'purposes mistook / Fall'n on th'inventors' heads' (V. ii. 366–7). Moreover, the Christian ideology of Hamlet's interpretation of his own history is at odds with the pagan ethic of revenge that has motivated his father's ghostly command to 'Revenge his [the father's] foul and most unnatural murder' (I. v. 26). What are we to make of the paradox that Hamlet sees himself as having finally achieved that objective not by his own active intervention but by submitting himself passively to the will of the Almighty?

Hamlet's greatest uncertainty has to do with knowing when to act and when to pause and reflect. As Dowden and others have seen, the answer is far from simple, so much so that Hamlet's hesitation need not be explained away as driven by a paralysis of the will. Hamlet berates himself for inactivity, and he does urge himself forward to act; but when he hears the voice of a man concealed behind a curtain in his mother's private chambers and assumes rationally enough that the perfect moment is at hand to slay his hated uncle, his forthright action of stabbing through the curtain produces a baleful result: Hamlet kills the concealed Polonius instead of the Claudius he had supposed to be there. He at once finds meaning in this tragic mistake: 'heaven hath pleased it so / To punish me with this, and this with me, / That I must be their scourge and minister' (III. iv. 180–2). In other words, as Fredson Bowers explains, Hamlet understands now that he must justly suffer heaven-sent punishment for his having killed the wrong person, just as Polonius also must pay for his officious snooping.

Later, too, in his conversation with the Captain of Fortinbras's army, Hamlet perceives on every hand how the question of when to act and when to desist from action is profoundly complex to the point of cosmic irony. 'Examples gross as earth' exhort one to act, Hamlet observes, even though the reward may be nothing more than 'an eggshell', a matter of finding 'quarrel in a straw / When honor's at the stake' (IV. iv. 47–57). If that is true of Fortinbras and his campaign to conquer parts of Poland that no sane person would wish to farm, it is also true of Laertes, who acts forthrightly in the name of a code of revenge demanding that he slay Hamlet as the killer of his father. Hamlet did indeed slay Polonius, but Laertes's implacable pursuit of his duty as a revenging son leads only to his falling into Claudius's dishonourable trap of using secret poison and an unbated sword against Hamlet. Perhaps Hamlet is right, then, in the view of Bowers and others, to perceive that 'Our indiscretion sometime serves us well / When our deep plots do pall' (V. ii. 8–9). 'Rashness' has a rightful place in the scheme of things, but an appreciation of the conundrum does not always guide one as to when to act or when not to act in any given situation.

Biographers and other writers on Shakespeare have often tried to explain these dilemmas in *Hamlet* by analysing Hamlet's penchant for delay as a symptom of melancholic distress. Johann Wolfgang von Goethe, in 1778, saw Hamlet's delay as 'the key to Hamlet's whole procedure'. Stunned by the perception that he is unequal to the task of accomplishing what his father's Ghost has demanded, Hamlet, in

Goethe's view, is overwhelmed by 'amazement and sorrow'. His 'beautiful, pure, noble, and most moral nature' cannot carry him through the crisis of a loss of nerve. August W. von Schlegel, in 1809, similarly sizes up Hamlet as a man whose brooding mentality 'cripples the power of acting'. In England, Samuel Taylor Coleridge championed in 1808 the view of Hamlet as one who 'vacillates from sensibility, and procrastinates from thought, and loses the power of action in the energy of resolve'.

More recently, this reading has commended itself to classically trained scholars, who see in Hamlet's delay the 'hamartia' or 'tragic flaw or mistake' demanded by Aristotelian dramatic analysis, and to psychoanalysts, notably Sigmund Freud and his disciple Ernest Jones, who in 1910 argued that Hamlet is driven by a subconscious incestuous longing for his mother of such intensity that he finds he cannot punish Claudius for having done the very thing that Hamlet himself incestuously desires. Hamlet's own confession to Rosencrantz and Guildenstern that he has lost all his mirth, 'but wherefore I know not' (II. ii. 296–7), seems to such critics to underscore the seriousness of the psychological problem. Yet other critics have observed that when Coleridge describes Hamlet he is really describing himself. 'I have a smack of Hamlet myself, if I may say so', Coleridge confessed (*Table Talk*, i. 59, 24 June 1827; quoted and discussed in Gary Taylor, *Reinventing Shakespeare*, 102–3). Coleridge, notoriously, could never carry through his great designs. Wells (*Shakespeare: A Dramatic Life*, 300) enlarges the point: 'Coleridge is not the only one to have fancied he had "a smack of Hamlet" himself.' The warning applies generally to analyses of Hamlet's delay as pathological.

Despite such warnings, some recent biographers have wondered if the supposed portrait of nearly pathological delay may reflect some torment that Shakespeare himself was undergoing in 1600–1. To Greenblatt (p. 308), Shakespeare 'had every reason' to be shaken by the failed rebellion attempt and execution in 1601 of the Earl of Essex, especially since the Earl of Southampton, an active supporter of Essex and Shakespeare's one-time patron, was also imprisoned and in danger of being beheaded. Shakespeare's acting company had had to explain why they had agreed to perform *Richard II* on the very eve of the rebellion attempt. Or was the problem something deeper and more personal involving the death of an only son some four years earlier and the death of the father in September 1601? Shakespeare could have been worried about his father's health prior to that event, especially if, as Greenblatt speculates, father and son had talked about the afterlife and had wondered if the whole business about Purgatory was perhaps not true (p. 317). Did Protestant denial of the existence of ghosts confront Shakespeare with a personal anxiety that Anglican doctrine could not assuage? If Shakespeare played the part of the Ghost in early performances, as stage tradition maintains, was he able to conjure up within himself 'the voice of his dead son, the voice of his dying father, and perhaps too his own voice, as it would sound when it came from the grave' (Greenblatt, 320–2)?

Weis incorporates the whole family in his analysis of Shakespeare's 'obsessive need' to write *Hamlet*: in that play, writes Weis, 'he seems to have worked through various obsessions and anxieties about his mother, his brothers, his dead son, and the Earl of Southampton' (p. 328). Kay hears in *Hamlet* echoes of new responsibilities and worries heaped upon Shakespeare by his father's death: 'final responsibility for property, tenants, business interests and dependents far away in the town of his birth', and the like. 'After 1601', writes Kay, 'the merry-cheeked old man was no more. There may have been in Shakespeare's mind as he approached his play—or as he returned to revise it—a powerful sense of obligation to his father, to see that his memory was properly served' (p. 230).

A counter-argument is to propose that Hamlet, though he does of course employ delaying tactics in his contest of wills with Claudius and in his urgent wish to find out if the ghost he has seen is real, does not delay unnecessarily. He faces a profoundly ethical conflict, one that is made all the more acute, as Ackroyd argues (pp. 202–3), in the context of his Christian faith. Hamlet is a Christian who is also powerfully drawn to the teachings of Stoicism. He is eloquent in praise of his friend Horatio, who is prepared to endure misfortune through stoical resolve and passivity. Horatio, as Hamlet sees him, 'is not passion's slave'. He is 'A man that Fortune's buffets and rewards / Hast ta'en with equal thanks'. His 'blood and judgment are so well commeddled' that he is not 'a pipe for Fortune's finger / To sound what stop she pleases' (III. ii. 65–71).

Hamlet rightly perceives that classical Stoicism teaches indifference to the rewards of Fortune as well as the strength to withstand adversity. The two ideas are the two sides of one coin. If one does not crave worldly success and good luck, one cannot be disappointed when the capricious goddess Fortune turns her inexorable wheel. Hamlet longs to be like Horatio in his stoical resolve. The two men love to argue about ideas as fellow students at Wittenberg. They love to disagree. Horatio is the sceptic, the rationalist, who must see a ghost before he can believe in one; Hamlet is the Christian who insists to Horatio, when they have in fact seen and heard the Ghost, that 'There are more things in heaven and earth ... Than are dreamt of in your philosophy' (I. v. 175–6). Horatio's reading of Hamlet's story is profoundly different from Hamlet's Christian interpretation: to Horatio, the story is not providential but instead one of 'accidental judgments, casual slaughters', and 'purposes mistook / Fall'n on th'inventors' heads' (V. ii. 364–7).

These many differences leave *Hamlet* strikingly open to varying interpretations. The result is that, though biographers disagree as to whether Shakespeare himself embraces Christian providentialism or secular historicism, or some admixture of these creeds, he is undoubtedly fascinated with huge philosophical uncertainties that have not been as evident in his earlier plays and poems. Shapiro argues that the revisions of the *Hamlet* text 'suggest a degree of uncertainty on Shakespeare's part, as if he were not quite as sure as he had been in *Julius Caesar* or *As You Like It* where his characters and plot were heading'; Hamlet's tortured soliloquies derail the revenge plot, resulting in an incoherent resolution (*1599*, 307–12).

Calvinism also engages with the question of human choice and of God's determination of events. As another burning topic of Shakespeare's day, it surfaces in *Hamlet*. Many Anglican clerics preached a Calvinist theology that was strongly oriented to the Genevan Bible (Schoenbaum, *Compact Documentary Life*, 56; Nuttall, 21–2). These Protestant ministers, forced into exile during the reign of the Catholic Queen Mary, 1553–8, had taken refuge in Geneva, and had then returned to England in 1558 inspired by the teachings of Jean Calvin. Cambridge University especially became a centre of Calvinist ideology. The emphasis on salvation through faith rather than works was common to Lutheranism and other forms of Protestantism, but Calvinist teaching stressed a predetermined salvation for the Elect and damnation for those who were not. Since God is all-powerful, all-knowing, and eternal, Calvin reasoned in his *Institutes* and other writings, all events must take place as God wills. No human can earn salvation, since we are all innately prone to evil after the Fall of Man in the Garden of Eden. Salvation is the gift of the Supreme Deity. It is His to give or not give as He chooses, and it does not behove us, in our ignorance and fallen condition, to question His mysterious wisdom. Nor can we deduce from this that God is somehow the author of evil; we are responsible for our own failures. If Calvin's teachings seem paradoxical, that is no more than to say that all profound religious truths are paradoxical.

Calvinist influence in *Hamlet* suggests itself to Shakespeare biographers at several points. 'Why wouldst thou be a breeder of sinners?' Hamlet asks Ophelia. 'I am myself indifferent honest, but yet I could accuse me of such things that it were better my mother had not borne me: I am very proud, revengeful, ambitious, with more offenses at my back than I have thoughts to put them in, imagination to give them shape, or time to act them in. What should such fellows as I do crawling between earth and heaven? We are arrant knaves all; believe none of us' (III. i. 122–30). When Polonius assures Hamlet that he will see to it that the players visiting Elsinore Castle are entertained properly, 'according to their desert', Hamlet fires back, 'God's bodikin, man, much better. Use every man after his desert, and who shall scape whipping?' (II. ii. 527–30).

These are the premises not just of Calvinism but of Augustinian teaching and of late medieval Christianity generally, to be sure, but they take on a more polemical edge in the play's contrasting portraiture of Hamlet Senior and Claudius. 'Look here upon this picture, and on this', Hamlet lectures his mother, as he shows her the likenesses of her former and present husbands. One image shows 'Hyperion's curls, the front of Jove himself', while the other is 'like a mildewed ear, / Blasting his wholesome brother' (III. iv. 54–66). To set them side by side thus is to contrast 'Hyperion to a satyr' (I. ii. 140). This antithesis between the two brother kings is, as Honan (p. 284) and Harold Jenkins (pp. 128–32) cogently argue, at the heart of the play's dramatic and moral structure. Claudius is a textbook case of the unregenerate sinner, incapable of extricating himself from his damnable predicament despite his knowing precisely what he would have to do to save his soul: give up 'My crown, mine own ambition, and my queen', the things for which he murdered his brother. 'May one be pardoned and retain th'offense?' he asks rhetorically, knowing that the answer has to be, No, one cannot be pardoned on those terms (III. iii. 55–6). Claudius lacks the will to save himself from eternal damnation. We will come back shortly to Shakespeare's fascination with the issue of predeterminism vs. free will when we look at *Macbeth*. Our interest at the moment is in the way *Hamlet* reflects the pessimism, newly highlighted in Shakespeare's work, that seems to some observers to require biographical explanation.

Shakespeare's fascination with Stoicism manifests itself in *Julius Caesar* (1599), a play nearly contemporary, as Shapiro (1999) observes, with *Hamlet*. Brutus shows himself to be an adherent to Stoic principles in his oddly bifurcated response to the news that his wife, Portia, has committed suicide by swallowing fire, in her grief at her husband's ill fortunes after the assassination of Caesar. (Plutarch reports that she 'took hot burning coals and cast them in her mouth, and kept her mouth so close that she choked herself'.) Brutus's first response is muted but intense. He and his fellow general, Cassius, now in Asia Minor where they are awaiting battle with the forces of Mark Antony and Octavius Caesar, have just quarrelled bitterly over the management of their military operation. Cassius asks Brutus how he could have given way to such anger as he has just displayed, saying: 'Of your philosophy you make no use / If you give place to accidental evils.' By 'your philosophy' Cassius means Stoicism, which should teach a man to bear misfortune with equanimity. Brutus's answer shocks Cassius with its unexpectedly devastating news: 'No man bears sorrow better. Portia is dead.' Cassius, recognizing an 'insupportable and touching loss', agrees with Brutus to speak no more of Portia and to 'bury all unkindness' in a toast of wine, their partnership having been restored in good part by their quiet and understated sharing of grief (IV. iii. 146–61).

But then more officers arrive, one of them (Messala) with news, reluctantly uttered, that Portia 'is dead, and by strange manner'. Brutus now cuts off further discussion or expressions of sympathy with a textbook stoical response: 'Why, farewell, Portia. We must die, Messala. / With meditating that she must die once, / I have the patience to endure it now.' Brutus has evidently prepared himself for this moment of semi-public revelation of Portia's death, and has resolved to have his comrades see him face it like a man and a Stoic. Messala is suitably amazed. 'Even so great men great losses should endure', he comments. Cassius, who of course knows what has just transpired more privately between himself and Brutus, adds his appropriately admiring astonishment at Brutus's Stoical calm. 'I have as much of this in art as you', he says to Brutus, 'But yet my nature could not bear it so.' That is, I too have striven to acquire the fortitude of Stoical teaching, but I could not practise it with the philosophical equanimity that you have just displayed. 'Well, to our work alive', says Brutus, and no more is heard of Portia (IV. iii. 188–95).

The seeming duplication of these two episodes was once regarded as a textual problem resulting from the printing of a rewritten passage that Shakespeare intended to be cancelled, but is now interpreted as a telling two-pronged insight into the psyche of a Stoic thinker. (See Nuttall, 184–5.) Should a true Stoic respond with bland self-control to the news of the death of a wife or child or other family member? The problem offers a classic challenge to Stoicism by asking if that philosophical system borders on the inhumane. Does Shakespeare invite admiration or criticism for Brutus as a Stoic thinker? The question spills over into other potentially troubling aspects of Brutus as arguably the tragic protagonist of the play: his sense of family pride, his unwillingness to compromise with his fellow conspirators, his inability to see into his own inflexible self-assurance, his blindness to his susceptibility to flattery, and in all these his ironic resemblance to the would-be tyrant whom he helps to assassinate. (See Rabkin, *Shakespeare and the Common Understanding*, 105–19.) Shakespeare shows us what there is to applaud in Brutus and what there is to deplore.

Stoicism thus looms in Shakespeare as a great idea against which the dramatist invites each member of the audience to assess his or her own philosophical resolution or lack of it. If Shakespeare's depiction in *Julius Caesar* of 'the assassination of a self-willed and childless autocrat by a younger faction' reminded its audience of Essex's stirring up of disaffection against Queen Elizabeth that was to culminate disastrously in his ill-fated rebellion attempt of 1601, as Duncan-Jones proposes, it did so in a fashion that 'in no way endorsed their conspiracy' (p. 108). No doubt Elizabeth 'was increasingly asking to be viewed as a god', like 'the frailly human Caesar', and promoted Accession Day celebrations that were analogous to the Feast of

Lupercal in Act I of Shakespeare's play (p. 116), but the dramatist is careful throughout to assess dangers and weaknesses on all sides. Shakespeare's ironies 'mock his audience' as well (Honan, 272).

The problem plays present similar challenges to the writing of Shakespeare's biography. *Troilus and Cressida*, close in time to *Hamlet*, is highly sardonic in its depiction of the Trojan War. Analogies to England's situation in 1601 must have seemed painfully relevant to Shakespeare's audience. The mood in the last years of Elizabeth's reign was often one of disillusionment and anxiety. The queen's decline, and the illness of Lord Hunsdon, the Lord Chamberlain, meant that the future of the Lord Chamberlain's acting company was uncertain (Honan, 287). Biographers have speculated that Achilles is a portrait of the Earl of Essex, perhaps with Southampton as his 'masculine whore' (V. i. 17), his Patroclus (Weis, 262, 331). James Bednarz and James Shapiro see a parallel in Shakespeare's play to the so-called War of the Theatres (a theatrical quarrel particularly among Ben Jonson, John Marston, and Thomas Dekker that may also have involved Shakespeare), with the burly and temperamental Ben Jonson as composite of Achilles and Ajax.

The early publishing history of *Troilus and Cressida* is a vexed one. When a quarto edition finally emerged in 1609, it did so in two successive versions, one offering the play 'as it was acted by the King's Majesty's servants at the Globe', and the other insisting that it had never been 'staled with the stage, never clapper-clawed with the palms of the vulgar' or 'sullied with the smoky breath of the multitude'. This latter assertion, set forth not in Shakespeare's own words but in a publisher's blurb, has been viewed by Gary Taylor and others as an attempt to offer to sophisticated readers a play that had not succeeded in the theatre but that was a collector's item in its own right as a literary masterpiece. Possibly the play was staged in two locales, at the Globe (as stated on one title page) and at the Inns of Court (Taylor, '*Troilus and Cressida*: Bibliography', 99–136, and Schoenbaum, *Documentary Life*, 216–17). With its ambivalent and experimental mix of history, tragedy, and dark comedy, its war-weary mood, and its pessimistic reflections on a universal breakdown of order and degree (see Bate, *Soul of the Age*, 61–3), *Troilus and Cressida* strikes biographers as adroitly poised at the *fin de siècle* turn of Shakespeare's career towards the dark side of human experience.

So do *Measure for Measure* and *All's Well That Ends Well*. Though they end, nominally at least, as comedies (as *Troilus and Cressida* does not), the marriages at the end are notoriously problematic, and the means used in both plays to achieve comic resolution are fraught with ethical dubieties. The 'old fantastical Duke of dark corners', as Lucio calls him (*Measure for Measure*, IV. iii. 164), is an enigmatic and whimsical figure as he goes about choreographing, in the guise of a friar, the lives of his subjects. His leaving Vienna to the tender mercies of Lord Angelo, whom he knows to be a 'seemer' (I. iii. 54) and a breaker of his promise to marry Mariana because her dowry was lost at sea (III. i. 215–25), strikes many critics as capricious. In modern productions he is sometimes seen as tyrannical. The play was seldom performed in the nineteenth century, in good part because its aura of sexual dissipation was regarded as so unseemly. Indeed, the doings of Mistress Overdone, Pompey, Froth, Lucio, and the rest are unlike anything seen in earlier comedies. The choice of prison as the location of several long and central scenes (II. iii; III. i; III. ii; IV. ii; IV. iii) is also something new in Shakespearean comedy. If the portraiture of the Duke as not loving to 'stage' himself to the 'loud applause and *aves* vehement' of the people (I. i. 67–70) glances at the reluctance of England's new monarch in 1603, James I, to court the popular voice (see, for example, Honan, 307), the play's problematic character becomes all the more evident.

Most of all, the tense encounters of Angelo and Isabella are drawn to such extremes of polarity that these two characters seem fashioned more for tragedy than for comedy. Isabella is on the point of entering the convent, and her choice seems partly determined by a devout wish to isolate herself from the indolently sensual world of Vienna that surrounds her on all sides. Even her brother Claudio, whom she loves dearly and depends on after the loss of their now-dead father, has conceived a child out of wedlock—with the woman to whom he is engaged to be married, to be sure, but nonetheless with the result that both Claudio and Juliet feel ashamed at having surrendered to the importunities of sexual passion.

Biographers like Greenblatt (p. 141) and Weis (p. 279) have posited a resemblance of this situation to that of Shakespeare and Anne Hathaway in 1582 when they discovered that Anne was pregnant and that the laws on marriage left them few choices other than to hasten to the altar. The enervating atmosphere of Vienna encourages a permissiveness that few can escape. Angelo, newly appointed deputy in the Duke's apparent absence, is determined to remedy the situation by draconian enforcement of an existing but heretofore neglected statute forbidding fornication and adultery under penalty of death. In his discussions with his colleague Escalus about how to proceed, Angelo concedes that his programme of inflexible enforcement of the law will no doubt punish with extreme severity some like Claudio who are in a sense only minimally guilty, but Angelo has a ready answer: if the law is applied with perfect consistency, without regard to whom it sweeps up under its provisions, the effect will be to deter criminality in others. In a sense it will actually be merciful by issuing a clear and unmistakable warning. Greenblatt and Weis, among others, ask whether this debate about law and carnal desire gives dramatic form to Shakespeare's own troubled recollection of a sexual longing that led to long-lasting consequences. If so, what are biographers to make of Angelo's discovery, to his own intense dismay, that he is as prone to sensual desire as any other male, so long as he believes he can get away with the intended sexual act? Is Shakespeare probing the dimensions of his own carnal desire? Or does Shakespeare mean to criticize Angelo as a puritanical hypocrite, as Honan (p. 307) and others have suggested? What did Shakespeare make of Puritanism as it applied to his own life experience? The word 'precise' is applied to Angelo by the Duke in the sense of being one who 'scarce confesses / That his blood flows or that his appetite / Is more to bread than stone' (I. iii. 50–3). 'Precise' is a term widely and satirically applied to Puritans at the time.

Angelo succumbs to desire, not for any of the women in Madam Overdone's bordello, but for Isabella, a virtuous virgin on the threshold of a life of religious seclusion. The sheer perversity of such a desire to 'raze the sanctuary' and to desire Isabella foully 'for those things / That make her good' (II. ii. 178–82) disgusts him. As observers have noted, he is like the poet-speaker of the Sonnets, revolted by his own depraved sexuality and yet unable to do anything about it; see, for example, Sonnets 129–44, and Greenblatt's suggestion that we here see evidence that Shakespeare himself 'could not find what he craved, emotionally or sexually, within his marriage' (pp. 254–5). If the Duke is testing Angelo to see how he will behave when all institutional restraints are apparently removed from him, the test is devastating in what it reveals, for Angelo learns to his horror that he is a monster in his own eyes, guilty of the very thing he most abhors and condemns in others. Only by the ethically dubious means of the bed trick (being duped into making love to Mariana in the dark of the night when he thinks he is lying with Isabella) can Angelo be forced to confront the consequences of his own carnality.

Angelo's enforced marriage to Mariana in Act V, and Isabella's betrothal to the Duke, have struck a number of biographers and other critics as bizarre and deliberately unsatisfactory, of a piece with Lucio's being obliged to marry Kate Keepdown (III. ii. 194; V. i. 521–2). Modern directors and actors even doubt that the union of the Duke and Isabella actually takes place; ever since John Barton's production for the Royal Shakespeare Company in 1970, with Estelle Kohler as a hesitant and bewildered recipient of the Duke's unexpected proposal (see Wells, *Shakespeare for All Time*, 120), actresses in the part have felt free to practise the option of remaining single. A common assumption is that Shakespeare is exploring his own troubled feelings; see, for example, Greenblatt, who sees this play and *All's Well* as 'the expression of a deep skepticism about the long-term prospects for happiness in marriage, even though the plays continue to insist upon marriage as the only legitimate and satisfactory resolution to human desire' (p. 136).

This last note of the accepted necessity of marriage does afford for some biographers and critics a significant glimmer of hope in this play written at a pivotal moment in Shakespeare's career as a dramatist, and presumably at a key point in his development as a sensitive human being. Even though *Measure for Measure* wallows at times in carnality, and even though the Duke's means of coping with Vienna's waywardness are truly bizarre, a critic like Arthur Kirsch (pp. 71–107) can nonetheless present a humane and moving argument for seeing the play as a comedy. Christian teaching plentifully acknowledges the intransigence of humankind's fallen condition (as explored earlier in *Hamlet*), but it also celebrates Isabella's deeply Christian charity in forgiving Angelo while still supposing that he has ordered the execution of her brother Claudio. The Duke withholds knowledge of Claudio's being alive to see what Isabella will do. He offers her the opportunity for what might seem a justifiable revenge; indeed, he insists that he will proceed with the execution of Angelo no matter what she might say. In the face of this temptation to be revenged, Isabella kneels in petition for Angelo's life in part because she realizes that Mariana still wants Angelo to be her husband, and in part because Isabella is persuaded, as she says, that 'A due sincerity governed his [Angelo's] deeds, / Till he did look on me' (V. i. 454–5).

Isabella's act of forgiveness, and that of Mariana as well, atone for much in this play, as earlier, for example, in Hero's willingness to forgive Claudio in *Much Ado*. The Duke's testings have also obliged Angelo to confront his own potential for evil—surely a self-examination that is needed before any person can hope to amend. Isabella must learn too, no matter how painful the realization is bound to be, that she can uncharitably wish for her brother's death; conversely, her brother must face the dismaying fact that his courage in facing death collapses when he learns that he could save his life through his sister's shame. These are hard things to learn, hard but necessary. The biographical thesis of Greenblatt and others supposes that these coming to terms with human weakness provide Shakespeare with an artistic means of transmuting his own personal struggles and anxieties into a lasting work of art.

To see the play as a 'comedy of forgiveness', in Robert G. Hunter's useful phrase, is to perceive that Shakespeare's deeply problematic approach to marriage can find room for forgiveness. Such a reading also leaves open the possibility that Isabella, whose 'real desire' has indeed been, as Greenblatt says, 'to enter a strict nunnery' (p. 136), now embraces marriage in all its imperfections as the better choice. As Benedick says, in *Much Ado*, by way of explaining his own overcoming of reluctance to marry, 'The world must be peopled' (II. iii. 237).

All's Well confronts biographers with similar problems, intensified if anything by what Greenblatt (p. 136) calls Bertram's 'loutish' disposition that leaves many readers and audiences wondering why Helena would wish to have anything to do with him. Then, too, Helena is a schemer in a way that Isabella is not in *Measure for Measure*; in that play, the Duke thinks up the trick of substituting Mariana for Isabella in Angelo's bed, whereas in *All's Well* Helena is the one who proposes that she take the place in bed of the young Diana whom Bertram is hotly pursuing. In other ways, too, Helena seems calculating in her desire to catch a husband who is socially above her, especially when she asks the French King to award Bertram to her as her prize for curing the King's fistula, knowing as she does that Bertram will be offended at the perceived indignity. She shows a comparable ingenuity in meeting the terms of Bertram's riddle specifying that she may call him husband only when she can get the ring on his finger 'which shall never come off' and 'show me a child begotten of thy body that I am father to' (III. ii. 57–9).

At the same time, *All's Well* suggests a more positive reading as comedy of forgiveness: Helena certainly has much to forgive, and arguably (as Wheeler notes in *Shakespeare's Development*, 34–45) Bertram has much to learn about his own immature sexuality. He is ultimately weaned from the male and misogynistic camaraderie of the boastful Parolles and comes to acknowledge, through the paradox of the ring, that a male must accept the physical consequences of his sexual being. Having conceived a child, and having been tricked and cajoled into admitting that the child is his, Bertram also accepts that the child's mother is his wife. Even if the lesson is grudgingly learned, and even if it perhaps reflects the author's own uneasy feeling of having been obliged to marry as the result of an unplanned pregnancy (see Greenblatt, 136), the mood of forgiveness (including self-forgiveness), and the acknowledgement that the demands of maturity must be acted on, lend to this bittersweet comedy an aura of emotional realism that suits well a turning point in Shakespeare's career as dramatist.

Othello presents biographers with an intriguing challenge. Shakespeare certainly did not kill his wife, and even those biographers who assume that Shakespeare was unhappily married hesitate to suggest that he fantasized the killing of Anne in jealous rage. Yet we do have the Sonnets, with their stark portrayal of the poet-speaker's jealousy at having his dark-complexioned mistress stolen away from him by the young man to whom most of the sonnets are addressed. Why has Shakespeare chosen to focus so intently on jealousy now in his artistic career? He could have made other choices. *Othello* is based on an Italian short story containing the essential plot elements; it is about a Moorish commander who, falling from loving his Venetian wife into uncontrollable jealousy under the malign tutelage of a resentful junior officer, conspires with him to murder the wife. What drew Shakespeare to this particular account at this juncture in his artistic career?

Viewed in this light, *Othello* seems biographically comprehensible as a further exploration of a topic with which Shakespeare appears to have been increasingly concerned. Sexual jealousy is indeed a major theme of the late sonnets, written perhaps in the years around the turn of the century. Othello's jealousy is like that of Claudio in *Much Ado* (1598–9), now intensified into murderous rage as Shakespeare turns to tragedy in the early 1600s and thereby confronts in full the misogyny and fear of women that we also see in *Hamlet* ('frailty, thy name is woman!', I. ii. 146) and the problem plays. This perception raises for biographers and other students of Shakespeare (for example, Nuttall, 277–84, and Holden, *Life and Work*, 218–22) the question of how to explain Othello's fall into homicidal jealousy, and why this matters so greatly to Shakespeare at this stage in his writing career. Why is Othello, and by implication many other men, so fearful that their peace of mind and sense of manhood can be destroyed by a woman?

The problem is made all the more acutely puzzling by the fact that Othello appears to be utterly happy with Desdemona in the play's opening scenes. He has courted her, at her implied invitation, by telling her of his adventures, his 'hairbreadth scapes i'th'imminent deadly breach' (I. iii. 138), and all the rest. She has proved to be the perfect audience for him: admiring, astonished, deeply concerned. Their elopement takes some courage, for they know that her father will do what he can to thwart their marriage. Othello's defence of his courtship of Desdemona fully convinces the Venetian Duke and other senators that Othello has used no witchcraft. Her consent is well-informed and deeply willing. Yet soon after their arrival in Cyprus, in the course of a single conversation with Iago, the love and trust that Othello feels for Desdemona dissolve into hatred and mistrust. Why is this great general and noble human being so vulnerable to jealous fears?

A significant clue has been discerned, by Arthur Kirsch (pp. 16–18) and others, in what Othello says to the Venetian senate about the relationship that he and Desdemona have developed in their courtship. 'She loved me for the dangers I had passed', he says, 'And I loved her that she did pity them' (I. iii. 169–70). Othello prizes Desdemona because she admires his manly deeds and pities the dangers he has encountered. She makes him feel like a man. So far so good, but the problem implicit in such a relationship soon surfaces under Iago's cross-examination: suppose Desdemona is only pretending to love Othello? Suppose she really prefers a man of her own ethnicity and age and social class, such as Cassio? To the huge extent that Othello's love for Desdemona is a response to the way she makes him feel so good about himself, that love for her is fragile. It depends on a statement of conditional fact: If she loves her husband, then all is well. If perhaps she does not, then her purported virtue turns out to be, in the tortured mind of her husband, worse than valueless.

Desdemona, for her part, does not express her love for Othello in these implicitly conditional terms. Her love for him is unconditional. Her heart is 'subdued / Even to the very qualities of my lord'. She sees 'Othello's visage in his mind', and so she has consecrated her soul and fortunes to his (I. iii. 253–7). As Kirsch observes, her love for her husband is one in which she has harmonized the instinctual and spiritual in their brief life together, uniting beautifully 'the religious and psychological commitments of marriage' (pp. 16–18). Accordingly, her love for him is not vulnerable to insinuation in the way that his is for her.

Whether or not some event in Shakespeare's life may have triggered the writing of *Othello*, biographers have more plausibly seen the play as a kind of response to the Sonnets and *Hamlet* and *Measure for Measure*. Shakespeare's intense exploration of sexual jealousy in *Othello* grows out of the misogyny, pessimism, and anxiety that are so engrossingly a part of his view of the human condition in the early years of the seventeenth century.

Iago is, under such circumstances, the ultimate embodiment for the Shakespearean biographer of a psychological and spiritual affliction to which men are unhappily prone as an inherent condition of their being male. Iago's uncontrolled jealousy needs no objective facts to justify its raging existence. His wife Emilia may fantasize what it would be like to make love to some other man (IV. iii. 66–80), but she has never been untrue to her marriage vows. She understands jealousy with the clear-eyed perception of a woman who has experienced at first hand the jealous rage of her husband. She knows that at bottom it is simply irrational. Men are 'not ever jealous for the cause, / But jealous for they're jealous', she tells Desdemona (III. iv. 161–2). Iago's own fantasies, especially when he pictures himself lying abed with

Cassio and being kissed by him 'As if he plucked up kisses by the roots' (III. iii. 438), betray a psychotic temperament that psychoanalytic observers like Stanley Hyman usually classify as that of a latent, paranoid homosexual. Honan (p. 315) and Nuttall (p. 280), among others, concur in the diagnosis.

Can any of this be applied factually to Shakespeare's own life? Weis does speculate that Shakespeare may have been motivated to write *Othello* by his having been involved with 'the real Emilia', Emilia Bassano Lanier, 'a Jewish Venetian woman' and a musician. Weis is further convinced that Iago's latent homosexuality glances at King James I's well-known fondness for personal favourites at court, and that Shakespeare may have played the part of Iago on stage (pp. 288–90). As we saw in Chapter 3, several biographers are persuaded that Shakespeare himself had bisexual and homoerotic tendencies. Even without indulging in heady speculation of this sort, biographers have wondered if the story that Shakespeare dramatizes so grippingly may reflect, at some distant perspective, the inner life of an author who dwelt apart from his wife and family and whose writings in the 1600s especially seem to express what Greenblatt calls 'a deep skepticism about the long-term prospects for happiness in marriage' (p. 136).

Misogyny runs deep in *King Lear* (*c.*1605–6) as well. A related concern here is the play's fascination with unorthodox ideas about the place of humankind in a potentially godless universe. As Kay (p. 265) and Honan (p. 337) argue, the play manifests the sceptical and questioning influence of Montaigne. Jonathan Bate (*Soul of the Age*, 58–66) thinks it altogether likely that Shakespeare was acquainted with the work of Thomas Digges (d. 1595), the greatest English astronomer of his time, who, in *A Perfect Description of the Celestial Orbs According to the Most ancient Doctrine of the Pythagoreans, Lately Revived by Copernicus* (1576), freely translated Copernicus's *De revolutionibus orbium coelestium* 1543) and thereby confronted English readers with the challengingly unorthodox theory of a sun-centred solar system.

Whether or not Shakespeare actually knew Digges and Copernican theory, he does seem to be obsessed, as William Elton argues in *King Lear and the Gods*, with dramatizing the plight of humans who plead in vain for divine intervention in their lives. 'O heavens', King Lear pleads, 'If you do love old men, if your sweet sway / Allow obedience, if you yourselves are old, / Make it your cause; send down, and take my part!' (II. iv. 190–3). Lear's petition is based on traditional theology equating heavenly power and wisdom with hierarchy among mortals; respect for age and obedience to authority should provide the foundation for human society. Yet in this play the gods, if they exist at all, do not come to Lear's rescue. To the contrary, he seems more vulnerable to misfortune than are those cynics who flout morality.

Frustrated hopes for divine intervention are no less central to the play's second plot of the Earl of Gloucester and his sons. Gloucester's traditional view that 'late eclipses in the sun and the moon' portend mutinies, treason, discord, and other disruptions in human society merely earns him the contempt of his bastard son, Edmund, who is a thorough-going sceptic. Edmund believes that the gods should 'stand up for bastards', and by 'gods' he means the goddess Nature, presiding over a naturalistic world in which the race goes to the swiftest. Edmund is an intelligent sceptic, scornful of those like his father who lamely make guilty of their disasters 'the sun, the moon, and stars, as if we were villains on necessity, fools by heavenly compulsion, knaves, thieves, and treachers by spherical predominance, drunkards, liars, and adulterers by an enforced obedience of planetary influence, and all that we are evil in by a divine thrusting on'. Edmund makes us uncomfortable because his ideas are so unnervingly revisionary and free of humbug. He confidently believes that he is who he is by his own volition, not because some star twinkled at the moment of his bastardizing (I. ii. 1–136). He agrees essentially with the creed of Iago in *Othello* that ''Tis in ourselves that we are thus or thus' (I. iii. 322–3).

These challenges to orthodoxy are all the more disturbing in that they are embodied in a plot that Shakespeare borrowed from Sir Philip Sidney's *Arcadia* and added to the legendary story of King Lear. This material thus represents a conscious choice on Shakespeare's part to highlight his analysis of sceptical doubts about the traditional view of a god-centred universe.

What is particularly threatening in *King Lear*, presumably to Shakespeare as to us, is that Edmund's scepticism as a self-made man beholden to no deity (see Bate, *Soul of the Age*, 363–72) takes him so far towards worldly success. Edmund effortlessly deceives his father into banishing his older and legitimate brother, Edgar, as a would-be parricide. He ingratiates himself with the powerful Duke of

Cornwall as a means of condemning his own father, Gloucester, as a traitor, and then, after Cornwall's death at the hands of a servant, becomes the new Duke of Cornwall himself by taking up with Cornwall's widow, Regan. By having an affair with the Duke of Albany's wife, Goneril, Edmund puts himself in competition with the most powerful lord in the kingdom. He becomes co-general of the British forces, with Albany, against the French invasion. Edmund is within a heartbeat of mounting to the British throne as supreme ruler. The virtuous persons in the play are at an inherent disadvantage in worldly terms because they restrain their acts within the bounds of conventional morality, while those who regard such moral imperatives as a myth are free to kill or deceive or supplant whom they please. Down to the last moment, at least, the gods, if they exist, do not seem to show any concern. To biographers and critics like Elton, Shakespeare would appear to be asking himself the ultimately challenging question as to whether the universe is divinely ordered or existentially proceeding on its own naturalistic course. The question seems to arise inevitably out of the pessimism and misanthropy of the plays Shakespeare has just been writing.

Edgar is a crucial figure in Shakespeare's grappling with such portentous issues, as Stanley Cavell demonstrates in his essay on 'The Avoidance of Love: A Reading of *King Lear*' (*Disowning Knowledge*, 39–123). Edgar is in many ways as much a sceptic as his villainous brother. Whereas well-meaning persons like Albany keep looking for reassurance, in the face of devastating evidence to the contrary, that heavenly 'justicers' really are 'above' and that they stand ready to avenge speedily 'these our nether crimes' (IV. ii. 79–81), Edgar teaches himself not to be deceived by vain hopes. He is a Stoic in the best and most realistic way possible. When he assumes at one point that things cannot possibly get any worse for him as a hunted man with a price on his head, he encounters his blinded father, and perceives at once that he has been fooling himself again: things *can* get worse (IV. i). The wisdom of folklore, proclaiming that it's a long road that has no turning, that what goes down must eventually come back up, etc., is all very well as a mythology but has no necessary relation to the brute facts of human existence. Edgar has few illusions. As Cavell puts it, Edgar perceives 'that all appeals to the gods are distractions or excuses' (p. 74).

Yet Edgar does not use his sceptical intelligence to take advantage of others in the way that Edmund does so heartlessly. Edgar implicitly spots a defect in Edmund's existentialist philosophy: if the race goes to the swiftest, if no gods are watching and holding us in check, one need not therefore choose to be villainous. Other reasons urge us to practise patience and charity; human beings are happier in the last analysis if they choose to live charitably, even if they are likely to suffer at the hands of the unprincipled. The practice of narrow self-interest in *King Lear*, as Shakespeare chooses to dramatize the story, is ultimately self-defeating: it leads finally to Edmund's death at the hands of the brother and to the edifyingly unhappy demises of Cornwall, Oswald, Goneril, and Regan. Edgar's compassionate scepticism prompts him to devise a bogus mythology for his suicidal old father, catering to Gloucester's need to believe in fiends and miracles with a tale of how a monster with a thousand noses and eyes like two full moons has tempted the old man to throw himself off the cliffs of Dover, only to be saved by divine intervention (IV. vi).

Edgar's role as inventor of a cosmology can be interpreted biographically as paralleling Shakespeare's own role as the deviser of this highly inventive and original story. Both Shakespeare and Edgar acknowledge the seemingly illusory nature of divinity without yielding to the temptation (to which Edmund readily succumbs) of forsaking any call for compassion and generosity. It is as though Shakespeare, confronting the ultimate challenge of a godless universe, feels impelled to find some remnant of hope. He shows us the charitable responses of those virtuous few (especially Edgar, Cordelia, and Kent) who can fully comprehend what is existential about the universe and yet find the humane decency in themselves to persevere in goodness. The hope may strike some readers of *King Lear* as no less illusory than the older orthodoxies of Gloucester and Lear, but the idea of belief in some kernel of human decency is nonetheless Shakespeare's choice. He chooses it in place of the conventional happy ending to the story of King Lear as it had been told in earlier versions and was to be reintroduced in the later seventeenth century.

Biographers generally agree that *King Lear* need not represent a serious breakdown in Shakespeare's own family relationships. The very fact that he chooses the name 'Edmund' for his chief villain is perhaps indicative; 'Edmund' was the name of his youngest brother, of whom, says Duncan-Jones, he seems to have been particularly fond (p. 199). Yet on a more thematic level the play takes up issues that must have seemed pressing to Shakespeare as he approached old age. *King Lear* is his most unsparing depiction of the existential nightmare of human existence. At the same time, it is a story that the author refuses to tell without reflecting also on the consolations of caring that can bind human beings to one another. As Cavell puts it, the play 'throws our redemption into *question*, and leaves it up to us' (p. 74). We shall return to the issue of ageing in the next chapter.

Macbeth similarly avoids the narrowly autobiographical while engaging in issues of terrifying import. Shakespeare did not need to kill a king in order to be able to write this play. He was not married to a wife who might goad him on to commit such a crime. Yet he chose to analyse, in his ongoing exploration of human beings' penchant for evil, the mind of a man who finds that he cannot resist doing what he knows to be horribly wrong. In this, Macbeth is like Angelo in *Measure for Measure* and Claudius in *Hamlet*. He kills King Duncan knowing full well that the act is damnable and that it will lead only to disaster for him.

As biographers have observed, Macbeth sums up the case for and against committing the murder by seeing that the reasons for not acting outweigh overwhelmingly those for going ahead. Duncan, he concedes, has come to stay the night in Macbeth's castle 'in double trust: / First, as I am his kinsman and his subject, / Strong both against the deed; then, as his host, / Who should against the murderer shut the door, / Not bear the knife myself' (I. vii. 12–16). The crime he is about to commit is thus the murder of a close relative, the murder of a reigning monarch, and a gross violation of the sacred obligations of hospitality. No crime could strike more at the heart of all that civilization attempts to uphold. As Wells points out (*A Dramatic Life*, 285), the murder of Duncan 'is compared to sacrilege, to the desecration of a temple'. Duncan is a gentle, gracious king whose 'virtues / Will plead like angels, trumpet-tongued, against / The deep damnation of his taking-off'. In other ways as well, the deed will surely be self-defeating. If an act could 'trammel up the consequence' by ending with the performance of the deed, that would be one thing, but in fact history teaches us that 'in these cases / We still have judgment here, that we but teach / Bloody instructions, which, being taught, return / To plague th'inventor. This evenhanded justice / Commends th'ingredients to our own lips' (ll. 4–10). Macbeth knows that he will destroy his own happiness, and will have to pay the full consequences.

On the other side of the argument, Macbeth admits that he has 'no spur / To prick the sides of my intent, but only / Vaulting ambition, which o'erleaps itself / And falls on th'other' (ll. 25–8). The image he chooses to characterize his ambition is deliberately humiliating: he sees himself as a rider mounting the horse of his ambition with such ineptitude that he flies over the saddle and lands ingloriously on the ground. How could a person see with such clarity the huge imbalance of the choice facing him and yet go ahead? Clearly, like Claudius, he is an unregenerate man in the grip of an obsession. In some way that he does not fully understand, he is destined to commit this crime. It will be an act of his volition, and yet it is predetermined. How else could the Weird Sisters know to greet him, at their first encounter, 'All hail, Macbeth, that shalt be king hereafter!' (I. iii. 50). Theirs is a 'supernatural soliciting' that 'Cannot be ill, cannot be good' (ll. 131–2). As Macbeth writes to his wife, 'they have more in them than mortal knowledge' (I. v. 2–3). Paul Jorgensen (p. 45) astutely observes that 'every appearance of *fair* in the play, must, according to the Witches' equation, in a darker sense be also read as *foul*'. 'Fair is foul, and foul is fair', they chant (I. i. 11), to be echoed shortly afterwards by Macbeth in his first entry: 'So fair and foul a day I have not seen' (I. iii. 38). 'Good sir', Banquo asks him when they have heard the Weird Sisters' three-part prophecy of promised kingship, 'why do you start and seem to fear / Things that do sound so fair?' (ll. 51–2).

The paradoxes of predestination and free will have puzzled and fascinated virtually all those like A. C. Bradley and Paul Jorgensen who have written about *Macbeth*. The paradoxes of Calvinist theology, with roots also in Stoic philosophy, apply here as in *Hamlet*: predestination and free will are somehow both at work in human destiny. In His infinite wisdom, according to this view, God knows all that will happen, and yet the individual must take responsibility for his or her choice. *Macbeth*, like Marlowe's *Doctor Faustus*, focuses on the dark side of this paradox, on the terrifying fate of the sinner who cannot help being who he is and who yet will be held accountable. Paradox is essential to all great religious insight. It cannot ultimately be explained; it demands faith in the impossible. Why does Calvinist theology seem so important to Shakespeare at this juncture in his life when he was writing one astounding tragedy after another?

One possible approach taken by biographers is to note that Shakespeare meaningfully contrasts his protagonist in *Macbeth* with a man, Banquo, who is able to resist temptation. Why is it that some men can withstand the blandishments of the devil while others cannot? The contrast is like that of Claudius and Hamlet's father in *Hamlet*, or Doctor Faustus and the Old Man in Marlowe's *Doctor Faustus*. Banquo knows how to pray to 'Merciful powers', begging them to restrain in him 'the cursèd thoughts that nature / Gives way to in repose' (II. i. 7–9). He acknowledges that he is prone to evil, as are all humans; that is why he seeks divine assistance. He is thus able to ask the Weird Sisters what they can foresee for him; since he will 'neither beg nor fear / Your favors nor your hate', and understands well that 'to win us to our harm / The instruments of darkness tell us truths, / Win us with honest trifles, to betray 's / In deepest consequence' (I. iii. 60–1, 123–6), Banquo is armed against their assault. Macduff is another instructive opposite to Macbeth. So is King Duncan, unlike his counterpart in Scottish history.

Why it is that some men can resist evil and others cannot remains a dark mystery. That mystery is essential to the pessimism and gloom that pervade Shakespeare's great tragedies from *Hamlet* and *Othello* to *King Lear* and *Macbeth*. Yet these plays also provide the consolation of spiritual hope, as depicted in the lives of those who suffer at the hands of evil men but persevere in goodness. That is the positive side of the Calvinist equation.

As biographers and critics have noted, the Calvinist paradoxes of predestination and free will are also at the heart of *Macbeth*'s topical allusions to the years around 1606–7 in which the play was written and produced. The drunken Porter's wry description of 'an equivocator, that could swear in both the scales against either scale, who committed treason enough for God's sake, yet could not equivocate to heaven' (II. iii. 8–11) alludes to the hated tactic used by Jesuits like Henry Garnet in England as a way of equivocating under examination for spying (Ian Wilson, 314–20, Duncan-Jones, 197–8). (*King Lear* similarly makes use of Samuel Harsnett's exposure of Jesuit exorcist practices in his *A Declaration of Egregious Popish Impostures*, 1603.)

Macbeth also implicitly alludes to the infamous Catholic Gunpowder Plot of 5 November 1605 to blow up the houses of Parliament (Honan, 330; Holden, *Life and Work*, 231–3). The '*show of eight kings*' that the Weird Sisters present to Macbeth, ending with a procession in which some carry 'twofold balls and treble scepters' (IV. i. 111–21), evidently points to the coronation of James VI of Scotland and I of England at Scone and then Westminster (hence 'twofold') and to the triple title that James claimed of Great Britain, France, and Ireland.

By choosing to dramatize the story of an eleventh-century Scottish king, and by rewriting the story freely in such a way as to adapt it to current religious controversy and politics, Shakespeare surrounds the momentous events of the early seventeenth century in England with an aura of malevolent inevitability. The witches are always present, foreseeing and ensuring what will happen. Even if Scotland is restored to political order at the end of the play, the shadow of cosmic nightmare hovers over the scene by incessantly reminding us that human attempts to resist an insidious inner evil are by no means assured of success.

What then might be the play's estimate of England's reigning monarch in 1603 and afterward? Does Shakespeare implicitly regard James I as a force for good, or as perhaps prone to the spiritual evil that the play so hauntingly invokes? Not surprisingly, biographers are divided on this critical issue. An entire book by Henry N. Paul, devoted to what he calls *The Royal Play of 'Macbeth'*, makes the case for the play as an extended flattery of James as a descendant not of Macbeth but of Banquo. James's *Daemonology* (1597) contains denunciations of witches that are similar to those of Banquo when he insists to them that he will 'neither beg nor fear / Your favors nor your hate' (I. iii. 60–1). Greenblatt sees the play as honouring James 'not for his wisdom or learning or statecraft but for his place in a line of legitimate descent that leads all the way from his noble ancestor in the distant past to the sons that promise an unbroken succession'. The play is 'a collective ritual of reassurance' (pp. 335, 337). Shakespeare was, after all, a member of the King's Men. James I was his royal patron.

Yet other biographers (such as Honan, 307) offer a more critical approach, arguing that the royal abuses of authority to which Macbeth is increasingly prone are not unlike those for which James I was blamed. James autocratically insisted, for one thing, that the union of Scotland and England should take place in his own royal person from the moment he was crowned, and needed no act of Parliament; the claim was vigorously resisted. James was no friend of the Puritan wing of the church. He was extravagant, and his personal habits proved distasteful to many. Yet biographers agree that, whether *Macbeth* supports the new Stuart regime or offers implicit criticism, or is impartial in its analysis, the play undoubtedly bespeaks a fascination on Shakespeare's part with the profound issues of predestination and the capacity of humankind for spiritual failure. *Macbeth* is in this sense the culmination of the dark themes that have captured the imagination of Shakespeare during the years when he wrote his greatest tragedies.

7

On the Heights

Edward Dowden's biographical account of the phases in Shakespeare's career proposes, as we have seen, that the dramatist's sojourn in the 'depths' of pessimism and misogyny gave way after 1607 or so to a return of hope and affirmation, especially in the so-called romances or tragicomedies: *Pericles, Cymbeline, The Winter's Tale,* and *The Tempest.* Having completed his 'inquisition into the mystery of evil', having studied 'those injuries of man to man which are irreparable', having 'seen the innocent suffering with the guilty', Shakespeare entered on 'his last period of authorship', one in which he 'remained grave—how could it be otherwise?' but in which 'his severity was tempered and purified' (pp. 360–1). Dowden's model remains influential today. René Weis remarks in 2007, for example, that 'After the bleakness of *King Lear* and *Macbeth*, the luminosity of *Antony and Cleopatra* comes almost as a shock. Something must have happened in the autumn of 1606 to brighten Shakespeare's mood' (p. 316). *Antony and Cleopatra* is thus another luminous feature of the presumed late phase. Park Honan organizes his 1998 biography into four phases, of which the last two are 'The Maturity of Genius' (including 'The Tragic Sublime') and 'The Last Phase'. Peter Alexander similarly arranges his study of Shakespeare's life and art into four phases, ending with 'The Final Period'. In the metaphoric view of Dowden and other biographers, Shakespeare emerges out of the depths onto the heights.

Actually, a chronological dividing line between the 'tragic period' and that of the tragicomedies or romances is hard to fix with any accuracy. It cannot be seen to coincide precisely with the King's Men's new practice of performing in the Blackfriars Theatre as well as at the Globe. To be sure, Richard Dutton (pp. 141–3) defines 'the last major redirection of Shakespeare's career' as having been initiated by the King's company's occupying the Blackfriars in 1608, enabling them to perform plays like *Cymbeline*, *The Winter's Tale*, and *The Tempest* indoors to audiences of a more select nature than those at the Globe, especially during the inclement months of the year. Yet Dutton observes that *Pericles* was published in 1609 'as it hath been divers and sundry times acted by His Majesty's servants at the Globe on the Bankside'. Shakespeare's company did not begin acting at Blackfriars until 1609, whereas *Pericles* was entered in the Stationers' Register in May 1608, and is sometimes dated as early as 1606, before the usual date assigned to *Coriolanus* (*c.*1608). (See Wells, *Dramatic Life*, 329.) The dating of *Timon of Athens* is hard to determine, but it too may have overlapped with *Pericles* and *Antony and Cleopatra*.

Dutton notes, moreover, that *Cymbeline* and *The Winter's Tale* were seen at the Globe by the astrologer/doctor Simon Forman, *The Winter's Tale* on 15 May 1611, and *Cymbeline* also presumably in that same year, since Forman died suddenly on 8 September. *Henry VIII* was certainly performed in the Globe (under the title *All Is True*), as evidenced by the burning of that theatre on 29 June 1613 during a staging of this play. In fact, no surviving record attests to any performance of Shakespeare's plays at the Blackfriars other than the play he wrote collaboratively with John Fletcher, *The Two Noble Kinsmen* (1613–14), which, as Wells observes (*Dramatic Life*, 288), declares on its title page that it was performed at the Blackfriars, with no mention of the Globe. Some others must have been put on there. Stylistically, Shakespeare's romances are not as oriented to court tastes and fashions as is sometimes supposed, even if Fletcher, Shakespeare's successor as chief playwright for the King's Men, was undoubtedly influential with his well-publicized definition of tragicomedy as a genre lacking deaths but bringing its characters near to it. No clear distinction between the two houses is evident until the 1630s.

Biographers have been careful not to suppose that Shakespeare had to finish his work in tragedy before he could start thinking about where to turn next. Nor do they generally suppose, with Weis, that 'something must have happened' to lighten Shakespeare's mood at some particular point. As Duncan-Jones puts it, the claim 'that some personal life crisis provoked him to write tragicomedies and tragedies' now 'seems far too simple, in separating Shakespeare from the complex social, economic and political environment in which he lived and worked' (p. 181). *Timon of Athens*, in some ways the most mordantly misanthropic play that he (with Middleton) ever wrote, may have been composed at a time when Shakespeare had become substantially wealthy. Schoenbaum notes that Shakespeare invested £440 in July of 1605 to procure half-interest in a lease of tithes on grain in three hamlets adjacent to Stratford, along with the 'small tithes of the whole of Stratford parish' (*Documentary Life*, 192). As Duncan-Jones comments, these investments would have procured for Shakespeare and his family a considerable income extracted from the labourers and lease-holders of his native town. *Coriolanus*, no less a product of these prosperous years, dramatizes such an explosive danger of food riots and civil unrest that it may have proved unstageable, as we saw in Chapter 4 (Duncan-Jones, 204). If he wrote *Coriolanus* after the death of his mother in September of 1608, as Weis (274) and Garry O'Connor (259) suppose, that might explain something, but we cannot be sure of the date of the play.

Allowing then for imprecisions in the sequencing in the plays, *Antony and Cleopatra* (early 1607) does strike most biographers and critics as representing a significant change in Shakespeare's approach to sexuality and to the very nature of dramatic genre. 'It is impossible to read *Antony and Cleopatra* without feeling that the thrifty poet had been raised to his poetic summit by the imagined spectacle of riotous indulgence', writes Ivor Brown. 'He surrendered to the splendour of these passionate squanderers' (p. 58). The play is a tragedy in that its title figures suffer defeat and death, and yet its transcendent ending seems to raise them up in the imagination to the status of demigods triumphing over their worldly adversity. (George Bernard Shaw, to be sure, demurs from the generally held view; to him, *Antony and Cleopatra* demonstrates Shakespeare's remarkable ability as a poet to bestow on a tale of besotted sexual transgression an aura of transcendent splendour that it surely does not deserve.)

The issue of sexuality is particularly striking for most critics. The relationship of Antony and Cleopatra is of course a stormy one: a highly romantic meeting on the River of Cydnus (historically in 41 BC), his marriage with Octavius's sister Octavia, his return to Cleopatra, the defeat of Antony and Cleopatra at Actium by Octavius in 31 BC, their quarrelling, his bungled suicide, and much more. Their famous love affair is presented as beset by difficulties. The Roman view, as expressed in Scene i by Philo, is one of sad disapproval of a once-great general whose 'captain's heart... reneges all temper, / And is become the bellows and the fan / To cool a gypsy's lust' (I. i. 6–10). This is indeed the judgement of Plutarch, whose *Life of Antony* (as translated by Thomas North) provided Shakespeare with his main source for the play. Octavius Caesar, in Shakespeare's play, is dismayed, even disgusted, by the news he receives of how Antony 'fishes, drinks, and wastes / The lamps of night in revel; is not more manlike / Than Cleopatra, nor the queen of Ptolemy / More womanly than he' (I. iv. 4–7). To be sure, the famous revels in Egypt, with gargantuan meals and epic bouts of love-making, are given their due in the play; Enobarbus, for one, is captivated by the superabundant vitality of a life that contrasts so richly with the restraint of the Roman ideal. John Southworth (p. 249) speculates that Shakespeare, drawn to Enobarbus's 'distinctive characteristic of detachment' and 'witty, intelligent, and perceptive' observation of the action throughout, might have chosen to play that character on stage. Still, in his sober moments Antony knows that 'These strong Egyptian fetters I must break, / Or lose myself in dotage' (I. ii. 122–3).

What seems to many observers (including Janet Adelman, in *The Common Liar*) particularly liberating in the story, despite its fearful cost in practical terms to the protagonists, is the triumph the lovers achieve over the Roman ideals of compulsive self-discipline and pursuit of mundane success above all else. When Cleopatra, as she is about to commit suicide, declares that her act will enable her to 'call great Caesar ass / Unpolicied' (V. ii. 307–8), she means that the unstable vision of mutual love to which she and Antony have dedicated themselves in their deaths will amount to a refutation of all that Octavius Caesar represents.

Octavius is no doubt correct in his own terms to deplore the Egyptian debaucheries of which he is told, but his revulsion suggests that he is disturbed by the very idea of easy-going sensuality. It bothers him to think of a fellow Roman choosing 'to tumble on the bed of Ptolemy', 'To reel the streets at noon, and stand the buffet / With knaves that smells of sweat' (I. iv. 17–21). These details stick luridly in his imagination, like Hamlet's obsessive picturing to himself of his mother and his hated uncle living 'In the rank sweat of an enseamèd bed, / Stewed in corruption, honeying and making love / Over the nasty sty' (*Hamlet*, III. iv. 93–6). Octavius prefers to remember an Antony of old who was hard as nails, crossing the Alps in wintertime under such straitened circumstances that he was driven by thirst to 'drink / The stale of horses and the gilded puddle / Which beasts would cough at' and to 'eat strange flesh, / Which some did die to look on' (*Antony and Cleopatra*, I. iv. 62–9). Aboard Pompey's ship off Misenum in southern Italy, Caesar is reluctant to join in the festive drinking; when Antony proposes a toast to him, Caesar replies, 'I could well forbear't. / It's monstrous labor when I wash my brain / And it grows fouler' (II. vii. 99–101).

Control means everything to Octavius Caesar: control of political negotiations, of military encounters, of drinking and eating and love-making. He is not married, so far as we are told. His one personal attachment is to his sister Octavia, and yet she is for him a pawn in high-level diplomacy: he marries her to Antony in the expectation that Antony will prove unfaithful to Octavia and thereby provide Octavius an excuse to break his alliance with him. Octavius's view of women is deeply cynical. 'Women are not / In their best fortunes strong', he tells Thidias, 'but want will perjure / The ne'er-touched vestal' (III. xii. 30–1). His motive in sending Thidias to Cleopatra is to inveigle her into accepting a political arrangement with Octavius that will cut Antony out of her life entirely. Cleopatra astutely surmises that his wish is to take her back to Rome as a prize in his triumphal entry into that city, thereby bringing the unruly woman back under strict male control, where, in Octavius's view, she belongs. He must contain her threatening and transgressive sexuality; she is a repudiation of all that Roman imperium stands for. He will humiliate her by uplifting her to the view of 'Mechanic slaves / With greasy aprons, rules, and hammers' who encloud her with 'their thick breaths, / Rank of gross diet' (V. ii. 211–12). As Greenblatt observes (p. 170), that is why Cleopatra is so determined to repudiate what he has to offer and to align herself in death with the vision of a man whose 'legs bestrid the ocean' and whose delights 'Were dolphinlike; they showed his back above / The element they lived in' (pp. 81–9).

Antony and Cleopatra are at their best, in the view of most biographers and critics, when they dare to cross the boundaries between male and female that Octavius finds so necessary. Antony embraces the hedonistic life of matriarchal Egypt; Cleopatra, as she prepares in death to meet Mark Antony again, declares that 'I have nothing / Of woman in me. Now from head to foot / I am marble-constant' (V. ii. 238–40). Together they tell the world that 'It is not worth leave-taking' (l. 298). In this mutual triumph of the spirit, unstable though it must be, they seem to answer much that is destructive about the relations of men and women in the earlier tragedies and problem plays: Hamlet's taunting Ophelia as to why she would wish to be 'a breeder of sinners' (*Hamlet*, III. i. 122–3), Othello's homicidal jealousy of Desdemona, Angelo's self-hatred in his lusting after Isabella, Troilus's fury at beholding how 'The fragments, scraps, the bits and greasy relics' of Cressida's 'o'ereaten faith' are now bound to Diomedes (*Troilus and Cressida*, V. ii. 162–4), Bertram's choosing the life of a soldier over that of hugging 'his kicky-wicky here at home, / Spending his manly marrow in her arms' (*All's Well*, II. iii. 281–2), Goneril's giving her body adulterously to a manly man (Edmund) to whom 'a woman's services are due' rather than allowing her 'fool' husband Albany to usurp her body (*King Lear*, IV. ii. 26–8), Lady Macbeth's frightening prayer to the 'spirits / That tend on mortal thoughts' to 'unsex me here' (*Macbeth*, I. v. 40–1), Timon's sardonic plea to Phrynia and Timandra to 'Be whores still' and sow consumptions 'In hollow bones of man' and 'mar men's spurring' (*Timon of Athens*, IV. iii. 142–55), Coriolanus's saying to his mother Volumnia that in persuading him to spare Rome she has won a happy victory for the city but has prevailed with her son 'Most dangerously' (*Coriolanus*, V. iii. 84–7), and much more.

This is not to say, of course, that Shakespeare has succeeded once and for all, in his art or in his private life, in achieving a freedom from sexual inhibition, or that René Weis (316–17) is correct in supposing that Shakespeare was having an emotionally satisfying affair at this time with Jane Davenant, the wife of a wine merchant who, at 38, was some five years younger than Shakespeare. (Weis compares Antony at 43 with Cleopatra at 28.) The late plays offer abundant evidence that the problems of sexual inhibition and shame do not go away for Shakespeare. Still, as a vision, *Antony and Cleopatra* testifies to the strength and cogency of a longing to come to terms with one's own repressions.

Antony's triumph of the spirit is all the more significant because he suffers throughout the play from what our modern world might call a midlife crisis. He longs for sexual achievement on an epic scale, and Cleopatra knows how to feed and share his appetite. 'O thou day o'th'world', Antony greets Cleopatra as he returns to Alexandria from a military victory over Octavius, 'Chain mine armed neck; leap thou, attire and all, / Through proof of harness to my heart, and there / Ride on the pants triumphing!' (IV. viii. 13–16). Such great moments are needed, it seems, to assuage Antony's anxiety about growing older and thereby losing his sexual advantage to younger rivals. He is only too aware that grey hairs 'Do something mingle with our younger brown' (l. 20). In his jealous fears he bids Cleopatra 'To the boy Caesar send this grizzled head' in hopes of reward (III. xiii. 1–19). He refers sardonically to Octavius as one who 'wears the rose / Of youth upon him' (ll. 20–1).

As biographers have noted, this fear of ageing is a notable theme in the late plays. Duncan-Jones characterizes Shakespeare's 'tragedies of survival' as explorations in 'the misery of living too long' (p. 183). Othello is persuaded to mistrust Desdemona's professed loyalty to him in part because he is black and does not have 'those soft parts of conversation / That chamberers have', but in part also because he is 'declined / Into the vale of years'—perhaps 'not much', but still enough perhaps to be of concern (*Othello*, III. iii. 279–82). In *King Lear*, according to Greenblatt, Shakespeare's 'bad dream' is of 'a loss of power and the threat of dependency posed by age' (p. 369). Lear mockingly implores Regan, 'Dear daughter, I confess that I am old. / Age is unnecessary. On my knees I beg / That you'll vouchsafe me raiment, bed, and food' (*King Lear*, II. iv. 152–4). The Earl of Gloucester is afflicted with a similar anxiety that his son and heir appears to wish him dead (I. ii. 47–79). Macbeth mourns that 'My way of life / Is fall'n into the sere, the yellow leaf, / And that which should accompany old age, / As honor, love, obedience, troops of friends, / I must not look to have' (*Macbeth*, V. iii. 22–6). Instead of fruitfulness in his advanced years, he sees only that 'all our yesterdays have lighted fools / The way to dusty death' (V. v. 22–3). Timon rages, 'Pity not honored age for his white beard' (*Timon*, IV. iii. 114).

When therefore Enobarbus says praisingly of Cleopatra that 'Age cannot wither her', he is suggesting that what she offers to Antony above all else is an 'infinite variety' that 'makes hungry / Where most she satisfies', enabling him for a time to affirm his youth and manhood (*Antony and Cleopatra*, II. ii. 245). This preoccupation with ageing and its concomitant diminution of sexual potency does not surprise Shakespeare's biographers; the dramatist was in his forties when he wrote these plays, and had less than a decade still to live. How specifically autobiographical the insight may have been cannot easily be determined, but Shakespeare's absorption in the topic is chronologically appropriate.

The struggle to achieve serenity in old age has great dramatic potential in a dramatist of Shakespeare's stature. His biographers are in accord that ageing forms a major topic in his late plays, and that it is linked with concerns that are both domestic and professional: a man's relationship with his daughter, his concern about retirement from his profession, his anxiety about reunion with a wife from whom he has been separated for so long, and his thoughts about the approach of death. 'His last plays do not convince us that he has found peace of mind', writes Hesketh Pearson, 'much though he longed for it' (p. 167).

How well do these concerns about ageing and career and family fit the known facts about Shakespeare? He was only 52 when he died in 1616. The date of his return from London to Stratford is uncertain. Documentary records place him in Stratford in September 1611, October 1614, September 1615, and March and April 1616 (Eccles, 131), but he may also have spent substantial amounts of time there earlier, in the years 1603–10, since, as J. Leeds Barroll and Jonathan Bate (*Soul of the Age*, 335) note, the theatres were closed in London for months at a time, adding up to a total of more than four years during this troubled time of plague. Sometimes the closings were more a consequence of the London authorities' hostility towards theatre than actual outbreaks of plague, but the result in either case was a ban on theatrical performances. Conceivably, as Bate speculates (pp. 337–8), Shakespeare may have lived principally in Stratford in semi-retirement after 1604, doing his writing there, collaborating by correspondence with other dramatists like Middleton and Fletcher. He seems not to have been active on stage, and cannot be shown to be in residence in London during these years, whereas several documents seemingly imply his presence in Stratford in 1605 and 1608–9. If he did move back to Stratford in 1604 or shortly after that, he would have been only 40 years old—hardly what we regard today as aged. Yet people did age quickly in the early modern period, owing in part to poor diet; Shakespeare's very prosperity may have meant that he was able to eat protein-rich fare. He seems not to have been in good health in his last years.

At all events, biographers posit that Shakespeare had plenty of reasons to meditate on his mortal condition. As a gifted and famous writer, he might well wish to consider the shape of his career as the end drew near. As a family man he evidently had much on his mind. He was the father of two daughters, of whom one, Susanna, seems to have been the favoured child after Hamnet's death. Her marriage to the successful physician John Hall in June of 1607 appears to have flourished, and tradition reports that Shakespeare helped the couple obtain a handsome house (now known as Hall's Croft) not far from New Place (Schoenbaum, *Documentary Life*, 237). Holden (*Illustrated Biography*, 303), supposing Susanna to have been literate while Judith was not, speculates that Shakespeare 'may have taken more pride in his more refined, worldly-wise, locally respected older daughter', even though 'he knew that he had not been much of a father to either'. Judith did less well than Susanna when, at the ripe age of 31, she married Thomas Quiney on 10 February 1616, shortly before her father died. Prior to the marriage, Quiney (aged 27) had impregnated Margaret Wheeler, who then died with her infant in childbirth a month or so after Judith's marriage to Quiney (Schoenbaum, *Documentary Life*, 238–41).

Given these circumstances, biographers generally have seen Shakespeare's last years as an especially promising area in which to look for connections between his plays and Shakespeare's own life story. The late romances revisit family history with a repeated emphasis on father and daughter, the disappearing and sometimes reappearing wife, the lost son or sons, retirement, and preparation for death (see, for example, M. C. Bradbrook, 224). In all but *The Tempest*, Shakespeare dramatizes an existing plot source, so that the search for autobiographical connection must assume that Shakespeare's choice of what story to tell had a personal meaning for him. Because the family story varies significantly in its retelling, analysts must assume either that Shakespeare's feelings about his family history varied from time to time during these years, or that Shakespeare's imaginative creativity can help account for at least some of the variations. Germaine Greer usefully reminds us (p. 115) that functional marriages are almost never shown in imaginative literature; dysfunctional marriages are invariably more interesting. Nonetheless, some biographers find it useful to approach the late plays as a series of personal fantasies in which, from a perspective distance provided by dramatic fiction, Shakespeare provides for himself an opportunity to meditate on last things, even while he is also, of course, entertaining and edifying an audience.

Pericles is generally accepted to be a work of collaborative authorship, probably with George Wilkins, containing some uneven writing and bizarre inconsistencies in an imperfectly preserved text. Yet the play was immensely popular during Shakespeare's late years and afterwards, and was widely ascribed to him (see Duncan-Jones, 204–5, and Bradbrook, 231). A consensus view gives to Shakespeare at least the lively comic scenes in the bordello and the play's finale, so that the play's ideas about family can be considered his. At heart, the story is of a romantic hero, Pericles, Prince of Tyre, who crisscrosses the eastern Mediterranean in search of adventure and of a wife. He narrowly escapes the tyrannical clutches of the incestuous King of Antiochus and his daughter; happily marries Thaisa, the daughter of the genial Simonides, King of Pentapolis; is obliged to commit the body of his wife to the sea when she seemingly dies in a storm; gives his infant daughter, Marina, born in that terrible moment at sea, to the care of Cleon, Governor of Tarsus, and his homicidally envious wife, Dionyza; is eventually reunited with his daughter, now a young woman, in Mytilene, where she has been sold into prostitution by pirates but has managed to convert her customers (including the Governor, Lysimachus) to a life of pious decency; and is then instructed in a vision by the goddess Diana to find his long-lost wife, Thaisa, at Diana's temple in Ephesus, where she has been placed by a lord of Ephesus named Cerimon who revived her when her body floated ashore in a coffin during the terrible storm of years ago.

This romance tale, with all the characteristics of its genre—travel, adventure, hair's-breadth escapes, separation, and reunion, all highly improbable and thrilling—provides biographers with a number of suggestive configurations. Incest is a major theme. It takes an outwardly inviting guise, but is deeply threatening. As Honan says, Pericles 'seems in flight from himself and also from a recognition of the possibility of incest' (p. 367). Incest bespeaks the way in which fathers can all too easily become possessive of their daughters and hostile to young suitors who come to woo. The King of Antiochus professes to offer his daughter in marriage to the most competitive candidate, but secretly he plans to destroy them all and continue to live incestuously with the daughter.

As Wells observes, this episode stands in vivid contrast to the play's 'portrayals of ideal virtue' (*Dramatic Life*, 334). Simonides of Pentapolis at first seems to be another incestuous father; he bridles at Pericles's attentions to Thaisa, accuses him of having villainously bewitched her, and brands him as a traitor (II. v. 49–55). He does so, however, as a test and as a humorous contretemps. Every love story needs an encounter with adversity, usually in the form of parental opposition (as in *A Midsummer Night's Dream*, for instance), and so Simonides jocosely plays the role of the irate father only to sweeten the pleasure of his finally giving consent for their marriage. In this he anticipates the role played by Prospero in *The Tempest*, who threatens Ferdinand with harsh servitude and frightens Miranda with his choleric behaviour even while he informs us as audience in a series of asides that he is only doing this to make sure that the young couple think seriously about their commitment to each other.

It is as though Shakespeare is repeatedly pondering, in these late plays, how a father should behave and think when he finds himself on the point of giving up a daughter to a younger man. As Greenblatt says (pp. 389–90): 'It cannot be an accident that three of his last plays—*Pericles*, *The Winter's Tale*, and *The Tempest*—are centered on the father–daughter relationship and are so deeply anxious about incestuous desires.' (To which he might just as well have added *Cymbeline*, as we shall see below.) Fathers in earlier plays have repeatedly failed to learn how to let go: Egeus in *A Midsummer Night's Dream*, the Duke of Milan in *The Two Gentlemen of Verona*, Shylock in *The Merchant of Venice*, Brabantio in *Othello*, and King Lear especially (Greenblatt, 127). Some early instances here are examples of the parental opposition that one expects to find in romantic comedy, but the later instances represent what Freud would call an incestuous resistance—not in a fully physical sense but as an emotional attachment that the father may not fully understand in himself.

Is Shakespeare attempting personally to come to terms with such feelings? We cannot be sure, but biographers have taken note of an important date: Shakespeare's elder daughter Susanna married John Hall in June of 1607, presumably close to the time of his working on *Pericles* and *King Lear*. Charles Nicholl, observing that Susanna and Judith were roughly the same age as Mary Mountjoy, in whose house on Silver Street in London Shakespeare had lived, speculates that Shakespeare's absorption in father–daughter conflicts over dowry and the like may have been partly inspired by what he had earlier witnessed at first hand in the troubled Mountjoy household (pp. 268–9).

The seeming death of Thaisa in *Pericles* inaugurates another motif that will be a feature of the late plays. Like Hermione in *The Winter's Tale* (see below), Thaisa only seems to be dead. Her grieving husband consents to her being thrown overboard in a coffin because of a sailors' superstition that the raging storm will not subside 'till the ship be cleared of the dead' (III. i. 48–9), but when her coffin washes ashore at Ephesus she is revived by Lord Cerimon. He talks as though he has brought her back from the dead: 'Death may usurp on nature many hours', he says, 'And yet the fire of life kindle again' (III. ii. 84–5). Onlookers speak of having witnessed a miracle. Pericles, meanwhile, knowing nothing of Thaisa's revival, continues on his adventures. Just as he is about to be reunited at last with the daughter whom he saw only momentarily after her birth at sea and whom he has left for many years in the care of Cleon and Dionyza, Pericles is a sadly changed man. He dresses in rough clothing, has allowed his hair and beard to grow untrimmed, and is so withdrawn into a deep, catatonic melancholy that no one can get through to him.

What is the cause of Pericles's sorrow? Helicanus says only that he is 'a goodly person, / Till the disaster [i.e. the loss of his wife] that, one mortal night, / Drove him to this' (V. i. 37–9). Perhaps Helicanus implies, as David Hoeniger argues (*Pericles*, 1963), that Pericles is tormented with guilt about his role in consigning his wife to burial at sea. Necessity compelled, and yet, in a sense, Pericles did abandon his wife and has chosen to live apart from his only daughter. The restoration to him of them both is something so miraculous that he can scarcely credit it. 'This is the rarest dream that e'er dull sleep / Did mock sad fools withal. This cannot be' (ll. 166–8), he exclaims when Marina gives him reason to believe that she is indeed his long-lost daughter.

The story of *Pericles* thus translates rather persuasively into a parable with potential autobiographical relevance about a man who has left his wife and daughter for a long enough time to allow the child to reach sexual maturity. Shakespeare lived in London, apart from his family for much if not most of the time, from 1590 or so to as late as 1610 or thereabouts, a comparable span of years. He left when the children were young. Much later, he had to learn how to accept and perhaps rejoice in the marriage of his daughter Susanna to John Hall in 1607, much as Pericles celebrates his family reunion by giving his blessing to the marriage of Marina to Lysimachus (V. i. 264–6). Shakespeare returned in 1610 or so (perhaps somewhat sooner) to a domestic relationship with the wife from whom he had lived apart, except presumably for periodic visits, for roughly the same interval of time.

Even if Germaine Greer is right to insist that Shakespeare did not abandon his wife—a criminal act, 'punishable in both the ecclesiastical and civil courts' (p. 146)—Shakespeare, in the view of some biographers, could have sought out fictions like the story of Pericles and Thaisa in which to explore imaginatively the emotional burdens placed on a husband who may have felt some remorse or anxiety about his own separation from his family. Pericles is grateful to the gods for the seemingly miraculous restoration of Thaisa; as he embraces her, he bids her to 'be buried / A second time within these arms' (V. ii. 44–5). The embrace thus supplants and atones for the earlier consigning of the wife to her watery grave. The present kindness of the gods 'Makes my past miseries sports' (ll. 41–2), says Pericles. The play ends happily, as a romance should do (see *Pericles*, ed. Gossett, 153–61), but not without its sombre reflections on what the husband has done to bring down misfortune on himself and how little he can hope to deserve the happiness given him by the gods at last.

The family in *Cymbeline* (*c*.1609–10) presents biographers with a different possible perspective on autobiographical imaginings. As Duncan-Jones argues, the play is preoccupied with royal lineage and genealogy expressed through the image of a great cedar tree whose branches represent children 'first lost and apparently lopped, then eventually found' (pp. 233–5). King Cymbeline's two sons have disappeared in their infancy, leaving him as possible heir only a single daughter, Imogen, who then frustrates her father's dynastic hopes by marrying beneath her social station. Posthumus Leonatus is, in the King's eyes, unworthy to be the consort of a queen, however well endowed with personal virtues. Cymbeline's rage against Imogen is 'psychopathic', says Duncan-Jones (p. 210), like that of Lear, and of Leontes in *The Winter's Tale*. This ungovernable anger sets in motion the tragic phase of the tragicomedy, which ends eventually in reconciliation and forgiveness, like that of Pericles and Marina in *Pericles* and Leontes and his wife and daughter in *The Winter's Tale*.

A significant variant here is that Cymbeline, a recent widower, has married a second time, to a frighteningly domineering and evil woman who attempts to destroy Imogen and eventually the King himself. Her witless but menacing son, Cloten, whom both she and the King wish to see married to Imogen, is a further extension of the Queen's all-encompassing churlish and envious nature. As a reincarnation of Dionyza in *Pericles*, Goneril and Regan in *King Lear*, Lady Macbeth, Volumnia in *Coriolanus*, or, further back in Shakespeare's writing career, Joan of Arc in *1 Henry VI* and Queen Margaret in the tetralogy of plays from *1 Henry VI* to *Richard III*, the Queen in *Cymbeline* is the enduring nightmare vision in Shakespeare of a threatening maternal presence. She is like the mythic figure Althaea, who, told by the Fates that her son Meleager would live so long as a brand on the fire was not consumed, snatched it away from the fire and preserved it until Meleager killed her brothers in a quarrel, whereupon she threw into the fire the fatal brand. Cymbeline's Queen is, in other words, the mother figure who both gives and takes away life. She is the embodiment of what men fear most in women and wrongly imagine in Hero, Helena, Desdemona, and other maligned heroines in Shakespeare's plays. As Janet Adelman puts it, '*Cymbeline* suggests the radical instability of a masculine identity inevitably defined by the female' (*Suffocating Mothers*, 199).

Some biographers have asked if this disturbing and recurring female presence in Shakespeare's plays and poems owes something to the part played in his life by his mother, Mary Arden Shakespeare. Weis, for example, wonders if Shakespeare as a son 'had striven ceaselessly to please Mary Arden above all, but felt that she never quite reciprocated his devotion' (p. 330). Purported evidence for such a speculation is to be found in *Coriolanus*'s portrayal of 'a mother–son relationship that is suspect and destructive', and in similarly fraught situations. 'The treatment of mothers in his last plays suggests that the relationship between Shakespeare and Mary Arden was never resolved', writes Weis (p. 329). Hence, in Weis's interpretation, the absence of mothers in *Twelfth Night*, *Othello*, *King Lear*, and *The Winter's Tale*, among others. Honan's view is that 'The most tangled and contradictory of his [Shakespeare's] relationships, one suspects, was always with his mother. His troubled attitudes to women are too deep to be of anything but early origin. There is no biographical evidence that he abhorred women, but in relation to female sexuality he had become fastidiously self-protective' (p. 358).

Greenblatt, to be sure, cautions that one must be wary here of too facile a linking of Shakespeare's writings to his life, since Mary Shakespeare in her late years was 'not, as far we know, either mad or tyrannical' (p. 356). Still, at the level of the artistic imagination one can note that the innocent and recovered mother in *Pericles* and then in *The Winter's Tale* is replaced in *Cymbeline* by a dragon lady of fearsomely destructive power. In any event, biographers do wonder if it is only coincidental that Shakespeare appears to have written this Queen into *Cymbeline* at about the time of Mary Arden Shakespeare's death in September of 1608.

The Queen in *Cymbeline* is, moreover, a wife as well as mother. Her disappearance at the end of the play by means of suicide, after having confessed to aiming at the lives of Imogen and then the Queen's royal husband (V. v. 27–61), is unhappily suggestive of an authorial design to exclude the wife from the play's happy conclusion. *Cymbeline* ends with a family reunion that restores the daughter and her husband and brothers to the King, but without the mother. This Queen is not Imogen's true mother, to be sure; she is a wicked stepmother. As in 'Hänsel and Gretel' and other such tales, this substitution of step-mother for mother barely conceals ambivalent feelings of anger and fear of rejection towards the biological mother. *The Tempest* ends, like *Cymbeline*, with no wife-mother. In *Pericles* and *The Winter's Tale*, on the other hand, she is fully incorporated in the happy ending. Scholars like Stephen Orgel have wondered if this varying strategy reflects an ambivalence on Shakespeare's part towards the wife he had left behind him in Stratford for decades and with whom he was now planning to share his years of retirement.

Cymbeline is unique among the four late romances in that its restored family in Act V includes two long-lost sons, one of them (Guiderius) the proper heir to Cymbeline's throne and thus an ideal opposite to the cowardly and hateful Cloten, whose sexual and political aspirations are a consistent target of ridicule in the play. As we have seen in Chapter 6, Shakespeare's own loss of his only son and heir, Hamnet, in 1596, at the age of 11, seems to have prompted a surprisingly late response, if it was indeed a response, in *Twelfth Night*, *c.*1600, with its tale of identical boy-girl twins (Hamnet was Judith's twin) of whom the lad, Sebastian, is thought to be drowned and is replaced throughout most of the play by his look-alike boy-impersonating sister, Viola, in her disguise as Cesario. Sebastian is then in effect brought back to life and is reunited with his sister. If this is dreamwork on Shakespeare's part, it takes the not uncommon form of coping with such a disaster by imagining that the dead son can somehow be recovered.

In the plays that follow *Twelfth Night*, Brabantio, Lear, Pericles, and other fathers have no sons. Cymbeline, on the other hand, has sired two sons. Their having been taken from him and their presumed demise help set in motion much that is potentially tragic in *Cymbeline*: the King's ill-considered remarriage, his pinning his hopes on Cloten as an heir, his turning in wrath on Imogen for having married a husband of non-royal lineage, and all the rest. Yet here the tragicomic pattern resolves itself into the discovery of that which has been lost: a true heir to the throne. As Leah Marcus puts it, 'Through the discovery of lost children, the ancient kingdom of Brute is finally reunited' (p. 135). Down to the last minute, Cymbeline foolishly attempts to undo his happiness by sentencing Guiderius to be executed for having slain Cloten, until he is informed by old Belarius of Guiderius's true royal identity. All is finally resolved in what A. D. Nuttall calls the play's 'extraordinary dénouement' (p. 339). Cymbeline's happiness is all the more rich for being undeserved.

Cymbeline is blessed too with a recovered lost son in another sense of the term: he now embraces without hesitation the son-in-law, Posthumus, whom earlier he banished. Since Imogen is no longer heir to the throne, Posthumus is no longer a threat to Cymbeline's dynastic hopes. The son-in-law as an allowable substitute for the lost or non-existent son is a motif that will figure prominently in *The Tempest*. Pericles finds comfort in a son-in-law, Lysimachus; so does Leontes in *The Winter's Tale* in Florizel. (The word 'son' in Shakespeare regularly means both 'son' and 'son-in-law'.) These happy resolutions have prompted biographers to wonder if Shakespeare is thinking of John Hall, the successful physician to whom Susanna was married in 1607 (see, for example, Duncan-Jones, 266–70; Honan, 356; Weis, 326–7; Greenblatt, 144). In *Cymbeline*, containing as it does the motif of the recovered sons and son-in-law, along with the daughter, we have a family constellation that is more complete than in any of the other late romances, but with one truly notable exception: the mother has been scapegoated as the wicked Queen and then erased from the story's happy ending. No such figure is to be found in Shakespeare's main sources for the play; she is the fairy-story-like invention of his imagination.

The Winter's Tale, written in 1610 or so, after Shakespeare seems to have chosen to return to Stratford and 'to his neglected wife in New Place', ends, as Greenblatt says, 'with the moving reconciliation of a husband and wife who had seemed lost to one another forever'. Does this mean, asks Greenblatt, that Shakespeare 'had finally achieved some loving intimacy' with Anne? 'Perhaps this was indeed Shakespeare's fantasy for his own life, but if so the fantasy does not seem to correspond to what actually happened' (p. 144). In his will, in 1616, Shakespeare would leave the great bulk of his estate to Susanna and John Hall, with provision for Judith and also for Shakespeare's one surviving sibling, Joan, along with modest remembrances to friends and neighbours and the town's poor. To Anne he left nothing at all, until in a last-minute codicil he specified the gift 'unto my wife' of 'my second best bed and furniture'. Other than that the document does not name her; it contains none of the customary endearments of 'my beloved wife' and the like that are to be found in comparable wills (Greenblatt, 145). Nor does Shakespeare leave her any jewels or keepsakes that might have sentimental value.

Honan describes how Shakespeare was intensely wary of Anne's ambitious relatives, especially her brother Bartholomew, prompting Shakespeare to exclude all of them from his will and empowering

Susanna to act as executrix in a way that would ensure the carrying out of his intent (pp. 232–4). Earlier, in 1613, when Shakespeare bought his first property in London, the Blackfriars gatehouse, he arranged matters in such a way that 'Anne Shakespeare was denied a dower right in the gatehouse, even if her husband died intestate' (Honan, 378–9). Sidney Lee (488–9) comments that 'Such procedure is pretty conclusive proof that he [Shakespeare] had the intention of excluding her from the enjoyment of his possessions after his death' (quoted in Schoenbaum, *Documentary Life*, 223). Duncan-Jones suspects that 'conjugal relations between William and Anne ceased some time in the 1580s, and by the time of Hamnet's death [in 1596] were quite extinct' (p. 91); the antagonism between the Shakespeares and the Hathaways 'may go right back to the time of his reluctant marriage' (p. 150). Opinions on this important matter vary, to be sure. For counterarguments by Greer and others defending the marriage and Shakespeare's last will and testament, see Chapter 3 above.

If then *The Winter's Tale* pursues a fantasy that did not in fact materialize in Shakespeare's life in retirement, this unhappy thought might seem to confirm the pointed absence of reconciliation with a wife in *Cymbeline* and *The Tempest*. In no way, however, does it lessen the potential poignancy for biographers of such a fantasy as expressing what Shakespeare could have dreamed and perhaps hoped to await him on his return to his native town. Leontes, King of Sicilia, though blessed with a virtuous and beautiful wife, is pathologically driven into a fear that his wife is 'slippery', a 'hobbyhorse . . . As rank as any flax-wench that puts to / Before her trothplight' (I. ii. 272–7). Leontes is convinced beyond any doubt that he is being cuckolded by his oldest and dearest friend, King Polixenes of Bohemia, upon no real evidence other than that Polixenes has been a royal guest in Sicilia for nine months and that Queen Hermione is at the fullness of her term. Leontes's most loyal courtiers, especially Camillo, cannot persuade him to abandon his groundless accusation.

As Jonathan Bate points out (*Genius of Shakespeare*, 145), Leontes's jealousy is well motivated in Shakespeare's source, Robert Greene's *Pandosto*, where the Queen frequently visits the bedchamber of their royal guest to make sure he is comfortable and whiles away her time with him in private conversation in the palace garden. Shakespeare, conversely, has played up the irrational nature of the jealousy as utterly without foundation. The King persists in ordering a public and humiliating trial for Hermione, though agreeing to consult the oracle of Delphi, which, he is sure, will confirm his suspicions. He condemns the newborn child, Perdita, to be killed, but then relents to the extent of allowing a courtier (Antigonus) to carry the babe to a far-off shore and abandon it there. Too late, Leontes receives word from Delphi that 'Hermione is chaste, Polixenes blameless, Camillo a true subject, Leontes a jealous tyrant, his innocent babe truly begotten, and the King shall live without an heir if that which is lost be not found' (III. ii. 132–6). Almost immediately, news arrives that the crown prince Mamillius has perished 'with mere conceit and fear / Of the Queen's speed' (ll. 144–5). Next comes a report that the Queen too has died of consternation and shame. Mamillius is in fact dead, though we learn much later, in the play's final scene, that the Queen is alive after all. At present, however, Leontes seems to have lost everything through his own jealous folly.

As biographers have seen, the potential application to Shakespeare's own life story is more stark here than in any of the other late romances. Leontes is given no motivation or excuse for his wilful acts; the guilt is entirely his. The fantasy then is of a husband whose abandonment of his wife cannot be justified. He has not been given a difficult choice in the matter, like the sailors' insistence during a storm at sea that Pericles consent to having the body of his wife thrown overboard. No cunning tempter like Iago in *Othello* or Jachimo in *Cymbeline* has assisted in implanting jealousy in the husband's troubled mind. Leontes wantonly destroys his own happiness. The best that can be said for him is that he fully accepts the blame, asking only of his loyal critic Paulina that she ceaselessly remind him of his culpability.

Conversely, this play imagines a wife who is radiantly beautiful, royally born, and utterly loyal in her marriage. However much these circumstances may or may not apply to Anne Hathaway in whole or in part, they bespeak for biographers a fantasy in which the abandoned wife is a rich prize whom the erring husband has rejected insanely. 'Is it a coincidence', asks Jonathan Bate, that *The Winter's Tale* 'is about a man who asks his wife for a second chance after sixteen years of separation?' (*Genius of the Age*, 178). The wife whom Leontes ultimately recovers through the ministrations of Paulina is every bit as worthy and loveable as he could dream or hope. 'Oh, she's warm!' he exclaims as the seeming statue of Hermione in Paulina's house comes to life and steps down from the pedestal, being 'stone no more'. Hermione embraces her husband and hangs about his neck (V. iii. 90–113). Paulina and Leontes have noted admiringly that the statue represents Hermione not as she was an entire generation earlier, but 'As she lived now', 'As now she might have done' (ll. 31–2). Leontes is prepared to love his wife in her advancing years. She has forgiven him for doing what he knows was unforgivable, much as Cordelia forgives her father in *King Lear* (IV. vii. 77–8), Hero forgives Claudio in *Much Ado*, Helena forgives Bertram in *All's Well*, Mariana forgives Angelo in *Measure for Measure*, and Imogen forgives Posthumus in *Cymbeline*.

This memorable scene of the statue coming to life, like Leontes's irrational jealousy, is not to be found in Shakespeare's main source for *The Winter's Tale*, Robert Greene's *Pandosto*. In that account, Pandosto, the equivalent of Leontes, 'calling to mind how first he betrayed his friend Egistus [Polixenes], how his jealousy was the cause of Bellaria's [Hermione's] death, that contrary to the law of nature he had lusted after his own daughter, moved with these desperate thoughts he fell into a melancholy fit and, to close up the comedy with a tragical stratagem, he slew himself'. Shakespeare deletes not only the protagonist's suicide but the incest between father and daughter that had so fascinated him (and his collaborator) in *Pericles*. The fantasy in *The Winter's Tale* is carefully sanitized, and may seem all the more deeply personal for that reason. If, as Greenblatt asks, it does indeed represent the dramatist's artistic imagining of what life might be like for him in Stratford in retirement, the gap between imagined hope and the seeming reality is all the more poignant. Such an analysis, Jonathan Bate proposes (*Genius of Shakespeare*, 145–6), can perhaps help explain how Leo Tolstoy managed to read *The Winter's Tale* so unsympathetically, condemning it as a piece of overblown and improbable fiction.

That the wife is absent from *The Tempest* might seem to confirm a glum assessment of Shakespeare's prospects for a renewed marriage. *The Tempest* is, as Jonathan Bate observes, 'a work that concerns itself deeply with a father's attitude to his daughter's prospective marriage but which has almost no interest in the figure of the wife of a man who lives by "potent art"' (*Soul of the Age*, 178). Prospero's wife, as

Stephen Orgel points out, is alluded to only once in the play, and that one instance takes the form of a familiar anti-feminist joke. 'Sir, are not you my father?' Miranda asks Prospero, who has mystified her by telling her that, twelve years ago, 'Thy father was the Duke of Milan and / A prince of power'. He assures her that he is referring to himself in the third person and that Miranda is indeed his daughter: 'Thy mother was a piece of virtue, and / She said thou wast my daughter; and thy father / Was Duke of Milan, and his only heir / And princess no worse issued' (I. ii. 55–9). The mother/wife is not named (just as Anne is not referred to by name in Shakespeare's will), and we learn nothing more of her.

The joke here reflects one of the oldest of male insecurities: that of being unsure who has fathered the child or children borne of a wife's belly. 'That thou art my son I have partly thy mother's word, partly my own opinion, but chiefly a villainous trick of thine eye and a foolish hanging of thy nether lip that doth warrant me', Falstaff pronounces with mock seriousness as he play-acts King Henry IV in his famous tavern scene with Prince Hal (*1 Henry IV*, II. iv. 399–402). Again, the mother is not named. When Don Pedro, in a scene of happy greeting in *Much Ado*, says to Leonato as he bows to the pretty young woman at Leonato's side, 'I think this is your daughter', Leonato replies: 'Her mother hath many times told me so.' Benedick cannot resist playing with the old joke. 'Were you in doubt, sir, that you asked her?' he interrupts, to which Leonato has the perfect put-down reply: 'Signor Benedick, no; for then were you a child' (I. i. 98–103). This is all we learn of the fleetingly named '*Innogen his* [*Leonato's*] *wife*' (I. i. 0 SD, mentioned also as 'wife' at II.1.0). Taken more seriously, this enduring male paranoia is at the heart of August Strindberg's *The Father* (1887).

The Tempest (*c*.1611) is widely regarded as Shakespeare's formal farewell to the theatre. The evidence is all internal and hypothetical, but cumulatively impressive. As Greenblatt (p. 373) and others have noted, it is the last play Shakespeare wrote entirely by himself; he evidently collaborated afterwards with John Fletcher, his successor as chief dramatist for the King's Men, in the writing of *Henry VIII* (1613) and *The Two Noble Kinsmen* (1613–14), as well as the now-lost *Cardenio* (1612–13), but *The Tempest* is his. It takes pride of first place in *Mr William Shakespeare's Comedies, Histories, and Tragedies*, the handsome volume known as the First Folio of 1623, as though the editors,

John Heminges and Henry Condell, wished to offer it as representing the very best work of their author. The text is carefully printed from a transcript by the noted scribe Ralph Crane, based seemingly in turn on a theatre playbook or a good Shakespearean draft that had been annotated for production.

The play has no known single source. Instead, it reads as an exquisite anthology of Shakespeare's trademark comic dramaturgy: a love story beset by (seeming) parental opposition, a nearly tragic backdrop of fratricidal rivalry and exile (as in *As You Like It*), separation and loss at sea (*The Comedy of Errors, Twelfth Night, Pericles*), shipwreck, reunion, buffoonish below-stairs characters, fantastic fairy-like creatures (*A Midsummer Night's Dream*), the intervention of the gods in human affairs (*Midsummer, Cymbeline*), and still more. As Duncan-Jones says, '*The Tempest* is a uniquely original work of synthesis' and also seems to be 'the most revealingly personal of all Shakespeare's plays' (p. 236). Weis agrees: Shakespeare 'is writing about his own creative genius in *The Tempest* and casting himself as Prospero' (p. 322). Weis finds it hard to doubt 'that Shakespeare saw himself as a wizard of language and books, who had for twenty years created airy nothings out of his imagination and become rich by it' (p. 337).

Most of all, *The Tempest* strikes biographers generally as a retirement play because of its insistent meditation on fathers and daughters, on the father's difficult role in relinquishing to a younger man his claim on the daughter, on the equally difficult role of laying aside his magical-like powers as an artist, and on the hardest thing of all, perhaps, preparing for death. *The Tempest* offers the perfect paradigm for all these considerations. Its fable is of a father and a daughter living together for twelve years with no other company than that of Caliban, who has become their slave. Father and daughter are a couple. Miranda presumably has learned to keep house for her father, like Desdemona for her father Brabantio in *Othello* or Jessica for Shylock in *The Merchant of Venice*. On the island, Prospero is in command through his magical powers in a way that he certainly was not in the dukedom of Naples.

The island of *The Tempest* is his theatre, his domain, where, as Alvin Kernan has shown, he can control the destinies of those who come to the island much as a dramatist shapes the fortunes of his characters in the theatre. The island exists apart from the fallen world of Italy, with its incessant political manoeuverings. The island is a kind of utopia, a place that exists only in the imagination of the artist and his audience. There Prospero is in charge, even though he is also reliant on a power of magical creativity that comes to him through Ariel, a spirit that serves him for a time but that must be freed at the end, because that spirit is eternal whereas Prospero is mortal. He must finally give up his power as artist because retirement and death are unavoidable. He must give up his daughter to a younger man because she must be free to live her own life as his own approaches its end.

All of this seems intensely pertinent to Shakespeare at the end of his career as a dramatist, not only autobiographically but in the larger sense of something that is shared by all humanity. The biographical connection seems all the more moving as an imagined story because it addresses and resolves so many of the problems that Shakespeare has grappled with in his earlier plays. The fathers in *The Merchant of Venice*, *Othello*, *King Lear*, *Pericles*, *Cymbeline*, and *The Winter's Tale*, among others, have not known how to deal wisely with their daughters' wishes to marry. That, perhaps, is why the incest motif in *Pericles* or in Shakespeare's source for *The Winter's Tale*, Greene's *Pandosto*, seems so compellingly relevant. These fathers have done their best to destroy their own happiness and that of their children by not knowing how to let go. Prospero, aware of the problem, takes charge. Through his magic he brings young Ferdinand ashore at precisely the spot on the island where he will encounter Miranda. Prospero is there, invisible, orchestrating their first meeting and the beginnings of courtship. He wishes it to happen, and it goes according to his plan. It satisfies his dynastic wishes as well as his emotional needs, for Ferdinand and Miranda will reconcile in their marriage the feud between Naples and Milan that led to Prospero's exile twelve years ago.

To be sure, Prospero says some very angry things to Ferdinand, and compels the young man to perform demeaning manual tasks like carrying logs that liken his condition to that of Caliban, Prospero's slave. Yet Prospero repeatedly assures us as audience that his show of anger is a part of his stratagem. A love plot needs parental opposition to give it the necessary artistic shape of complication and resolution, and so Prospero plays the expected role of the angry parent. Biographers can wonder if he is not also channelling some genuine feelings of anxiety and regret into this subterfuge, as he play-acts the father who must find a way to know himself more wisely. To A. D. Nuttall, 'the obvious explanation is that Prospero is fighting his own incestuous desire for his daughter' (p. 368). In any case, Prospero's role as accepting father provides artistic closure to those repeated earlier instances where fathers were their own worst enemies. We cannot know the extent to which Shakespeare may have coped with comparable feelings of incestuous longing in himself, but we can see how splendidly he has conceived of that struggle as deeply a part of human experience.

Biographers generally agree that *The Tempest* is a celebration of Shakespeare's art as dramatist. As Greenblatt puts it, concurring with Kernan, Wells (*Dramatic Life*, 362), Holden (*Life and Work*, 285–6), and others, Prospero 'is unmistakably a great playwright—manipulating characters, contriving to set them up in relation to one another, forging memorable scenes'. Indeed, his princely power is precisely the playwright's power to determine the fate of his creations, and his magical power is precisely 'the playwright's power to alter space and time, create vivid illusions, cast a spell' (Greenblatt, 372). As Jonathan Bate says, there is 'something in Prospero that seeks to usurp God's powers' (*Soul of the Age*, 129). In Duncan-Jones's words, magic is 'a metaphor for theatrical spectacle'. The island, with its elaborate props such as 'animal heads, artificial wings and a fake banquet, is obviously an image of the playhouse and its backstage equipment' (p. 238).

However intensely personal it appears to be, *The Tempest* also must have seemed politically topical in its presentation of two issues of current fascination in 1611–12: royal marriage as a key to dynastic stability, and exploration of the New World across the Atlantic. As Duncan-Jones observes, 'Marriage prospects for the King's eldest children, Prince Henry and Princess Elizabeth, were the subject of increasingly excited rumour' (p. 236). The play was staged at court in November of 1611 and then in February of 1613, as Honan (p. 373) and Schoenbaum (*Compact Documentary Life*, 275) point out, to help celebrate the wedding of the Princess Elizabeth to Prince Frederick, the Elector Palatine of the Rhine. Interest in the Virginia colonies is hinted at in the play when Ariel recalls how Prospero has bid his spirit to 'fetch dew / From the still-vexed Bermudas' (or 'Bermoothes', as spelled in the First Folio, I. ii. 229–30).

Though the island is nominally situated somewhere in the Mediterranean, to judge from the accounts of Prospero's having been put aboard a leaky vessel from the Italian mainland (I. ii. 144–8) and of the King of Naples's journey from his kingdom to north Africa to attend his daughter Claribel's wedding to the King of Tunis (II. i. 72–3) and then back towards Italy, the island is also an indeterminate and visionary landscape. Miranda speaks of a 'brave new world / that has such people in't' when she beholds many Europeans in the play's final scene (V. i. 185–6). Shakespeare appears to have read and borrowed from a published account of shipwreck off the Virginia coast by Sylvester Jourdain (1610) and a letter by William Strachey, written in the same year though not published until later. Caliban is a native of the sort that English audiences might expect to find in accounts of the Americas. Honan shows how *The Tempest* evenhandedly characterizes the two sides of a legal dispute as to whether 'Virginia had been settled by natives who therefore owned the land along the James River, and whom Europeans had no right to supplant', despite official Jacobean denials of native claims (pp. 371–2).

Perhaps the most clinching argument in favour of a biographical connection is that *The Tempest*, as Duncan-Jones says, 'seems like a farewell to power' (p. 240). In Greenblatt's phrase, the play is 'not about possessing absolute power but about giving it up' (p. 374). After having described his own magical ability to bedim the noontide sun and waken the dead from their graves, in hauntingly beautiful language borrowed from the powerful black magician, Medea, in Ovid's *Metamorphoses*, Prospero solemnly abjures such 'rough magic' and vows to break his staff, bury it in the earth, 'And deeper than did ever plummet sound / I'll drown my book' (V. i. 33–57). The renunciation of so much power involves spiritual turmoil, but it also seems to bring with it some relief in laying down an immense burden. Prospero forgives his enemies after struggling with the intense desire to revenge himself on the men now in his power, reconciles himself to Caliban as 'This thing of darkness' that 'I / Acknowledge mine', and prepares to return to Milan where secular authority will pass to Miranda and Ferdinand and where 'Every third thought shall be my grave' (ll. 17–315). Any biographer of Shakespeare finds it hard to imagine a more perfect ending, for a career, for a family story, for a life history of an incomparably great artist.

8

L'envoi

Many significant gaps remain in what biographers have been able to tell us about Shakespeare's life. The years 1585–92, after his marriage and the birth of three children, are almost a total blank, despite efforts to place him in Catholic circles in Lancashire, and the identification of legal documents placing him at least briefly in London in 1588–9 (see Chapter 2 above). His religion, and that of his parents and wife, remain the subjects of heated debate. Whether he was happily or unhappily married, and whether he retired contentedly to a life of domesticity with Anne for the last five years or so of his life after having lived in London without his family for about two decades, are still matters of uncertainty. The death of his only son Hamnet in 1596 must have been a severe blow, but we cannot be sure that the event is personally recorded in his writings.

Did some misfortune or change of mood afflict him at the time that he turned to the writing of his great tragedies in 1599–1600 and afterwards? Did his view on life brighten as he turned to the late romances? Are his poems and plays a chronicle of sorts of his own life experiences? If such a chronicle can be discerned in his writings, what parts of it can be located in specific biographical circumstances? What parts would seem rather to operate in the realm of his extraordinary creative imagination? We ask, and cannot be sure. Matthew Arnold says it wonderfully, in his sonnet to Shakespeare: 'Others abide our question. Thou art free. / We ask and ask: Thou smilest and art still, / Out-topping knowledge.'

Arnold goes on, in this same sonnet, to wonder that such a writer as Shakespeare, 'Self-school'd, self-scann'd, self-honor'd, self-secure', was thus able to 'walk on earth unguess'd at'. How could a young man from a provincial town, educated in the local school but denied an opportunity to attend Cambridge or Oxford, have written such immortal plays and poems? His not having gone to university was probably the result of his father's financial reversals and, even more importantly, of his own marriage at the age of 18, since neither university would admit married students and since his need to maintain a family was pressing.

An education at Cambridge or Oxford might not have seemed necessary in any case as preparation for a career as poet and dramatist; the curricula at those universities were heavily weighted towards texts in Latin, Greek, and Hebrew, since the universities' first mission, nominally at least, was to provide training for the ministry. Other dramatists besides Shakespeare, including Ben Jonson, John Webster, Thomas Kyd, Thomas Dekker, William Rowley, and Anthony Munday, were not university-educated. Some writers were sons of tradesmen, like Shakespeare: Webster was the son of a London tailor and was himself a freeman of the Merchant Taylor's company, and Christopher Marlowe, though educated at Corpus Christi College, Cambridge, was the son of a Canterbury shoemaker. Thomas Kyd began work as a scrivener, Munday as apprentice to a stationer. Ben Jonson's stepfather was a bricklayer. Shakespeare's career path was not unique.

For most biographers and students of Shakespeare, the wonder is not that a provincial lad lacking in higher education could have written the works we associate with Shakespeare, but that any mortal could have done so. The presumed importance of a university education is misunderstood here, in the view of most scholars: it is based anachronistically on a modern view, especially in the United States, of college as offering a broadly liberal education. Cambridge and Oxford no doubt afforded a lively intellectual atmosphere, then as now, but the curriculum was restricted. A 'liberal' education then meant education in the seven traditional branches of knowledge: grammar, rhetoric, and logic forming the *trivium*, and geometry, arithmetic, music, and astronomy making up the *quadrivium*. The study of contemporary literature, including plays, made up no part of the curriculum, though plays and other entertainments were often presented at the universities and Inns of Court. Shakespeare was better off, or at least not penalized, in the view of many (Jonathan Bate,

S. Schoenbaum, Stanley Wells, Peter Ackroyd, Park Honan, Anthony Holden, Stephen Greenblatt, René Weis, Katherine Duncan-Jones, and still others), by his proceeding to London, where he was able to act in and see plays, take part in the life of a bustling city, and read a lot on his own.

Shakespeare was 'self-school'd', in Arnold's phrase; the plays and poems bear witness to his extensive reading. Some of it, including Ovid, Plautus, Virgil, and Seneca, he would have encountered in his Stratford schooling. The quotations and allusions in his early plays especially are consistent with what T. W. Baldwin and others have demonstrated about the school curriculum. For other adventures in reading he turned to Holinshed's *Chronicles*, Plutarch's *Lives of the Noble Grecians and Romans*, Homer's *Iliad* (at least the first books), Livy's *Roman History*, Montaigne's essays, and still other texts. These were increasingly available in English translation: Arthur Golding's Ovid *The Metamorphoses* (1567), Thomas North's Plutarch (1579), George Chapman's Homer (seven books) in 1598, Philemon Holland's Livy (1600), and John Florio's Montaigne (1603). Holinshed's *Chronicles* appeared in a second edition in 1587, just in time for Shakespeare to begin work on his English history plays. Shakespeare also had access to new translations of Italian novellas and short stories, to long narrative poems by Chaucer and others, from which he could draw plots for his plays. Bate (*Soul of the Age*, 135) estimates that Shakespeare's personal library 'would have contained no more than about forty volumes and possibly as few as twenty (excluding his own)'. Shakespeare presumably read many more books than he owned.

A contrary view has been advanced of late by those who argue that the man from Stratford could not have written the poems and plays. The candidates to replace Shakespeare as the author have been many, beginning with Sir Francis Bacon, whose namesake, Delia Bacon, proposed in the latter half of the nineteenth century that a man who had been a viscount and lord chancellor, and had written many essays and poems, was better fitted than a country fellow to know the inner workings of the English court. Marlowe has been proposed also, and is still sometimes discussed as a viable choice, since he did go to Cambridge, led a picturesque life to say the least, wrote incandescent plays and poems, and was widely read in the classics.

The favoured candidate today is Edward de Vere, seventeenth Earl of Oxford, a student in Queen's and St John's colleges at Oxford, a prominent figure in Queen Elizabeth's court, a capable poet, an experienced traveller on the Continent, patron of a juvenile acting company, and the son-in-law of Lord Burghley, Lord High Treasurer and Elizabeth's chief minister from 1592 until his death in 1598. Who better than Oxford to produce such a deft sketch of that tedious old busybody Polonius in *Hamlet*? Or to be able to record with such telling accuracy the speech mannerisms and idiosyncrasies of the great and the near-great at court?

I need not here rehearse at length the arguments for and against the anti-Stratfordian position. The case for Oxford as the author is set forth by the Ogburns and in a more recent book by Richard F. Whalen, *Shakespeare—Who Was He? The Oxford Challenge to the Bard of Avon* (1994). A book-length reply to the candidacy of Oxford and others, written in the same year, is to be found in Irving Leigh Matus, *Shakespeare, in Fact*. Jonathan Bate's *The Genius of Shakespeare* offers the life record as a continuous refutation of the Oxford candidacy. James Shapiro has published an analytical history of the anti-Stratfordian movement entitled *Contested Will: Who Wrote Shakespeare?* (2010).

Briefly, the argument in favour of Oxford (or one of the other candidates) rests to a great extent on Shakespeare's lack of university education and on his presumed lack of access to a genteel lifestyle whereby a dramatist might observe and participate in the ways of the great. Polonius in *Hamlet*, according to this view, reads like a thinly-disguised satire of Lord Burghley, Oxford's father-in-law. Oxford had ample opportunity to travel in Italy and other parts of Europe where many of the plays are set. Details of his life story seem to offer intriguing analogues to the plays' depiction of marital strife (Oxford's marriage to Anne Cecil in 1571 was an unhappy one, especially for her), factional conflict at court (Oxford quarrelled with Sir Philip Sidney in 1579 and was exiled in disgrace in 1582–3 as a result of his violent temper), military campaigning (he served against the Spanish Armada in 1588, despite his having converted earlier to the Catholic faith), and so on. Meantime, no evidence attests to Shakespeare's ever having ventured across the English Channel or having taken part in any military action whatever. Oxford was a courtier and man of letters; Shakespeare was a country lad turned professional actor who has left behind him no papers, almost no signatures even (and those unevenly spelled), and no reflections on what it meant to him to be a writer. Oxfordians generally posit that the Earl, gifted and ambitious as a literary creator but wary of the stigma attached to the humble calling of playwright, secretly commissioned Shakespeare the actor to be his front man, his publicly assumed identity.

The Stratfordian reply begins by pointing out that Oxford died in 1604, well before the usually accepted dating of many of the plays, including some of the greatest: *King Lear* in 1605–6, followed by *Antony and Cleopatra, Coriolanus,* and the four late romances, among others. Anti-Stratfordians tend to argue either that the conventional datings are erroneous, or that Oxford's literary executors had been commissioned by the Earl to insert into already-written plays certain details of topical import with the intent of updating the topicality. The Earl did not wish his identity to be made known, at least while the persons who would remember him well were still alive. To Stratfordians, this scenario seems unnecessary at best and smacking of conspiracy theory at worst. How would it have been possible to bamboozle so many people, some of whom knew Shakespeare well?

Ben Jonson, Shakespeare's younger contemporary and a man of fierce pride as a literary lion, praised and blamed Shakespeare as a fellow writer in terms that bespeak intimate acquaintance with the work and the man. Why would Jonson sign on to a conspiracy of silence or else fail to see the fallacy in the case for Shakespeare's own candidacy? 'I loved the man ... this side idolatry', wrote Jonson in *Timber, or Discoveries* (1641), going on to explain what he meant by 'this side idolatry': Shakespeare was for him untrained as a classicist and on many occasions an egregious violator of the rules for great writing, but he somehow managed to be the best writer of tragedy the world had seen in the past century or so and the best writer of comedy for all time. Praise like this did not come easily from Jonson. Moreover, it perfectly describes the Shakespeare that this present book has endeavoured to describe, through the story of his biographers: a native-born Stratfordian who came to London and, 'self-school'd', made his way to greatness as a writer. Jonathan Bate (*Genius of Shakespeare,* 70–3) cites others who knew Shakespeare and cannot have been easily fooled: Francis Beaumont, William Camden, Sir George Buc, Leonard Digges, Francis Meres. The list could be extended. (On Digges's connections with

Shakespeare, and on Thomas Russell's position as the overseer of Shakespeare's will, see Leslie Hotson, *I, William Shakespeare*, 237–79.) Jeffrey Knapp, in his *Shakespeare Only* (2009), ably demonstrates how Shakespeare's own contemporaries idolized him as a writer of a unique authorial identity: a dramatist like them, but one who took the stage 'alone' and incomparable.

All signs point to irreconcilable differences between the Oxfordians (or the Marlovians) on one side and the Stratfordians on the other; few minds appear likely to change. The present book will not alter that. Perhaps, though, by way of conclusion to a book about Shakespeare's biographers, a counterargument can be offered to the Oxfordian position. That position argues that what we know of Shakespeare's life could not have prepared him to report the private conversations of the great. One answer might be put in the form of a question in modern terms: if one were to seek today for brilliant reporting of goings-on in 10 Downing Street or the White House or the Élysée Palace, would one choose to hear from some strategically placed cabinet member or from investigative reporters like Woodward and Bernstein at the time of Washington Watergate? The question answers itself, and is meant here to suggest that Shakespeare, as an outsider to high life and political shenanigans, was in a better position to see life steadily and see it whole (to quote Matthew Arnold again) than a biased insider like Oxford.

An answer still more pertinent to the present book is that the plays and poems attributed to Shakespeare do indeed conjure up for us the very sort of person that Shakespeare seems to have been. This is convincingly true at the level of the family. Oxford's family life was dysfunctional, largely because he was a brute who gave his poor father-in-law heartache until the day Burghley died, which is to say even some years after Anne, the daughter and wife, escaped the nightmare of her married existence by dying in 1588. Can one imagine such a man depicting the mutual fondness of Prospero and Ferdinand in *The Tempest*? Or celebrating tender and loving male friendship in the Sonnets? Or paying homage to women, both young and old, who, in play after play, show how to forgive one's persecutors?

No, the persona that emerges from Shakespeare's writings and from biographical studies is a better man than Oxford could have imagined. Even the weaknesses enumerated by Katherine Duncan-Jones in her study of *Ungentle Shakespeare* strengthen the case for seeing the man in his writings. He seems to have acted churlishly towards his wife in devising his last will and testament, and even before that. He may have experienced strongly ambivalent feelings of attachment to a young friend like the Earl of Southampton. Probably he was disillusioned about the end of the charismatic and self-destructive Earl of Essex. He seems to have felt great pride in himself as a writer while also cringing in self-abasement at the unsavoury reputation that attached itself to the calling of professional actor. He seems to have been acquainted with both euphoria and self-loathing in the sexual act. If he was faithless to his marriage during his many years of living apart from his family in London, as Weis assumes to be the case (p. 390), we can see an image of what that experience might have meant to him in Sonnet 129, or in Angelo's self-hatred for his uncontrollable lust in *Measure for Measure*, or in Antony's dismay at his having deserted his wife and children in *Antony and Cleopatra*. If he did not do as well by Anne as he might have wished, the plays offer ample opportunity for exploring the tortured psyches of husbands like Othello, or Posthumus Leonatus in *Cymbeline*, or Leontes in *The Winter's Tale*, who find it hard to forgive themselves for what they have done. If he brooded over the troubled feelings that could arise between a father and a daughter, we need look no further than *The Merchant of Venice* or *King Lear* for dramatic representations of how the participants might feel.

The death of an only son, the obtaining of a coat of arms for a father, the striving to be wealthy—all seem consistent not only with what we know of the man from Stratford but with the ideas and situations that are debated and dramatized in the plays and poems. Such, and much more, is what we can hope to learn from biographers about the inner life of the man who wrote some of the greatest plays that the world has ever seen.

My purpose here is twofold: to indicate my many indebtednesses to biographers of Shakespeare, and to offer suggestions for further reading on the topics I have addressed.

I refer repeatedly throughout the book to a number of recent biographical studies of Shakespeare. These include Jonathan Bate, *The Genius of Shakespeare* and *Soul of the Age*; Katherine Duncan-Jones, *Ungentle Shakespeare*; Stephen Greenblatt, *Will in the World*; Germaine Greer, *Shakespeare's Wife*; Park Honan, *Shakespeare: A Life*; S. Schoenbaum, *William Shakespeare: A Documentary Life* and *William Shakespeare: A Compact Documentary Life*; René Weis, *Shakespeare Revealed*; and Stanley Wells, *Shakespeare: The Poet and His Plays*. All these deserve careful reading. My indebtedness to them is greater than I can easily say.

Other general studies that I am happy to recommend include Peter Ackroyd, *Shakespeare: The Biography*; Ian Wilson, *Shakespeare: The Evidence. Unlocking the Mysteries of the Man and his Work*; Anthony Holden, *William Shakespeare, his Life and Work*; Michael Wood, *In Search of Shakespeare*; and Dennis Kay, *Shakespeare: His Life, Work and Era*. A new biography of Shakespeare by Lois Potter is to appear soon, and should be very rewarding, with plentiful insights about stage history.

On Shakespeare's life in Stratford, Mark Eccles, *Shakespeare in Warwickshire*, is deeply informative. Charles Nicholl, *The Lodger: Shakespeare on Silver Street*, offers intriguing glimpses into Shakespeare's life in London. A. D. Nuttall, *Shakespeare the Thinker*, studies the development of Shakespeare's ideas. James Shapiro, *1599: A Year in the Life of William Shakespeare*, offers a detailed look at one of Shakespeare's most productive years as a dramatist. Gary Taylor, *Reinventing Shakespeare*, gives an account of Shakespeare's ever-changing 'life' in the theatre, in literary references, in political life, and much else.

Please see the bibliography for further suggestions, and for a full listing of the books and articles to which I am indebted. I cite these works in parenthetical references throughout this book, with fuller information on date and place of publication in the bibliography.

Shakespeare citations are from my own edition of the *Complete Works*, 6th edition, 2009.

Bibliography

Ackroyd, Peter, *Shakespeare: The Biography* (New York: Nan A. Talese, Doubleday; London: Chatto & Windus, 2005).

Adelman, Janet, *The Common Liar: An Essay on 'Antony and Cleopatra'* (New Haven: Yale University Press, 1973).

—— *Suffocating Mothers: Fantasies of Maternal Origin in Shakespeare's Plays, 'Hamlet' to 'The Tempest'* (New York and London: Routledge, 1992).

Alexander, Peter, *Shakespeare's Life and Art* (London: James Nisbet & Co., 1939).

Aubrey, John, *Brief Lives* (London, 1898; ed. Oliver Lawson Dick, London: Secker and Warburg, 1949; Ann Arbor: University of Michigan Press, 1962).

Bacon, Delia Salter, *The Philosophy of the Plays of Shakespeare Unfolded* (1857). Delia Bacon was sister of the moderate abolitionist Leonard Bacon, author of *Slavery Discussed in Occasional Essays* (1840), a book that made an impression on Abraham Lincoln.

Bailey, John, *Shakespeare* (London and New York: Longmans, Green & Co., 1929).

Baldwin, T. W., *William Shakspere's Small Latine & Lesse Greeke*, 2 vols. (Urbana: University of Illinois Press, 1944).

Barber, C. L., *Shakespeare's Festive Comedy* (Princeton: Princeton University Press, 1959).

Barroll, J. Leeds, *Politics, Plague, and Shakespeare's Theater: The Stuart Years* (Ithaca: Cornell University Press, 1991).

Bate, Jonathan, *The Genius of Shakespeare* (London: Picador, 1997).

—— *Soul of the Age: A Biography of the Mind of William Shakespeare* (New York: Random House, 2009).

Bearman, Robert, '"Was William Shakespeare William Shakeshafte?" Revisited', *Shakespeare Quarterly*, 53 (2002), 83–94.

—— 'John Shakespeare: A Papist or Just Penniless?' *Shakespeare Quarterly*, 56 (2005), 411–33.

Bednarz, James P., *Shakespeare and the Poets' War* (New York: Columbia University Press, 2001).

Bevington, David, *Shakespeare: The Seven Ages of Human Experience* (Oxford: Blackwell, 2002; 2nd edn., 2005).

Bevington, David, *Shakespeare's Ideas: More Things in Heaven and Earth* (Malden, Oxford, and Chichester: Wiley-Blackwell, 2008).

—— (ed.), *The Complete Works of Shakespeare* (6th edn., New York: Pearson/ Longman, 2009).

Bloom, Harold, *Shakespeare and the Invention of the Human* (New York: Riverhead Books, Penguin/Putnam, 1998).

Boas, F. S., *Shakspere and his Predecessors* (New York: Scribner, 1896, 1904).

Bowers, Fredson, 'Hamlet as Minister and Scourge', *PMLA* 70 (1955), 740–9.

Bradbrook, Muriel C., *Shakespeare: The Poet in his World* (New York: Columbia University Press, 1978).

Bradley, A. C., *Shakespearean Tragedy: Lectures on Hamlet, Othello, King Lear, Macbeth* (London: Macmillan, 1904, 1916).

Brandes, Georg, *William Shakespeare* (London: William Heinemann, 1916, translated in 1898).

Brown, Ivor, *William Shakespeare* (London: International Profiles, 1968).

Brunkhorst, Martin, *Shakespeares 'Coriolanus' in deutscher Bearbeitung: Sieben Beispiele zum literarästhetischen Problem d. Umsetzung und Vermittlung Shakespeares* (Berlin, New York: de Gruyter, 1973).

Burgess, Anthony, *Nothing Like the Sun: A Story of Shakespeare's Love-Life* (London: Heinemann, 1964).

—— *Shakespeare* (London: Cape, 1970, and Harmondsworth: Penguin, 1972).

Calvin, Jean, *Institutes of the Christian Religion*, ed. John T. McNeill, trans. Ford Lewis Battles (Philadelphia: Westminster Press, 1960).

Capell, Edward, *Notes and Various Readings to Shakespeare* (London: printed by Henry Hughes for the author, 1779–83).

Cavell, Stanley, *Disowning Knowledge in Seven Plays of Shakespeare. An updated version* (Cambridge: Cambridge University Press, 2003); originally... *Six Plays* (Cambridge: Cambridge University Press, 1987).

Chambers, E. K., *The Elizabethan Stage*, 4 vols. (Oxford: Clarendon Press, 1923).

—— *William Shakespeare: A Study of Facts and Problems*, 2 vols. (Oxford: Clarendon Press, 1930).

Chute, Marchette, *Shakespeare of London* (New York: Dutton, 1949).

Coleridge, Samuel Taylor, *Coleridge on Shakespeare: The Text of the Lectures of 1811–12*, ed. R. A. Foakes (Charlottesville, Va.: University Press of Virginia, 1971).

—— *Specimens of the Table Talk of the Late Samuel Taylor Coleridge*, ed. H. N. Coleridge, 2 vols. (London: J. Murray, New York: Harper, 1835).

Cook, Ann Jennalie, *The Privileged Playgoers of Shakespeare's London, 1576–1642* (Princeton: Princeton University Press, 1981).

Dowden, Edward, *Shakspere: A Critical Study of his Mind and Art* (London: Henry King, 1875; new edn., New York: Harper, 1918).

Downes, John, *Roscius Anglicanus; or, An Historical Review of the Stage* (London: H. Payford, 1708).

Duncan-Jones, Katherine, *Ungentle Shakespeare: Scenes from his Life* (London: Arden Shakespeare, 2001).

Dutton, Richard, *William Shakespeare: A Literary Life* (New York: St. Martin's, 1989).

—— Findlay, Alison, and Wilson, Richard (eds.), *Region, Religion, and Patronage: Lancastrian Shakespeare* (Manchester: Manchester University Press, 2003).

Dyce, Alexander (ed.), *The Poetical Works of William Shakespeare and Ben Jonson, With a Memoir of Each* (Boston: Houghton, Mifflin, 1880).

Eccles, Mark, *Shakespeare in Warwickshire* (Madison: University of Wisconsin Press, 1961).

Ellis, John M., *One Fairy Story too Many: The Brothers Grimm and their Tales* (Chicago: University of Chicago Press, 1983), ch. 5.

Elton, Charles Isaac, *William Shakespeare, his Family and Friends* (New York: Dutton, 1904).

Elton, William R., *King Lear and the Gods* (San Marino, Calif.: Huntington Library, 1966; Lexington: University Press of Kentucky, 1988).

Empson, William, *Seven Types of Ambiguity* (London: Chatto & Windus, New York: New Directions: 1947; rev. edns. 1953, 1956).

Erne, Lukas, 'Biography and Mythography: Rereading Chettle's Alleged Apology to Shakespeare', *English Studies*, 79 (1998), 430–40.

Everett, Barbara, 'Reade him, therefore', *TLS* Commentary, 17 August 2007.

Fraser, Russell, *Shakespeare: A Life in Art* (New York: Columbia University Press, 1988 and 1992; New Brunswick, NJ: Transaction Publishers, 2008).

Fripp, Edgar I., *Shakespeare: Man and Artist*, 2 vols. (Oxford: Oxford University Press, 1938).

—— *Shakespeare's Stratford* (London: Oxford University Press, 1928).

Goethe, Johann Wolfgang von, *Wilhelm Meister* (1778, 1795), later translated by Thomas Carlyle.

Gray, Joseph William, *Shakespeare's Marriage, his Departure from Stratford and Other Incidents of his Life* (London: Chapman & Hall, 1905).

Greenblatt, Stephen, *Hamlet in Purgatory* (Princeton: Princeton University Press, 2001).

—— *Will in the World: How Shakespeare Became Shakespeare* (New York: Norton, 2004).

Greer, Germaine, *Shakespeare's Wife* (London: Bloomsbury, 2007).

Gurr, Andrew, *William Shakespeare: The Extraordinary Life of the Most Successful Writer of All Time* (London: HarperCollins, 1995).

Halliwell-Phillipps, James Orchard, *Outlines of the Life of Shakespeare*, 2 vols. (9th edn., London: Longmans, Green, 1890).

Harbage, Alfred, *As They Liked It: A Study of Shakespeare's Moral Artistry* (New York: Macmillan, 1947).

—— *Shakespeare and the Rival Traditions* (New York: Macmillan, 1952).

Hazlitt, William, *Characters of Shakespeare's Plays* (London: C. H. Reynell for R. Hunter and C. and J. Ollier, 1817).

Holden, Anthony, *William Shakespeare: His Life and Work* (London: Little, Brown, 1999).

—— *William Shakespeare: An Illustrated Biography* (Boston, New York, and London: Little, Brown, 1999; abridged edn., 2002).

Honan, Park, *Shakespeare: A Life* (Oxford: Oxford University Press, 1998).

Honigmann, E. A. J., 'The Second-Best Bed', *New York Review of Books*, 7 November 1991. The argument is further explored in Honigmann's 'Shakespeare's Will and *Testamentary* Traditions', in *Shakespeare and Cultural Traditions*, ed. Tetsuo Kishi, Roger Pringle, and Stanley Wells (Newark: University of Delaware Press; London and Toronto: Associated University Presses, 1994), 127–37.

—— *Shakespeare: The 'Lost Years'* (Manchester: Manchester University Press; Totowa, NJ: Barnes & Noble Books, 1985).

Hotson, Leslie, *I, William Shakespeare, Do Appoint Thomas Russell, Esquire* (London: Jonathan Cape, 1937).

—— *Shakespeare versus Shallow* (Boston: Little, Brown, 1931).

Hughes, Ted, *Shakespeare and the Goddess of Complete Being* (London: Faber and Faber, 1992).

Hunter, Robert G., *Shakespeare and the Comedy of Forgiveness* (New York: Columbia University Press, 1955).

Hyman, Stanley Edgar, *Iago: Some Approaches to the Illusion of his Motivation* (New York: Atheneum, 1970).

Jones, Ernest, *Hamlet and Oedipus* (London: Gollancz, 1949; New York: Norton, 1976). Revision of an essay published in 1910 in *The American Journal of Psychology* and then in Jones's *Essays in Applied Psycho-Analysis* (Vienna: International Psycho-Analytic Press, 1923).

Jorgensen, Paul, *Our Naked Frailties: Sensational Art and Meaning in 'Macbeth'* (Berkeley: University of California Press, 1971).

Joyce, James, *Ulysses* (New York: Modern Library, 1934; New York, Vintage, 1990).

Kay, Dennis, *Shakespeare: His Life, Work and Era* (London: Sidgwick & Jackson, 1992).

Kernan, Alvin B., *The Playwright as Magician: Shakespeare's Image of the Poet in the English Public Theater* (New Haven: Yale University Press, 1979).

Kirsch, Arthur, *Shakespeare and the Experience of Love* (Cambridge: Cambridge University Press, 1981).

Knapp, Jeffrey, *Shakespeare Only* (Chicago: University of Chicago Press, 2009).

—— *Shakespeare's Tribe: Church, Nation, and Theater in Renaissance England* (Chicago: University of Chicago Press, 2002).

Kott, Jan, *Shakespeare Our Contemporary*, trans. Boleslaw Taborski (Garden City, NY: Doubleday, 1964; New York: W. W. Norton, 1964). First published in Polish by Panstwowe Wydawnictwo Naukowe, Warsaw, 1964.

Laroque, François, 'The Jack Cade Scenes Reconsidered: Popular Rebellion, Utopia, or Carnival?', in Tetsuo Kishi, Roger Pringle, and Stanley Wells (eds.), *Shakespeare and Cultural Traditions* (Newark: University of Delaware Press; London and Toronto: Associated University Presses, 1994), 76–89.

Lee, Sidney, *A Life of William Shakespeare* (London: Smith, Elder, 1898; new edn., New York: Macmillan, 1931).

Levi, Peter, *The Life and Times of William Shakespeare* (London: Macmillan, 1988).

Lewis, B. Roland, *The Shakespeare Documents: Facsimiles, Transliterations, and Commentary* (Stanford: Stanford University Press, 1940).

Lewis, C. S., *English Literature in the Sixteenth Century Excluding Drama* (Oxford: Clarendon Press, 1954).

Marcus, Leah S., *Puzzling Shakespeare: Local Reading and its Discontents* (Berkeley: University of California Press, 1988).

Masson, David, *Shakespeare Personally* (New York: Dutton, 1914).

Matus, Irvin Leigh, *Shakespeare, in Fact* (New York: Continuum, 1994).

Milward, Peter, *Shakespeare the Papist* (Ave Maria, Fla.: Sapientia Press, 2005).

—— *Shakespeare's Religious Background* (London: Sedgwick & Jackson; Bloomington: Indiana University Press, 1973).

Munro, John, *The Shakspere Allusion-book: A Collection of Allusions to Shakspere from 1591 to 1700*. Originally compiled by C. M. Ingleby, Miss L. Toulmin Smith, and Dr. F. J. Furnivall, with the assistance of the New Shakspere Society: re-edited, revised, and re-arranged, with an introduction, by John Munro (1909), and now re-issued with a preface by Sir Edmund Chambers, 2 vols. (London: Oxford University Press, 1932).

Mutschmann, Heinrich, and Wentersdorf, Karl P., *Shakespeare and Catholicism* (New York: Sheed and Ward, 1952).

Nicholl, Charles, *The Lodger: Shakespeare on Silver Street* (London: Allen Lane, 2007).

Nuttall, A. D., *Shakespeare the Thinker* (New Haven: Yale University Press, 2007).

Nye, Robert, *Mrs. Shakespeare: The Complete Works* (New York: Arcade, 1993).

O'Connor, Garry, *William Shakespeare: A Life* (London: Hodder & Stoughton, 1991).

Ogburn, Dorothy, and Ogburn, Charlton, *Shake-speare: The Man Behind the Name* (New York: Wm. Morrow, 1962).

Orgel, Stephen, 'Prospero's Wife', *Representations*, 8 (1984), 1–13; repr. in Orgel, *The Authentic Shakespeare and Other Problems of the Early Modern Stage* (London and New York, 2003).

Paul, Henry N., *The Royal Play of 'Macbeth': When, Why, and How It was Written by Shakespeare* (New York: Macmillan, 1950).

Pearson, Hesketh, *A Life of Shakespeare* (London: Penguin, 1942, 1949; rev. edn., London, Hamish Hamilton, 1987).

Pequigney, Joseph, *Such Is My Love: A Study of Shakespeare's Sonnets* (Chicago: University of Chicago Press, 1985).

Pogue, Kate Emery, *Shakespeare's Friends* (Westport, Conn.: Praeger, 2006).

Rabkin, Norman, '*Coriolanus*: The Tragedy of Politics', *Shakespeare Quarterly*, 17 (1966), 195–212.

—— *Shakespeare and the Common Understanding* (New York: The Free Press, London: Collier-Macmillan Ltd., 1967).

Reese, M. M., *Shakespeare: His World and his Work* (1953; rev. edn, New York: St. Martin's, 1980).

Rosenberg, Marvin, *The Masks of Othello: The Search for the Identity of Othello, Iago, and Desdemona by Three Centuries of Actors and Critics* (Berkeley: University of California Press, 1961).

Rogers, Joyce, *The Second Best Bed: Shakespeare's Will in a New Light* (Westport, Conn.: Greenwood, 1993).

Rush, Christopher, *Will* (London: Beautiful Books, 2007).

Rowse, A. L., *Discovering Shakespeare: A Chapter in Literary History* (London: Weidenfeld & Nicolson, 1989).

—— *The Poems of Shakespeare's Dark Lady* (London: Cape, 1978).

—— *Shakespeare: The Man* (New York and London: Harper & Row, 1973).

—— *Simon Forman: Sex and Society in Shakespeare's Age* (London: Weidenfeld & Nicolson, 1974).

Sams, Eric, *The Real Shakespeare: Retrieving the Early Years, 1564–1594* (New Haven: Yale University Press, 1995).

Schlegel, August W. von, *Lectures on Dramatic Art and Literature* (1809), trans. John Black (1846; repr. New York, 1965).

Schoenbaum, S., *Shakespeare's Lives* (new edn.; Oxford: Clarendon Press, 1991).

—— *William Shakespeare: A Compact Documentary Life* (Oxford: Oxford University Press, 1977). An abridged version of *William Shakespeare: A Documentary Life.*

—— *William Shakespeare: A Documentary Life* (Oxford and New York: Oxford University Press, in association with the Scolar Press, 1975).

—— *William Shakespeare: Records and Images* (Oxford and New York: Oxford University Press, 1981).

Shakespeare, William, *Complete Works of W. Shakespeare*, ed. George Steevens (London, 1773 and 1778). A continuation of the 1765 edition of Samuel Johnson, with additional commentary by Steevens.

—— *Hamlet*, ed. Harold Jenkins (Arden 2; London and New York: Methuen, 1982).

—— *Pericles*, ed. Suzanne Gossett (Arden 3; London: Thomson Learning, 2004).

—— *Pericles*, ed. F. David Hoeniger (Arden 2; London: Methuen; Cambridge, Mass.: Harvard University Press, 1963).

—— *The Plays of William Shakespeare*, ed. Edmond Malone (London: J. Tonson, 1790).

—— *William Shakespeare: The Complete Works*, ed. Stanley Wells and Gary Taylor (Oxford: Clarendon Press, 1986).

—— *The Works of Mr. William Shakespear*, ed. Nicholas Rowe, 6 vols. (London: for Jacob Tonson, 1709).

Shapiro, James, *1599: A Year in the Life of William Shakespeare* (New York: HarperCollins; London: Faber & Faber, 2005).

—— *Shakespeare and the Jews* (New York: Columbia University Press, 1996). An earlier essay by Shapiro, also entitled *Shakespeare and the Jews*, was published as the Parkes Lecture, University of Southampton, 1992.

Shaw, George Bernard, *Shaw on Shakespeare*, ed. Edwin Wilson (New York: Dutton, 1961).

Siemon, James, '"The power of hope?" An Early Modern Reader of *Richard III*', in *A Companion to Shakespeare's Works*, ii: *The Histories* (Oxford: Blackwell, 2003), 361–78.

Southworth, John, *Shakespeare the Player: A Life in the Theatre* (Phoenix Mill: Sutton Publishing, 2000).

Stallybrass, Peter, 'Editing as Cultural Formation: The Sexing of Shakespeare's Sonnets', *Modern Language Quarterly*, 54/1 (1993), 91–103, repr. in Marshall Brown (ed.), *The Uses of Literary History* (Durham, NC: Duke University Press, 1996); and James Schiffer (ed.), *Shakespeare's Sonnets: Critical Essays* (New York: Garland, 1999), 75–88.

Stopes, Charlotte Carmichael, *Shakespeare's Family* (London: Elliot Stock, 1901).

Stopes, Charlotte Carmichael, *Shakespeare's Warwickshire Contemporaries* (Stratford-upon-Avon: Shakespeare Head Press, 1907).

Taylor, Gary, *Reinventing Shakespeare: A Cultural History, from the Restoration to the Present* (New York: Weidenfeld & Nicolson, 1989).

—— '*Troilus and Cressida*: Bibliography, Performance, and Interpretation', *Shakespeare Studies*, 15 (1982), 99–136.

Tiffany, Grace, *My Father Had a Daughter* (Auburn, Wash.: Berkley Books, 2004).

—— *Will* (New York: Berkley Books, 2004).

Vaughan, Virginia Mason, '*King John*', in *A Companion to Shakespeare's Works*, ii: *The Histories* (Oxford: Blackwell; 2003), 379–94.

Velz, John W., 'Undular Structure in *Julius Caesar*', *Modern Language Review*, 66 (1971), 21–30.

Wallace, Charles William, and Wallace, Hulda, 'New Shakespeare Discoveries: Shakespeare as a Man among Men', *Harper's Monthly Magazine*, 120 (1910), 489–510, and *Nebraska University Studies*, 1 (1910), 261–360.

Weis, René, *Shakespeare Revealed: A Biography* (London: John Murray, 2007).

Wells, Stanley, *Shakespeare: The Poet and His Plays* (London: Methuen, 2001).

—— *Shakespeare for All Time* (London: Macmillan, 2002; New York: Oxford University Press, 2003).

Whalen, Richard F., *Shakespeare—Who Was He? The Oxford Challenge to the Bard of Avon* (Westport, Conn.: Praeger, 1994).

Wheeler, Richard P., 'Deaths in the Family: The Loss of a Son and the Rise of *Shakespearean Comedy*', *Shakespeare Quarterly*, 51 (2000), 127–53.

—— *Shakespeare's Development and the Problem Comedies: Turn and Counter-Turn* (Berkeley: University of California Press, 1981).

Wilson, Ian, *Shakespeare: The Evidence. Unlocking the Mysteries of the Man and his Work* (New York: St Martin's Griffin, 1993).

Wilson, Richard, *Secret Shakespeare: Studies in Theatre, Religion, and Resistance* (Manchester: Manchester University Press, 2004).

—— 'Shakespeare and the Jesuits', *The Times Literary Supplement* (London), 19 December 1997. A revised version of this paper forms the basis of ch. 2 in Wilson's *Secret Shakespeare*.

—— *Will Power: Essays on Shakespearean Authority* (Detroit: Wayne State University Press, 1993).

Wood, Michael, *In Search of Shakespeare* (London: BBC Worldwide Ltd, 2003).